T0354480

MAN PROPOSES— ROSE DISPOSES

Life, Love and other misadventures.

Rosemary Mason

BALBOA.
PRESS
A DIVISION OF HAY HOUSE

DEDICATION

For my two daughters, Sherrell and Jennifer and my brother Michael, who came to the fore with many suggestions and corrections.

Also, for my family and friends, who went into peals of laughter when I described events in my life and urged me to write a book – so here it is!

Balboa Press books may be ordered through booksellers or by contacting:

Balboa Press
A Division of Hay House
1663 Liberty Drive
Bloomington, IN 47403
www.balboapress.com.au
1 (877) 407-4847

Print information available on the last page.

ISBN: 978-1-5043-1288-2 (sc)
ISBN: 978-1-5043-1289-9 (e)

Balboa Press rev. date: 05/17/2018

TABLE OF CONTENTS

PROLOGUE

"NOEL!!! THERE'S A "NIGGER" IN MY BEDROOM!"

Rose and Noel leapt out of bed – "What did Mom say? She never uses the word "Nigger"!

Half awake, Noel grabbed his FN pistol and staggered down the passage. Rose turned and ran into the children's room to make sure they were unharmed. Switching on their light she saw all was well and ran to Dora's room behind Noel who got there in time to see a large black body take a mighty leap like a gazelle out of the opened window and disappear.

As for the thief, the sight of a white faced, white sheeted apparition, shouting and rearing up out of the darkness, must have made him sail out of the window thinking that the ghost of a Tokoloshi was out to get him "Yah! Weh!" and he was off.

Noel rushed out to check the rest of the house. Rose ran into Dora's room, switched on her light and ran over to the bed. There lay her beautiful mother, propped up on several pillows, wearing a delicate, lacy white nightdress and looking perfectly calm and unruffled She said it must have been the strong smell of a nervous native man that woke her, and, in the bright streak of moonlight she was horrified to see one in the middle of the room staring at her. She hadn't been on the stage for nothing and she sat up and shouted as loud as she could.

All the windows in the house had been opened wide by the thief as a means of getting away and none of them had bars. Rose quickly closed them. It was half past two in the morning and the police were on their way to take a statement. Noel checked the locked caravan and saw his son Christopher through the window, fast asleep and undisturbed. Noel returned bearing a long, sharp, pointed knife he had found in the creeper outside Dora's window. Only then they realized the extent of the danger she had been in.

Noel fetched his tools and secured all the window latches to open slightly for air and Rose made tea. Sherrell had woken and joined them in her grandmother's room. She was fourteen and wide awake but ten-year-old Jenny slept on. The policemen came and left at four taking the knife with them. So, with all the doors locked and the windows secured they went back to bed for a short sleep if possible. Rose was uneasy, so she was up at six and in Morny's room. The children called Dora 'Morny' as she didn't like 'Granny'. They searched the house and found nothing stolen except Sherrell's cardigan.

Morny habitually woke before six and waited for morning tea. The servant came in at six thirty and made it. Noel was up and away early and then there was an orderly rush for the bathroom and loo as all children got ready for school. Christopher first, as he had to cycle to school. Sherrell and Jenny travelled with Rose, dropped at their various schools on her way to work. Sherrell couldn't find her new school cardigan – worn only once and laid out on the bed to wear in the morning. It was a school project, started two years before and only just finished that week! Why that article of all things, Rose wondered?

Knitted on small needles in fine wool, it had been a nightmare of dropped stitches and errors, needing much undoing and causing much frustration until Rose and Morny came to the rescue, doing the sleeves and fronts while Sherrell finished the back. They vowed that they would not do that again, so Rose bought her one in town that morning. At least, the school mistress had seen the finished project.

"I'm surprised that you called him a nigger, Mom. That must have been what sent him leaping out of the window. I'm surprised he didn't stab you."

Mom laughed. "Actually, I surprised myself. I never say it, as you know. Somehow, I don't think a chatty 'there's a black gentleman in my bedroom' would have brought you running.

Rose laughed and had to agree.

ONE

ROBERT AND DORA: THE LATTER-DAY PIONEERS.

1880 – Monomatapa, the dark and dangerous hinterland beyond the great Limpopo river, had been explored by David Livingstone and Stanley and a few intrepid peddlers, taking their wares over the Limpopo when the waters subsided sufficiently in winter to swim their mules and horses across and barter three-legged cast iron cooking pots, gaudy cloth and mirrors for gold nuggets, ivory and a scrawny chicken and goat. Some prospectors had also ridden in to try and find the source of the gold in ancient workings. They were frequently killed when discovered.

The natives were hostile and dangerous, armed with their bows and arrows, spears and knobkerries – trimmed tree roots with a carved, round knob one end which made a fearsome weapon to crack open a skull. Most of them had never seen a white man or a firearm fortunately, and they fled in superstitious terror at the strange power of this stick that thundered and could kill at such a distance. However, they still could creep up on a victim at night, squirming along the ground in the blackness, invisible, as they were black themselves. So many of the peddlers lost their lives.

1

A few missionaries had also braved the dangers. Some survived and tried to convert the pagans, building huts and trying to understand the strange languages of the blacks around them, bribing them with gifts and handing them items of clothing to cover their ungodly nakedness. Two arm lengths of cheap cotton material formed a wrap for the women and their immediate conversion to Christianity – whatever that weird mumbo jumbo was, which was all that the strange white people wanted back from them! After all, the natives, too, had lots of invisible ancestors around. They could add the white man's Father in Heaven quite happily and this wicked white devil of theirs must be the brother of the evil and destructive black tokoloshi! Yah Weh! Help us!

And so, with persuasion and without any force, the Missions expanded in size and the black people gathered there for what they could get out of them. They worked at building large huts with open sides that they found strange indeed. Their own huts had no windows, only a small door for safety. But the 'penga murungu' – the 'mad white people' - wanted them that way! They were made for something called a school, whatever that was.

In 1883, in Cambridge, England, there was born to Robert James Mason and his wife, an only son whom they christened Robert James Barber Mason. In 1889 this lad started his education at the Perse Grammar School, two months before he turned seven. No more is recorded about his childhood except that, at the age of fourteen, he suffered an ear infection and had a mastoid operation. This was long before antibiotics were discovered and all his life he would be troubled with the same ear problem.

In 1890 In Monomatapa, the Union Jack was raised in Fort Salisbury and the country was renamed Rhodesia in honour of its founder, Cecil John Rhodes, who had claimed all the land north of the Limpopo River and as far East and West as he could for Britain, trying to reach the sea. Unfortunately, the British government stopped him fighting his way to the east coast, just a tantalising 180 miles away through Portuguese claimed territory. In the west was the vast expanse of Portuguese west territory called Angola, which Rhodes considered enough for them. Thus, Rhodesia became a land locked country. Her exports and imports were subject to the tariffs and diplomatic agreement of her neighbours. Much later, Rhodesia would be punished via sanctions, compromised, endangered and finally abandoned by her own motherland, Great Britain.

In 1893, in Durban, Natal, up on the Berea at 52, Manning Road, there lived Wharton Plowright, recently emigrated from Britain, his wife Lillian and three of their small children still living. They mourned the loss of one and Lillian was pregnant with a fifth child. This child died at birth. By 1898, all six children had been laid in the grave. No one knew that mosquitoes carried the malaria virus, and whooping cough, diphtheria, measles and even polio were plagues that carried children away almost inevitably. By then, Lillian was in permanent black mourning and she was deeply depressed.

Wattie, as she called her husband, was fast becoming a wealthy and prominent citizen. He owned a building in the centre of the city in Plowright Lane which ran between Smith and West Street, both one-way streets to and from the Marine Parade on the sea front. He was the managing director of his own business. He had his club to go to, so he seldom got home before seven or eight at night.

Lillian stayed at home alone, as all Victorian wives did. She had a cook and a housemaid, but she had the painful duty of dismissing the children's nanny. The house was a silent and lonely place of weeping for Lillian and she was heading for a complete breakdown, when one day, feeling off colour, she went to consult her doctor. To her astonishment, she found she was pregnant again. After months of fear, joy and dread because of her stillborn children, a healthy son was born. He was christened Herbert and they called him Bertie.

In 1898, in the Transvaal, South Africa a group of pioneers, both British and Dutch, were preparing their wagons, oxen, horses and supplies to travel into the unknown together, protected by a contingent of British South African Police.

The leader of this expedition was Cecil John Rhodes, empowered by the British Government to negotiate with the powerful Matabele King Lobengula in his kraal, a few hundred miles inside Monomotapa. This he had done, and Lobengula added his seal to the Rudd Concession paper after being wined and dined by Queen Victoria in London.

Wearing nothing but a top hat and a 'moochi' - a loin cloth, with a full leopard skin cloak draped round him, he was bedazzled by all the wonders of civilized London. Gifts of guns and everything he could wish for, given morphine for his gout by Leander Starr Jameson, the doctor accompanying Rhodes, plied with potent wine, he was befuddled enough to agree.

He appended the special seal of approval to the document. He couldn't read or write so this seal was made for him. It had a large elephant in the centre that he could relate to. In an ignorant, drunken and somewhat befuddled way, he apparently understood what he was doing as no sooner had he returned to his royal kraal of Bulawayo, he back-tracked, accusing the British of tricking him. The British were also deviating from the written terms which did not include colonizing the whole of Monomotapa and it was in this dangerous state of insecurity that the first wagons crossed the rocky sands of the wide Limpopo river in the dry season, swimming their animals through the deep, crocodile-infested pools to reach the promised land on the northern bank before the water rose.

The scouts set off ahead to seek the best way forward through the dense bush, hacking their way through the small trees of the Lowveld to allow the wagons to move, so it was slow, backbreaking toil. They were careful to keep their rifles with them all the time, in case they were attacked by marauding kaffirs or wild animals. The name 'kaffir' came from 'Kafir', the Arab word for unbeliever. The Arab slavers had thus dubbed the natives (and any other race for that matter) who did not worship Allah. The natives had their own spirit world and weren't interested in Allah.

Slowly, the remaining pioneers covered the hundreds of miles until they reached Fort Victoria. Some chose to take their chance of survival along the way when they reached open ground that looked suitable for farming. They had brought packets of seed and sacks of maize, some for grinding into meal, some to plant. Also, herded along with the cavalcade, they tried to bring a few cattle, sheep and poultry, most of which perished on the way, eaten by lions or leopards, or died of rinderpest, tick fever and the unknown tsetse fly bite that caused sleeping sickness.

Mostly, they were Dutchmen on their own but there were one or two with wives and families. The Dutch Boers had done this before in the Cape, as they trekked up north to reach new land. They knew how to avert disaster and they were the bravest of the group, lucky to survive at all.

The main contingent of British South African Police (BSAP) and troops had advanced some three hundred miles north of Fort Victoria and settled in an extensive, swampy plain in the highlands of Mashonaland. The Union Jack was raised in this place. They named it Fort Salisbury. In honour of Cecil Rhodes, the whole of Monomotapa was renamed Rhodesia.

In 1890, in England, Robert Mason Jnr started his ten years of schooling.

By 1898, Salisbury had been mapped out into a central business area with industries already springing up in the south and, west of that, an extensive satellite township was reserved for the native workers flocking in from the bush. There was the white residential area surrounding and spreading north, east and west.

The town planners had a quaint way of dealing with accommodating the growing numbers of mixed race people who called themselves "coloureds". With British reserve at the fore, the new government cordoned off an area just beyond the railway line in front of the industrial area and the native township, creating a colour grading, because the Indians and other designated "non-white" races were lumped together there. The British colonialists believed very firmly in segregation.

In no time, brickworks were firing thousands of bricks, a cement works was established, lime quarries were dug, and corrugated iron was imported so the buildings were mainly brick under iron. Beautiful red tiles were soon to be roofing the government buildings and banks. There was plenty of work for the thousands of black people drifting in from the bush, and Salisbury mushroomed rapidly.

The Municipality had a large town planning section carefully mapping out the future streets and quarter acre plots, fanning out in every direction. They could hardly keep up with the wave of colonists wishing to purchase business, industrial and home sites.

Government offices were built. One of the main sections dealt with Native Affairs and anyone British who had worked in India with tribesmen was welcomed. Those employed in the Native Department had to be trained to work with the local tribespeople and learn their languages and their ways. The main languages were Chishona in Mashonaland and Sindebele in Matabeleland where Lobengula's Matabele were still restive and troublesome.

Pioneers under attack in Matabeleland

THE FORMIDABLE
MATABELE
WARRIOR

Sketch of Bert as a BSAP officer

The whole country was being divided and planned. It was an enormous undertaking, deciding how to apportion land fairly, separating large sections in every province into farmland, government forest area and protected indigenous sections which encompassed approximately forty per cent of the land, as much of it as possible where the natives were already settled.

The indigenous sections became known as the Tribal Trust Lands and by law only the natives could live there. No "European" person could purchase or develop any part of this protected land or occupy it. Likewise, the rest of the land could not be purchased or settled on by the native tribes. Those already settled there were moved to the closest tribal trust land. This caused considerable unrest, as could be expected. Finally, the natives revolted, and extra British South African Police (BSAP) forces were brought in to quell the unrest.

At the turn of the century, Rhodesia was a dangerous country to settle in. South Africa was equally dangerous as the two main white groups were fighting and killing each other in the Boer war. Britain sent out troops to support and protect the English settlers and the Dutch farmers took to the bush with their guns and horses. They had the element of surprise and defeated the British in many battles with little loss of life as they melted into the surrounding bushland. This was mainly because they wore khaki clothes, the colour of the sand and dry veldt. The British troops wore red uniforms and white helmets and were targeted from miles away.

In 1899, Robert Mason left school and joined his father's painting and decorating business. He disliked the work and applied to the British South Africa Company that was on a recruitment drive for the BSA Police. They wanted men like him who were skilled with guns and were able to ride horses to join the mounted police and emigrate to South Africa. Unfortunately for Bert, they refused him and said he should apply again when he was twenty. He was too young.

In Durban, in 1899, Lillian Plowright gave birth to a baby girl, a beautiful, auburn haired sister for Bertie and they called her Doreen Lillian, shortened to Dora.

little Dora about
aged 2 years.
Bertie 5 y 9 months

They were still living in troubled times. One morning, the doorbell rang, and Lillian went to open the front door. There stood her sister, Betty. "Here! Take the child!" said her sister, thrusting her baby into Lillian's arms. Then she fainted on the wooden veranda.

This wasn't surprising, because once she had been revived and Lillian had got over the shock, it turned out that she had travelled all the way from Kimberly by train, without any food for two days and with a full set of silver cutlery hidden in her corsets round her midriff. Once she had relieved herself of these, fed and settled baby Maurice, she told her story over a much-needed luncheon.

The fighting had intensified near Kimberley and it was decided that the women and children, both English and Afrikaans, were to be evacuated by train immediately. Betty strapped her precious silver cutlery under her corsets, grabbed a loaf of bread, some napkins, baby bottles and a tin of condensed milk for Maurice, wrapped him in his shawl and was taken to the station just in time to board before it left.

She was horrified to find that a huge, belligerent Afrikaans woman with her six small children were in the same compartment. At least, the children behaved well but their mother sat opposite Betty glowering at her and not speaking. After some time, the train stopped. Maurice needed a bottle and Betty had to get out of the carriage carrying Maurice and walk down to the engine to beg for some hot water. The engine driver filled the bottles for her which was a relief.

Climbing back, she went into the carriage to open the condensed milk tin and found that the Dutch woman had stolen it and the loaf of bread. She had no food for her children. Betty told

Lillian dramatically "I said to her - you can keep the bread for your children, but I beg you to give me back the condensed milk for my baby." This the woman had the grace to do.

The train had been delayed on the line because there was fighting ahead but finally they were off again, arriving in Durban the next morning, so Betty was exhausted and weary. Her husband, Jack Kimberley would be following when he could, and Betty asked whether Lillian and Wharton could put them up until they could get established.

Lilian and Wharton had just built a complete unit up next to the garage. This comprised two rooms, a kitchen, bathroom and toilet. They were going to house two servants there so that they would be on hand early and not have to commute from the township and arrive at work at about ten in the morning. They now had a houseful, the three bedrooms being a nursery for Dora, a small room for Bertie and a double room for themselves, so they offered the new quarters to the Kimberleys.

This was received with gratitude. Some months later, Jack managed to sell his property in Kimberly and they bought a house in Durban and moved away. Unfortunately, by then they had decided that it had been an insult for the Plowrights to give them servants quarters to live in. They could have put Bertie in the nursery with Dora and given them the third bedroom. They didn't speak to them again for eighteen years!

This unfortunate impasse only ended when Maurice died in France just before Armistice day in World War One. It was then that Lillian felt such compassion for her sister's loss of her only child that she went to see her, and the rift was repaired.

Dora started in kindergarten school and began her first

piano lessons. She then went to the Durban Ladies College and moved into Standard One. There, she met another little girl called Dolly Rippon and they became close friends. They remained best friends for most of their lives.

Back in England in 1905, Bert was finally accepted into the British South African Police and he emigrated and set foot in Rhodesia.

There, in 1908, Bert Mason married and by the end of the year, he had a son. They named him Kenneth but called him Paddy. Three years later, another son was born, named Richard. They called him Dick.

In 1911, Bert decided to buy his way out of the Police Force because he had been offered a position of Location Superintendent. The salary was much higher and included a free house with stables, set on two acres near the Police Commissioner's house. He was tired of living in the police married quarters and he wanted to get himself a horse. A friend of his had shot a baboon in his mealie fields and clinging to its dead mother was a small baby. He was going to have it put down, but Bert decided to rescue it.

The family moved into the house and Bert bought a horse. The little baboon was quaint and clinging but, as it quickly grew, it became too dangerous and had to be chained to a pole at the back of the house. Bert saw to it, that the chain was long, and the pole was high, with a platform on top. It was set in concrete near a massive gum tree, and the baboon, which he named Ardonnis, could shin up the pole and jump over to one of the branches. Under the tree he had a small shed.

His chain was attached to a thick leather belt that was firmly strapped round his body, just above his back legs.

The boys were not allowed to go into the enclosure fencing Ardonnis away from the rest of the property. They had teased him, and he had started to bite. In no time, his eye teeth were about an inch long and he was dangerous. Bert's wife was afraid of him and hated him. She demanded that Bert got rid of him or she would leave. This wasn't the only matter causing a rift between her and Bert. Finally, Ardonnis managed to undo his chain and jump over the fence, threatening the children in the front garden. She did no more but gather up her two boys, pack their belongings and leave. She moved to Bulawayo where her family lived and sued for a divorce.

In 1914, the divorce was granted. Bert stayed in the house. He had a horse called Dick and his baboon, Ardonnis, three cats, two dogs and a sow called Ermentrude. There was also a fowl run with several Rhode Island Reds supplying him with his fresh breakfast eggs every day. He missed the boys but enjoyed being footloose and fancy free. The name Ardonnis was Dutch for baboon, and it amused Bert to call him that. Nothing could be less like the beautiful god, Adonis, than his baboon.

The Palace theatre provided entertainment and he joined the Salisbury Club and the Royal Salisbury Golf Club. He knew many of the farmers in the district and was often invited to spend a weekend with one of them, so his life was pleasant. All he needed was a motorcar. He was thinking of buying a Model T Ford.

In 1916, Dora finished her schooling. She had also passed her piano teacher's examination and was accepted at the Royal Academy in London for further piano study. Bertie was going to Guy's Hospital as an intern, so Lillian decided to sail over to England and rent a house in Sydenham, London so that Dora would have a home to live in. Wharton Plowright was wealthy enough to afford this. He made the money and Lillian spent it. Several times in the past Lillian had sailed over to England and taken the children to Paignton in Devon for a holiday. Wharton preferred to stay in Durban.

Dora had a wonderful time in London. Bertie used to bring his intern friends to the house to hear her play and sing and he loved her to unpin her hair and let them see it. She had never cut it and it was a thick, rippling mass of shiny auburn, so long that she could sit on it. Usually, it was plaited and hung in a thick plait with a bow near the end. She had just been allowed to pile it up on her head in the Edwardian style the women wore. It was very bulky and heavy done that way.

Left and bottom left - Dora in teen years at the London Royal Academy

MUSICAL COMEDY COMPANY.
3. Jim Martin
(Bert Beswick).
4. Joy Carter.
(Miss Doreen Page, Miss Billie Browne's under study).
Photo for "S.A. Pictorial," by African Film Productions, Ltd.

Above: Dora as Doreen Page playing Miss Joy in the play "Oh Joy" with which she travelled to Rhodesia in 1921

One day, she was passing a couturier in Oxford Street and decided on impulse, to go in and have her hair shingled in the latest fashion. Out she went with a bag containing the hair, neatly bound at the top as the hairdresser said she may want to sell it. They thought it was worth a lot of money. Lillian was shocked, but she couldn't help admitting that Dora looked beautiful. Bertie took one look and wouldn't speak to her for a week! Only when his friends thought it was stunning did he grudgingly agree with them.

Bertie and his friends took her everywhere with them, to the Galleries, where they whipped off the fig leaves hung on the penises of the statues and waited to see the effect on old ladies. She went with them to all the Musicals in London. At the end of the year, she was awarded a bronze medal at the Academy.

Then the blow fell. Wharton wrote to say he could no longer afford to keep them all in London. He said that Bertie must continue at Guys, but Dora and her mother must not renew the lease. They would have to return home. Dora was devastated but she realized it was inevitable.

The moment she came in the door, Wharton was appalled. What had happened to the child he had kissed goodbye a year ago? Was this a Jezebel he had been nurturing?

To be fair to him, he had not spent the past two years in London. In Durban, he didn't mix with the fashionable city crowd. His club interested him and then he was off home alone. He enjoyed one hobby and that was woodwork. He spent hours creating miniature furniture for dolls houses out of wooden cigar boxes, making them perfect. When she was six, he had made Dora a beautiful little bedroom set of a bed, dressing table, chest of drawers and a wardrobe standing about eighteen inches high. The dressing table had a real mirror and there was one in the door of the wardrobe as well.

But in 1918, when she first returned, she was miserable and missing the Academy and Bertie and London. Dora and her father began to drift apart immediately. If she went out, dressed in her modern, short dresses, with the heavy black eye makeup of the fashionable London society which he had never seen, he was suspicious. Once, he stopped her at the front door and insisted that her pupils were distended. What, he demanded, had she been putting in them? Get back in the bedroom immediately and wipe all that off her face if she wanted to remain in his house any longer! She didn't! So, she immediately moved away, and he said she wasn't to darken his doorstep again. Poor Lillian had no chance to say a word.

Dora, who preferred to be called Doreen, joined the nursing service in the terrible Spanish Flu epidemic sweeping the world. It had reached Natal and people were dying in horrifying numbers worldwide. For such a young girl, this was a brave and dangerous step which was deeply appreciated. They were desperate for assistance but, as soon as the situation was brought under control, they wanted her to leave. In gratitude for risking her life, she received a little gold medal.

Dora had contacted friends in Johannesburg who arranged an interview for her with O.P. Wheeler himself, at His Majesty's Theatre. He saw real talent when she stepped on the stage and her future was mapped out there and then. Dora joined Wheeler's Company as Doreen Page, her stage name.

She joined the theatre company to see a bit of the world. They were going on tour to the new country of Rhodesia which seemed exciting. Dora fitted a good deal into her first twenty-one years of life. She spent 18 months in London, nursed in 1919 during the great 'flu epidemic and then, there she was in 1920, suddenly on her travels, a leading lady in musical comedy.

Here she was, now, in the Palace Theatre in Salisbury, in the musical "Oh Joy". She had her medal from the Royal Academy of Music and another for nursing; school certificates for advanced years of study which must have taken her to at least seventeen. She was a totally brilliant pianist, a performer, not a teacher for which she hadn't the patience, and she had a beautiful, trained voice.

There she was, in darkest Africa, where the darkest people were milling around in the bush surrounding Salisbury, the new settlement, rapidly growing and expanding in all directions, finally being pronounced the Capital of Southern Rhodesia. The formerly savage natives were swarming into the area, drawn to the bright lights and affluence described by any of their brethren who had had the good fortune to be employed in some menial capacity there. A satellite township called Harare was developing south of the planned industrial area. This was for the native workers, and orderly two roomed houses were being built in rows by the Government. They were each fenced and had small gardens. There were also long rows of single rooms with ablution blocks for single men.

These lucky souls returned to their huts and families in the bush bearing riches and bragging about their superior status and knowledge of the world of the 'murungu' – the white man. Riches included beads, salt, sugar and lengths of vivid, printed cotton cloth to adorn their women. Children normally ran bare, with a little string round their necks on which was a charm against the evil one. Other men set off to make their fortunes like their brothers in the great white man's city, and they were warned that the first thing they had to do was obtain a 'situpa', a sort of passport, from the Native Commissioner and then see the Location Superintendent – the white man in charge of all natives - as there was a curfew on all natives roaming about the city. They had to be in Harare by nightfall. The white man's law and order was being enforced totally from the time of the rebellion.

All Africans had been warned to be in the location by six p.m. and the Location Super was Bert. There he was, leaving his office at the end of the day, off to put on his evening suit and go to the new Palace Theatre to see the musical comedy "Oh Joy". There was an announcement before the curtain went up that the part of Joy Carter would be played by the understudy, Miss Doreen Page.

What vision should he see up there on stage but Dora, looking alluring and singing divinely. The one who swept her off her feet was a different handsome hero to the actor on stage: one Robert James Barber Mason.

Polly

Bert

He appeared at the stage door and made sure he was the first attractive male there for her to meet. Attractive he was indeed, with his square set frame and twinkling blue eyes; a man tall, dark, handsome and charming.

Robert Mason was supporting two young sons and an ex-wife, but he wasn't going to let this prize out of his sight! He loved her passionately for the rest of his short life and filled her life with all the style and comfort he possibly could. They were married for nineteen years, until his death.

How he managed to afford the style is anyone's guess. Dora, set on a pedestal, didn't have to lift a finger. She decorated his existence and he, hers! On a good but modest salary, Robert Mason went cheerfully into debt all round, like any lord of the manor. All Rhodesians did! Tradesmen didn't dare suggest they paid their bills until they felt like it! There'd be one hell of a row if they did and the shop keepers needed all the trade they could hang on to, so they waited. It was such a small community.

He was already thirty-seven when she first set eyes on him, tall, thickset and virile, with blue, blue eyes that crinkled up with laughter, black hair and an attractive small cleft in his chin. He was charming and popular, and she was duly bowled over. It was love at first sight.

She was only twenty-one, slim and beautiful, with green eyes and that mass of thick, auburn hair, so he was bowled over too! They married as soon as the banns were read. Doreen Page, as she was called in the theatre, was a distinct catch. There was no woman in Rhodesia who could hold a candle to her.

Bert told Dora about his past marriage and divorce and

she immediately went to see if she could make friends with Ardonnis. He eyed her standing there with Bert and decided that he had better respect this female who seemed to belong to his master. Dora held out two sugar lumps and Ardonnis took them. He was as tall as Dora when he stood up on his legs instead of loping along on all fours using the knuckles of his hands. He had a huge jaw with massive teeth. Bert would control him when he managed to loosen his chain and wander off. He would point his rifle at the truant ape and say 'Back! Ardonnis!' and Ardonnis would rush back to his perch and try to do up the chain, very obligingly.

Bert and Dora each had a horse and in the early morning, passed Ardonnis on the way to the stables to mount up for a ride. Dora wore jodhpurs and a beautiful silk shirt and in the top pocket she put two sugar lumps, feeding two to Ardonnis on the way and taking some to the horses. One day, she forgot Ardonnis and she fed the horses first. There was a great performance of jumping up and down from the baboon and loud barks and chattering. She went back so he could put his huge hairy hand in her pocket and get them, as he loved to do. In a blind rage, Ardonnis tore her shirt literally off her back. Luckily for him, he carefully didn't injure her. He knew this was his owner's woman!

He was dangerous. He was a man's ape, not a woman's and he was going to show her what a male does if a female misbehaves – ape style. They can cuff and bite their nearest and dearest quite regularly and they beat their children. He controlled himself with Dora and she was lucky. A baboon has almost human intelligence in many ways. They have a doglike look, with a long, protruding nose, and a hairy face; but the eyes are cunning and bright. They are clever and mischievous, also a little erratic, lunatic and feral.

Their minds do not stretch to recalling, when they run through a field of maize, that they have an armful of cobs and should get going with their booty. They continue stripping cobs and dropping the ones already under their arms, thus being an animal that is shot on sight by the farmers. In the hills and mountains round Umtali, amongst the huge granite rocks many leopards and baboons roved. The baboons were the main food source of the leopards and kept careful watch, but they often had to fight for their lives and lose. A leopard is an enormous, powerful beast.

In 1922, Dora was feeling unwell and queasy, so she went to the doctor who told her she was pregnant. Both Bert and she were delighted. As she began to show, Bert started to call her Polly after a cartoon in the newspaper about Polly Oolie and the bump. That became Bert's nickname for her. He immediately advertised for a companion help and along came a motherly old Englishwoman called Miss Hughes. They hoped for a girl and that is what they had. In March,1923, a beautiful, fair haired baby girl arrived, and they named her Patricia Yolande Nairn. They called her Pattie. The problem was, she couldn't be left outside in her pram in case Ardonnis got free, so the furthest they could put her was out on the veranda.

Polly invited some of her friends to see the new baby and she and Hughie baked cakes and made sandwiches and scones. The table was set under a Jacaranda tree in the front garden with a dozen garden chairs set in the shade. Just as Hughie was pouring the tea, around the corner sauntered Ardonnis, up on his haunches with teeth bared. All the women screamed and ran inside. Ardonnis sat himself at the table and proceeded to demolish the cake and scones, upsetting the milk and tea all over everything. Polly fetched the rifle and went out, pointing it at him.

"Back, Ardonnis, back!" she ordered. Ardonnis just stared at her and went on with his feast. "Back! Back Ardonnis!" said Polly more loudly. She approached, waving the gun in front of her. Ardonnis jumped off the table and stood high on his hind legs. He bared his teeth and ran at her and she turned tail and just beat him to the front veranda door.

Obviously, he wasn't taking orders from a chit of a girl like her. The garden piccanin had to run to the office with a note and Bert hurried back to deal with his pet. Bert knew that he would have to remove Ardonnis. He couldn't bear to have him destroyed and he knew the baboon would pine if he went to a zoo. He couldn't be released in the bush because he had been in captivity for so long.

When Pattie was three months old, they planned to travel down to Durban and show her to her grandparents. Bert asked a friend of his to come over each day to feed the animals and they set off in his Model T, taking Hughie with them to see to the baby in her wicker basket on the back seat. This was before seat belts were fitted but the top speeds were minimal and safe without them. They arranged for a neighbour to check on the animals each day.

Everything went well at the house until early one morning Ardonnis undid his chain. He sensed that Bert was not there, so he decided to go and find him. The servants had not yet come to work so Ardonnis sauntered down the road and ended up in the Police Commissioner's garden. He was looking in his mirror shaving, when to his horror, a huge baboon peered over his shoulder.

Not for one moment did the Commissioner think this was his friend's pet. He picked up his revolver, turned and shot Ardonnis point blank between the eyes. He did not know it was Ardonnis and thought it was a wild animal. Perhaps it was the best thing that could have happened because Ardonnis was gone before he realized what had happened. Once the Commissioner found the baboon was his friend's pet, he had a deep grave dug beside the gum tree and Bert's servants buried him where he had been most happy.

It was a week before Bert and Dora returned. They were both sad about Ardonnis but relieved as well that he wouldn't be around when little Pattie was in her pram outside or toddling about the garden. Bert carved his name on the trunk of his tree. The next animals to depart were the sows. They returned one afternoon from a visit to find Ermentrude happily sleeping on their bed. There was a similar fear that the friendly sows might harm Pattie in some way, knowing that pigs often ate their young.

The fowls, too, had their moments. One large Rhode Island hen insisted on laying her eggs on the piano. No matter what they did, sooner or later she would creep in, finding a window too widely open or a door ajar.

The city was expanding in all directions and Bert had to move the horses further out of the built-up area surrounding him. Finally, Bert decided to move to Penhalonga village in the beautiful Eastern Districts, with the town of Umtali ten miles away over the Christmas Pass.

TWO

REZENDE MINE - PENHALONGA

With all his experience in the Police and in running the Location, Bert had joined the staff of Lonrho Mining and Land Co. as a Compound Manager, in charge of the welfare of about five hundred native mine workers and the black servants, all housed in a village known as the compound.

In the early years of colonial rule, the natives were not housed in a 'kia' or cottage at the back of the main house. They had to obey the curfew and be in the compound by six p.m. and they all carried a 'situpa', an identification certificate that the police demanded to see if they were found in the urban areas any later than that.

As the towns and cities grew, the rules were altered, and the blocks were planned with a lane running down behind the properties. Houses had to be built a minimum of thirty feet from the front fence and a 'kia' built for servants set on the back boundary, in one corner with its own amenities.

Also, on the back boundary, at the other end, well away from the kia, was an outside lavatory for the white dwellers in the house. These had a large bucket covered with a wooden box seat with a hole in it, set in a little hut called a P.K. That was an abbreviation of 'Piccanini Kia', in English 'Little Room'.

The mine houses had no toilets for the servants and they had to go in the bush.

Bert's salary was higher on the mine and with it came a free house, electricity and water. Bert decided to oversee the humane slaughter of cattle for the mine butchery and stunned the animals himself to make sure the job was done efficiently and painlessly. For that, he had free meat and could choose his own cuts.

Bert loved huge Sirloin roasts, fillet steak, fresh liver, tongue and kidneys, oxtail, lamb and mutton, but never pork, except smoked bacon. Veal, they were averse to. Polly wouldn't eat offal, except in steak and kidney pudding and even then, she delicately picked out the kidney and left it on the side of the plate.

Penhalonga was in the Eastern Districts, set in a beautiful valley with mountains around three sides. A deep, swiftly running stream ran through it and the village boasted a hotel, a couple of small shops run by Greek families, a school and a swimming pool. It was a small, single roomed, junior school and all the mine houses clustered round this centre.

The mine manager, the compound manager and the doctor's houses were up a side hill in large grounds. The rest of the staff had smaller establishments in smaller gardens further down. The miners were housed in the lower end of the village. Even on a mine, there was a pecking order.

The native compound was situated out of sight, over the hill where the mine shaft and buildings stood. Bert had an office at the back of the main offices, near the compound and he rode his horse to work, down over the bridge and up over the hill. He also took his large revolver and a sjambok, as it was called - a hippo hide whip with a handle, thick and solid for about two feet, then tapering to a point so that it was flexible. This was in case he was attacked by any unruly natives he had to control. He was the only white man around in the compound and the workers were unpredictable.

Four decades before, most of them had been living in the bush and had never seen a white man. Some of them had drifted into the Missions and were astonished to see for the first time a white skinned human looking like their albinos – native children that were born devoid of dark pigment and usually smothered at birth. It was considered a work of the wicked spirit and the mother could be deemed to be a witch and stoned to death or burnt alive.

The native people had a simple agricultural culture and were superstitious. In their comfortable state of natural plenty, an ideal climate, endless vistas of virgin soil, an abundance of wild animals for food and coverings, they didn't have any need to use their brains. But, once they saw the European standard of living, they were bedazzled, envious and needy. They wanted to leap out of their iron-age existence and into the European twentieth century and only vaguely sensed their current inability and ignorance.

They came from kraals in the bush and had no knowledge of schooling. They lived in huts of poles and mud with thatched roofing, no windows or doors and sat and slept on the earth floors, cooking meal and meat in iron pots balanced over a wood fire. The men wore little more than a moochi, an animal skin pouch covering their genitals, and the women wore cloth wound round their bodies, usually waist high. The material and the iron pots were recent imports bartered from travelling carpet baggers on donkeys, wandering through bush hoping to barter gold and meat for the pot in exchange for cheap goods.

The natives carted heavy wood and pots of water from the river on the heads of the women or a rudimentary sleigh of wood poles held together with strips of bark to a cross piece on the necks of cattle and dragged behind the beasts of burden because they had not so far, invented a wheel. This caused heavy erosion of the soil in some places. They also spoke different tribal languages because they had no alphabet or written language.

The black witchdoctors, 'N'gangas', roamed about terrifying the villagers and 'smelling out' culprits when asked to do so. This entailed a gathering of everyone there at a ceremony. Kaffir beer would be brewed and an animal slaughtered, so all would be full of party spirit as the evening wore on. There'd be drum beating and cavorting with the witch doctor ending up in the middle of the circle. They would sit and watch him perform his choice of ceremony, for which, by the way, he had charged a goodly amount, paid in salt, chickens and other livestock, because they used a barter system.

After much evoking of invisible spirits, incantations, throwing of bones and sometimes a frothing at the mouth, a fit and a trance, a long, bony finger would be pointed at someone quaking in the crowd. He could put the fear of the devil into them. If some poor, innocent creature was 'smelled out' as having been the cause of another's death or some disaster such as drought, there'd be a banishment or even a killing.

Bert saw to it that these evil creatures were forbidden in

the compound. Still the workers came to him asking for leave of absence. The usual excuse was "My father is dead. I want to go home."

House servants were the same. It was no use stopping them because they would just disappear and return a few days later apologizing because they just had to go. Sometimes they were away for a long time and would suddenly turn up again. Sometimes, they just didn't return.

Dr. Alexander was employed by the mine to examine them for TB, VD any other diseases they might have but they didn't trust the white man's doctor or believe him as implicitly as the witchdoctor. There were many good witches who gathered herbs and roots in the bush and some of their remedies worked. On the other hand, some of these remedies killed and others were placebos. If an N'ganga put a spell on an African and told him he was going to die, he died.

Polly Mason soon made an impression in the village because she was so talented. The Penhalonga hotel boasted a large hall with a sprung dance floor and a stage. She began producing plays, concerts and recitals there, to full houses. People flocked to Penhalonga from Umtali and all the surrounding farms to hear her and attend the theatrical performances.

Bert spent much of his time at weekends prospecting and staking claims up in the surrounding hills when he struck a reef. He sold one claim he called the Gog and Magog to Lonrho for the princely sum of five hundred pounds, the equivalent of two year's salary. The claim was named after the hills near Cambridge where he was born.

This enabled him to purchase an Armstrong Siddeley motorcar, a very up market vehicle indeed, with real leather upholstery and luxurious fittings. It was the closest he could get to a Rolls Royce, with beautiful woodwork inside, little tables that pulled out behind the back seats and a Wilson gearbox. Just a small lever on the steering column could be set in any gear and one press on the clutch pedal changed the gears automatically. That luxury car gave him a certain cachet, making him feel as though he was living in the style he aimed for, which was rather lordly.

He was an unusual man indeed, demanding a high standard of living. This was the only family in Penhalonga that had companion helps and horses and an army of servants, at least half a dozen. Who wants to be a millionaire? Well! He did! He was determined to live like a lord, at any rate, even if it was mostly on tick! Most Rhodesians didn't pay their bills until they felt like it and woe betide anyone who sent them a demand.

Many years later, a grandchild he never saw, Christopher James Strever was determined to live beyond his means. Nothing less than matched BMW's for himself and his wife, a six-million-rand house, a racing yacht and an aeroplane satisfied Rose's son Christopher.

In 1926, Polly was pregnant again. Suffering the full heat of midsummer, three days after Christmas, she gave birth to a second daughter, this time a black-haired baby with rosy cheeks, long eyelashes and big blue eyes. They named her Rosemary Nairn.

Pattie was then three and a half and she immediately acted like a maiden aunt, responsible for the good behavior of this child. Hughie had retired and gone back to England. Pattie missed her beloved Hughie. Perhaps she died and that was the kindest way Polly could think of explaining her absence to Pattie. Irene Armitage was the new companion help by then.

They had scanned the local and South African papers for a replacement for Hughie. "There's something about this one. She seems a bit desperate, I think we should answer her," said Polly. There arrived by train from Johannesburg, Irene Armitage, a straight-laced Yorkshire woman in her late twenties. Her story was shocking. She was engaged to be married to a man in England just before he emigrated to South Africa.

Once he was settled there, she was to sail to Capetown and take the train to Johannesburg. They were to be married as soon as she arrived there. She left her parents and the vicarage that was her home, paid almost all she had for the fares and when she arrived, her fiancée booked them into a hotel for the weekend. On Monday morning he disappeared without trace. He had jilted her.

Left in a strange country, without any contacts and very little money left, she didn't have the means to return to England. She used what she had to pay the hotel bill and try to obtain work without success. Nobody else had answered her adverts. She was desperate and almost on the point of taking her life when Bert's letter arrived, enclosing the money for her train journey to Rhodesia.

She was a very plain, thin little woman but a perfect replacement for Hughie.

Both Hughie and Irene were there when Polly gave birth to her second baby. They called her Rosemary Nairn and once Polly was up, she brought the baby out to show her to the staff. Nest, cook, looked down at her and asked about her name. "It's Rosemary", said Polly. Nest smiled "Hello, Miss

Gooseberry". They all laughed. She had big blue eyes and long, thick eyelashes and Bert gave her many nicknames like Gogs and Gog's Roses and Rose Gogs. There was a popular song at that time "Where did you get those gogs? Where did you get those eyes?".

After that, whenever she did something naughty, Nest continued to call her Piccanini missus Gooseberry.

Ah! Ah! Miss Gooseberry!
What you do!

When Rose was small, she was sure she had known Hughie. There was a shadowy memory of an old lady in a long black dress carrying a little reticule in which was a magic bottle. It was a dark green one with a silver top. Open it, and you could take a tiny sniff – not too much! It contained smelling salts and old Hughie carried it everywhere.

This bottle was still in Polly's dressing table drawer. The other article remaining in the house was a little black embroidered silk dressing table runner covered in shiny silk flowers and birds, smelling strongly of moth balls. And so, an old Victorian lady left her stamp on two children.

They went for a picnic one day and Bert parked the car off the road on a hillside near the quarry. They left Rose, aged 11 months, sitting on the companion help's lap in the front seat of the car, while Bert, Polly and Pattie found a good picnic spot. Rose leaned forward and tried to grab the steering wheel and Sheila McNish held her back. Soon, she found that she could touch the hand brake with her foot and kick it. It suddenly snapped forward and the car began to move down the hill, gathering speed. Sheila screamed, and Bert turned and ran after it shouting, "Put the brake on!"

Sheila shouted back "I can't reach it. Should I throw the baby out?"

"No!" Shouted Bert, running as fast as he could to reach the car before it went over the edge. Rose could just recall bouncing up and down as the car hit rocks and everyone screaming. Suddenly, there was a mighty jolt and the car slewed round and stopped, right on the edge of the drop. The car had hit a large rock and the crank shaft had broken.

Soon, Polly was back in her stride, leaving the children in

the care of Irene and casting another play in the hotel hall. A tall Jewish man who looked a bit like Noel Coward was auditioning and Polly found him perfect for the leading man.

He was one of a large, loud and boisterous family of Jewish refugees from Europe with almost no money and no property that had turned up suddenly in Penhalonga looking for a place to settle. There was Momma and her two daughters, Sarah and Rachel and six sons, Mick, Benny, Hiam, Maurice and Jack. The mine manager had allowed two of the brothers to set up a small, corrugated iron store near the compound. It was full of cheap merchandise that they sold to the natives, giving them credit on the understanding that the bill would be covered by an advance drawing on their weekly wage.

Feeling sorry for them, Bert invited the two of them to dinner and they arrived, together with Momma, their two sisters and three more brothers. Polly disappeared as soon as she could to tell Nest and sort out plenty of extra vegetables and places at the table. The children were to eat early and go to bed.

In the sitting room, the drinks were going down rapidly, and all the brothers were shouting at each other and begging Momma to decide who was right. Polly had to play for them and Esther had to sing. Bert had to play too, they demanded to hear what he could play so he played "Do ye Ken John Peel" and sang it too, in C major, which made it easy.

The applause was deafening, and Polly had to play again. They wanted Rachmaninov. They were silent and listened with rapt faces and appreciation, questioning her afterwards about the Royal Academy and O.P. Wheeler. Like all Jews, they were very interesting and clever. Benny was a lawyer and ended up in parliament as Minister of Law. The sisters were both trained nurses working in Umtali Hospital.

Of course, feeling so welcome, they often descended on Polly and Bert in a wave of lively, shouting and gesticulating humanity. Momma was their star and they referred to Momma for approval about everything they said or did. They all talked at once and everything was chaotic when they arrived at the house.

They would be invited for tea and they always arrived early. Then they stayed on for sundowners and Polly slipped away to tell the cook, Nest, to prepare the extra. They made sure they stayed until they were asked for dinner and Bert and Polly didn't mind. They were so poor then, that it was a life saver. Also, they lifted everyone's spirits, being so intelligent, amusing, and artistic. Rachel begged to visit occasionally on her own, so she could practice her songs with Polly accompanying her.

At these times, the garden piccanin was ordered to take Peggy, the Airedale bitch, for a long walk on her lead. This was because Rachel only had to open her mouth and start singing and Peggy would raise her eyes to the heavens and let out loud, mournful howls outside the window. There was something about Rachel's voice that set Peggy off into a compulsory duet.

It was Rosemary, now aged four, who noticed a likeness of features suddenly when she was staring at the one brother's long curved nose. She stood beside his chair and suddenly burst out "We've got a goose called Hi...."

Stopped in her tracks by her mother's frantic order not to talk when the grownups are talking and go outside and play, she stumped off feeling frustrated. Why had mummy butted in and stopped her telling this man something she was sure he'd be interested to know? It wasn't fair!

In no time, the family had saved enough to buy a piece of farmland and were building a ranch house big enough for all of them. They made their own bricks and toiled with a few native labourers planting maize and tobacco. Eventually, they were multimillionaires, buying up more and more surrounding farms until they had one of the biggest ranches in the country.

The only one who ever married was the youngest. He fell from grace when he married a Christian girl and they had two sons. He had moved away from the ranch and bought his own farm and the family didn't have much to do with him. Three of them ended up running the estate, finally employing hundreds of black workers.

The native miners and the house servants lived in the compound, the servants setting out for work at five a.m. to get their employer's yards swept, light the wood stoves, start cooking breakfast and boiling water for early morning tea. They stoked the Rhodesian Boilers with wood and got it burning fiercely so there was hot water for the bathrooms.

Set at the back of the house behind the bathroom, the Rhodesian Boiler was an open brick structure, with iron bars set in half way up to hold the logs, and a forty-four-gallon drum on its side, securely balanced on top. The main water pipe filled it at the top and the boiling water was piped out to the bathroom from a tap welded on at the base of the drum. This was a very successful, economical system used on all the farms and mines because wood was plentiful and free. Rhodesia was a land of trees growing on the richly fertile plains with mountains of solid, towering granite rocks.

Nest and one "houseboy" started work at five thirty a.m. in the outdoors kitchen preparing trays, making porridge and setting the table in the dining room for breakfast. The tea tray had to be at the bedroom door at six a.m. Bert and Polly were dressed and out exercising their horses on the golf course by five, returning at six for early morning tea. Bert kept his horse saddled and after tea he took his gun and sjambok and went off to the office to see that all was well in the compound, returning for breakfast at eight.

Polly went back to her room and relaxed on the bed with her tea tray and her two children. They had an hour with her before they were washed and dressed for breakfast by Irene and the African nanny, Phoebe. At eight, they sat at the dining table for breakfast, Rose in a high chair until she could see over the top of the table. They always had a full English breakfast.

Cook brought a large tray holding a bowl of porridge, a jug of milk and a bowl of sugar which he set in front of Bert who sat the head of the table with Polly on his left, dishing it out into bowls. Then came a large plate of fried eggs and bacon and usually liver or kidney which Bert served out, asking each child what they wanted. Even Rosemary, aged three and perched on a cushion so she could see over the table top, was asked politely what she would like.

There was a toast rack on the table piled with hot toast with more to follow when the plates were cleared, and the waiter had removed them. Sometimes they had kippers or kedgeree, which they loved.

A large tray of tea came next and more toast. This they ate with butter and marmalade, sweet for the children and bitter for the adults. After that, children had to ask to be excused before they could rush out and play in the garden.

First, they had to visit the bathroom, clean their teeth and wash their hands. The children, supervised by their black nanny, played outside until morning tea time as the house boys were in the house sweeping, polishing and making beds. The children were not allowed to talk to the servants, only to Nest and their nanny. The bedroom boys and the gardeners were ordered not to talk to them.

Polly, meanwhile, was supervising the servants, cutting and arranging bowls and vases of flowers which filled the sitting and dining rooms and scented the whole house. Although Nest could make a plain cake, Polly showed him how to make several different cakes and scones and she ordered provisions and decided what Nest must prepare for lunch and dinner. He could make cottage pie and roasts without supervision, but Polly made the special dishes and cakes herself.

The children were called in for morning tea which was usually put on the veranda or in the garden under a shady tree. There would be scones and little cakes, cucumber sandwiches and milky, sweet tea and then they could play again, but only on the veranda because the sun was almost overhead. They had to wear their wide brimmed hats outside, even in the winter.

Bert returned for lunch at one and it was usually the remains of the roast, cold with salad, a macaroni cheese or cottage pie, a light meal by their standards. But dinner at eight was a full, classic repast of soup followed by meat and vegetables and then a pudding. Rose was a lusty child who loved food and she soon started to plump up.

Pattie was a lively, dancing child - a tomboy, always climbing trees. Rosemary, content to just watch Pattie rush around, surprised them by starting to sing before she was a year old. They recognized in her 'da, da-de-da, da-de-da', the rhythm and tune of 'Birth of the Blues' that was popular at the time.

When she reached the terrible twos, she showed a stubborn determination to do everything herself, tie shoe laces, dress herself, do up buttons and draw pictures, everything. Of course, her small fingers didn't work properly, and the frustration was enough to bring on a tantrum and a biting of the floor in rage. She knew what she wanted to draw on the page, but her little hands couldn't get the pencil to do it.

When she was four, she could sing Danny Boy, remembering all the words except her rendering of "kneel and say an Ave there for me." All she could make of that was "kneel and say, 'and are they there for me?'" which sounded correct to her. For some reason, Polly thought it was amusing and didn't put her right. She continued to sing 'and are they there for me' for many years.

She loved singing but dreaded being asked to sing for Polly's friends. Then she became singularly shy. The old Valentine aunts begged to hear Danny Boy and she only agreed to sing it if she could sit out of sight under the dining room table. Apparently, it would have them in tears.

They were very old and Victorian. Each carried a precious black silk umbrella with a decorated ivory handle. One afternoon, when they got up to go, one of the umbrellas couldn't be found. It was a mystery indeed. Their farming son drove in to collect them and they couldn't wait so Polly promised to find it and return it to them. After two days, the mystery was solved. It was spotted down the deep hole in the PK, of all places. Pattie had to own up! She couldn't resist throwing it in there. The PK was the outside lavatory and it had what was called a long drop.

Every house on the mine was equipped with an outside lavatory. A good way behind the house, a deep hole was dug and covered with a strong, wooden frame and box seat with a hole cut in it. This was housed in a little corrugated iron or brick room with an iron roof and, usually, a gap at the top of the walls for light and air. This establishment fascinated the children.

Smelly, insanitary and full of flies, termites and spiders, it was forbidden for the little ones to go there alone because they loved to lean in the hole as far as possible, trying to see the life that went on down in what Bert referred to as 'the bog'. Rose knew it by no other name. Down in the depths, there were all sorts of odd bits of rubbish and sundry broken bottles, tins and creepy crawlies including things wriggling about. There were huge spiders and possibly snakes lurking.

Down there, half submerged, they could just see a black thing with an ivory handle. Torches, long sticks and fishing tackle and various adults were engaged in the recovery. The children were banned from the scene and it was horribly exciting and frustrating. Finally, out it came, and Pattie was given a talking to behind closed doors. Rose was told that she was not, strictly not, to say a word about it to anyone or there'd be trouble.

There was a good deal of laundering in a tub in the back garden before a pristine black umbrella was 'found' under the sofa and Polly set off alone to the Valentine farm with it. The children were not permitted to accompany her, and Rose howled. She loved the Valentine farm. She didn't know that her mother was certain she would have come out with the truth.

When frustrated or annoyed, Rose howled when she didn't throw a tantrum. Apparently, she would put her hand on her brow, over her eyes and stand there with her feet apart and head forward. Then, two fat tears would squirt out forward and splash on the floor before the howl. This made everyone laugh which infuriated her even more. The adults would say "Wait for it!" and sure enough, they would be treated to the works. This was a drama queen in the making, of course, and later there was certainly drama in her life.

Her biggest problem was her 'stays'. Stays were little sleeveless cotton jackets, worn over a vest. They held up the knickers, having six large buttons at the waist and four or five small ones down the back to close the stays.

The knickers had no elastic; just an opening each side and four buttonholes front and back, so the side buttons did double duty. They were the hardest to undo and little fingers fumbled for ages with them. By then Rose was dancing up and down with her legs crossed or wetting the floor, a source of great anxiety for her.

The leg openings were fitted tight, so another problem arose when the child grew bigger, the knickers got pulled up into the middle, chafed, and it hurt. Rose would fiddle around trying to loosen them at the bottom. She'd be questioned by Polly who would give her that certain look – as if she were looking at a pile of dog sick.

"What are you doing? Don't do that! You're not to touch yourself down there! Go and wash your hands!" A whining complaint usually ended in bigger knickers appearing and there came a day when, at last, she was old enough for knickers with elastic. Joy of joys! Training pants hadn't been invented in those days.

The only thing you could say in favour of the tight button-on type was that rape was impossible. They were literal chastity belts. They proved their worth when Rosemary was four.

Pattie had gone off for the day, and Polly was visited by a friend who brought her teen age son to tea with her. Usually, he had Pattie there to talk to and Rose wasn't included by them. His name was Vernon and Rose couldn't quite say it. She called him Vermin which was never corrected by her mother. Polly thought it much more appropriate because she didn't really like him. He had shifty eyes.

This time, because Pattie wasn't there, he came over to her and took her hand. "Come, let's go and look at the garden." said he.

Rose was delighted. She suddenly felt important and liked by this friend of Pattie's. She began to gabble all sorts of things to interest him. He didn't seem to talk much. Then he took her hand and said, "Let's go down these steps and sit under those bushes."

Rose was only too ready to do so. How great! This friend of Patty's liked her after all! Settling under the flowering shrubs down on the lower terrace, Vermin sat close to her. He put his hand on her leg and slid it up to her knickers.

'What is he doing that for', she thought and carried on talking. There was much fiddling and fumbling going on with Vermin trying to work out the mechanics of her strange, tight underwear. He wasn't getting anywhere! Now and then, he jumped up and peered up at the house and then sat down again. Rose was very curious.

"What are you doing?" she asked.

"This is a secret. You're not to tell anyone. Promise!" said Vermin. She promised. 'How interesting! This big boy was sharing a secret with her. Nobody had ever asked her to keep a secret. How lucky that Pattie wasn't here'.

He didn't seem to answer her questions or even listen. Why was he pushing his fingers in her tight knickers, rubbing her in a place she wasn't to touch and moving up on top of her and what did he want?' She was beginning to feel uncomfortable about it.

Well, as aforementioned, rape was impossible! Just then, there was a call from the house. "Rosemary, where are you? It's tea time. Vernon, tea time, come along!"

Vermin jumped up, hastily adjusting his clothes. He took off rapidly round the bushes and vanished. She got up and went up the steps to the house. "Where were you? What were you doing? Where's Vernon?" She didn't know and said so. She also said she was doing nothing, which was true. She didn't do anything, Vermin did. Nobody asked her about the secret. She couldn't stop thinking about it and wondering what it was all about. It had been very interesting but a bit nasty.

She didn't see Vermin again that afternoon. The secret was a hot potato inside her head. It lasted until she and Pattie went to bed at six. Then she just had to tell. She made Pattie promise not to tell. It was a secret. Pattie crossed her heart. As soon as Rose whispered it all, Pattie, of course, told her mother.

There ensued a first-class inquisition with Rose feeling totally let down by Pattie and both parents grilling her over and over. She began to feel guilty of something as if she had done something bad, but she couldn't think why.

Finally, there were instructions not to let boys or anybody touch her and to tell her mother straight away if they tried, or she'd be in trouble. The interesting secret existed no longer! She never saw Vermin again and when his mother visited, he wasn't with her. She recalled her father remarking as he walked away "Vermin by name and Vermin by nature!" which didn't make sense until she was much older.

Pattie had a big tricycle with a stand at the back. She loved to hare round the huge polished veranda which went around three sides of the house. How Rose loved that tricycle and yearned to ride it. She often begged Pattie to let her but Pattie said "No! You can't! You're too small. You'll fall off. Daddy will shout at me if I let you." And that was that.

Pattie & Rosy stayed on the back of her tricycle and held on tight as they raced around the veranda biting off mouthfuls of grapes

Sometimes, she would let Rose climb on the back and hold on tight round her middle and she would race round the veranda with her. They would pass the front entrance doorway, where a large grape vine grew. Luscious bunches of long, green grapes were ripening there.

They tried to bite off a mouthful of grapes as they passed. Pattie was better at it. Then they stopped where the water filter stood and added a mouthful of water. No wonder they often had tummy aches. The grapes were bitten off as soon as they were big enough. Ripeness didn't come into it!

Pattie once saw some huge green elephant-caterpillars eating the grape leaves. These were about three inches long by then and bloated, with a little tail sticking up at the back and horns. Round orange spots in front made them look as if they had big eyes.

Pattie had a little sewing machine and she put the poor creatures through, under the needle and turned the handle so they ended up with cotton stitching all along their backs. It didn't seem to bother them when they went back on the vine. They just resumed their munching, albeit somewhat philosophically. They would have turned into interesting butterflies! Fortunately for the poor things, Pattie soon lost interest.

Rose loved and admired everything Pattie did and followed her about until Pattie would lose her temper. "Go and play somewhere else, with your own things!" It always disappointed Rose, because Pattie was her sun and shining star. She was seven and a half when Rose turned four, three days before New Year's Day, 1930.

They had no telephones in the houses on the Rezende Mine in Penhalonga. A small black piccanin would run with a note to summon a doctor or hand an invitation to tea to a neighbour or tell Daddy there was a snake in the house and come quickly.

As daddy was one of the managers, they lived next to the doctor's in a staff house, which was fortunate for Rose when she swallowed a large tiddly-wink she was holding between her lips as a tea tray, with small ones on top for plates. Her nose was blocked so she took a quick breath and it went down, stuck in her throat and partially stopped her breathing.

She was dragged by her mother, screaming and choking, all the way down a long drive, along the road and up to Dr. Alexander's house. He came out to see what the commotion was about and Rose, squalling and choking, flung her arms round his legs:

"Doctor, save me! Save me! I don't want to die!"

He told her she wasn't going die, just stop yelling, open her mouth and let him look. There was nothing there any longer. He said it just felt like it because it had stuck going down. He suggested a dose of oil and a use of the potty for a day or two. Rose felt saved! She fell in love with the doctor then and there.

Not many people on the mine had a car when Rose was small. They always had one because it was a passion of Daddy's. First was a large tourer, circa 1920 in vintage. She remembered the name Whippet. Then Daddy spent his all and owed a good deal on an Armstrong Siddeley, a beautiful monster with rosewood interior dashboard and sills and even pull out tables at the back. That was a 1926 model, second hand. When they went to town, it was considered a rare treat. All dressed up in their Sunday best they'd climb aboard with Rose and Patty in the back with the companion help and mummy in front. Seatbelts were unheard of then and Rose wriggled about, sitting back or up on the edge of the seat, sometimes leaning over daddy as he drove.

When they reached the Christmas Pass where daddy had to change down and watch the road as they climbed the steep mountain, turning sharp, blind corners, they were told, in just that certain voice, to sit back and behave and they did, with a tight tummy of fear. Going up was the worst, because the sheer drops were on mummy's side. She exuded nervous vibrations all the way and it was catching. They'd stop at the top and park where there was a look out picnic space. Having taken half an hour to reach there, out would come the picnic basket and they would all settle on the upper bank where the grass had been mowed and the bush cleared, leaving the beautiful Msasa trees for shade.

They'd be taken into the bush a little way by the companion help and instructed to relieve themselves. Returning, there'd be a hand wash from the water bag slung in front near the radiator before they joined mummy on the picnic blanket. Daddy would have the kettle boiled on the little wood fire he'd made, with three big stones round it, on which balance the kettle. Spoons of tea would be thrown straight in and the scent was unforgettable; the wood smoke and the steaming tea being poured in cups, with milk added from a wine bottle, stopped up with a twist of brown paper; this, up on the mountain in the fresh, crisp air was a treat. Then, there'd be the cracking of a hardboiled egg, one each, with a bread and butter sandwich and scones or cake to follow.

Always, there'd be a wary eye out for baboons. There were troupes of them in the mountains and hills around the town of

Umtali and with the baboons came the leopards, their main predators. The baboons could be dangerous, particularly if people had started feeding them. A large male baboon could stand five feet high if it reared up in a fighting mood and they had huge, jutting canines.

Once down the Pass, there was a short drive into town. There, they'd be taken to the shops and watch as mummy bought material or ribbons and cottons. Or they'd sit in the car and wait for daddy as he went into the barber shop. Perhaps, they'd go to the Indian shop, Kewada's, and see all the silks and smell the strange incense burning there. The women would buy silk to make underwear, petticoats and French knickers. Mummy bought lovely, gauzy soft muslin and made her blouses, long sleeved to cover her arms from the sun as she loved to garden and ride her horse.

There'd be a trip to Meikles store to see the toys there while mummy bought shoes. Perhaps little pinched feet would be treated to new shoes! Always, near Christmas time, new white socks and black patent leather shoes were bought.

Too soon, there'd be the call to come on, get in the car, it's getting late.

Then off they'd go again, back over the Pass, feeling quite tired and sticky and ready for a bath and their supper.

The sun would be going down by then - sundowner time - and Rose's parents never failed to respect the hour for sundowners, when drinks were carried out on a tray by Nest onto the veranda. There, they watched the sun go down in front of them, sitting back in the Morris chairs with a whiskey and soda for daddy and a brandy and ginger for mummy. The children had lemonade with a splash of beer in it.

The native tribes had settled down under white rule and Bert only had the Mission boys from St. Augustine's to contend with, trying to stir up political dissention. None of the other workers complained until they were filled with the Mission worker's opinions that they were deprived, overworked and underpaid. They got that from the priests teaching at the mission and were out to spread the word. Essentially, the workers were indeed underpaid. The British based company had no intention of shelling out more of its investments than it could possibly get away with. After all, it was for the glory of the Empire. In fairness to the company, the average worker did not understand the value of accommodation, food and medical attention, all provided free, plus an annual bonus.

Sometimes, there'd be an undercurrent of trouble, manifested when the weekend beer drink warned Bert. Normally, on a Saturday night, the party in the compound would begin at six. Bert and Polly, Irene and the children sat together on the veranda in summer time. It was sundowner time and they would watch the sunset and listen to the night sounds. A servant brought out the Tilley lamps and Bert pumped them until the centres glowed, then hung them from the rafters. The crickets and frogs would tune up and the veranda would be squirted with mosquito repellant from a flit gun. They all had to take quinine tablets which had to be swallowed quickly – pushed in the back of the mouth and without a moment's delay, a good half glass of water swallowed. They were burningly bitter on the tongue, but malaria had to be avoided at all cost. They slept under mosquito nets as well.

The kitchen was a separate room, built at the back of the house, a few steps away from the back veranda. This was because the stove was a wood burning, black iron one with four plates and a hob at the top and a hot oven. Nest understood the stove and could judge just where to set the pots for boiling rapidly or simmering. Out of the oven, wonderful cakes, scones, pies and roasts emerged, all cooked to perfection.

After having the afternoon off, Nest was in the kitchen preparing dinner. He was a Mahommedan and didn't drink. In his white uniform, wearing his red fez, he was a tall, imposing man. He brought out a large brass tray bearing various bottles of liquor and cut-glass tumblers and set them on the table and Bert would pour a drink for each of the family. Polly liked brandy and ginger ale, Irene had sherry and the children had a shandy, very pale and down to almost all lemonade for Rose. Bert liked his whisky and soda. There were no television sets to distract them, so they'd enjoy watching the sun disappear over the hills and listening to the night sounds. Sometimes they heard and saw an owl. The night jars had a whirring call. These were strange birds with whiskers at the sides of their beaks.

On Saturday night, when the wind blew from the northeast, they could hear the drumbeats from the compound; African drums sending messages or just tuning up for the dancing and feasting. The drinking began far earlier, as soon as the workers returned from the houses. Great drums of kaffir beer awaited them. Made of fermented grains and prepared by the women in the compound early each week. It was drinkable by the Thursday or Friday and freely sampled. An illicit brew of kachasu was bound to be added. This was smuggled in from hidden stills on the night and was as effective and poisonous as poteen.

Apart from the drum beats, there'd be the sound of eerie

wailing as the women shuffled, stamped the ground and sang, getting louder as they became more inebriated. Bert listened quite intently to this, occasionally hushing the children for a minute. If there was silence or too much shouting, he got up, saddled his horse and, dressed in his jodhpurs and riding boots, strapped on his belt and holster with his revolver and bullets, took his rifle strapped to the saddle and his sjambok and galloped off to the Police station for some support. This tiny band would enter the compound to enforce law and order on a large dangerous mob of drunken workers.

There'd be an anxious time at home, wondering what was happening and then relief at the sound of his horse returning. Sometimes, drums would begin beating again and all was well. Sometimes, there was an incident when a drunken brawl had ended fatally and a knobkerrie, a knife or a panga had been used.

Bert had to make arrests and sit in judgement in the morning.at the Police Station. Sometimes, he had to single out an agitator and have him jailed by the policeman to restore law and order. Usually, the agitators were from the mission and they were apprehended by the police and barred from the compound.

Thirty years later, the Roman Catholic and the American Methodist Missions in Rhodesia were found to be harbouring terrorists, funded, trained and armed by the Chinese and Russian communists. Bishop Lamont, the RC Bishop in Umtali was deported as the Rhodesian white rulers and their supporters both white and black, fought a sixteen-year civil war against the tide of political chaos and destruction.

Christmas 1929 came and three days later, Rose turned

four. Polly and Irene were sewing baby clothes and knitting beautiful little jackets and bonnets. Rose thought she may be getting a new doll, beautifully dressed, but she was given a little wheel barrow for Xmas.

They went to the Palmer's farm one afternoon in March and in the ploughed fields beside the road were lots of storks. Pattie told Rose to chant out of the car window "Stork, stork, bring us a baby brother," over and over. She knew, but Rose hadn't been told that Polly was going to have another baby, but not for another four months. Rose kept an eye on all the storks after that.

After they had finished their tea, she and Pattie went to play behind the farmhouse where the Palmers had made a cement sandpit for children. Rose took off her shoes and long white socks and Pattie had one of her bright ideas. She filled a sock with damp sand and buttoned a shoe on it. It looked just like a foot. She had another bright idea. She held it at the top and ran around to the sitting room where the adults were having tea, ran in and held up the foot. "Rosemary's cut her foot off!" There was a stunned silence, then Polly fainted and fell off her chair – right on her stomach! Pattie's joke fell exceptionally flat. She was in trouble again. Rose couldn't understand adults. They hardly ever found Pattie as funny as she did.

Rose spent quite a lot of time flat on the ground looking under the gooseberry bushes in the vegetable garden. It was said that babies were to be found there, but she was out of luck. Then, in May, she was playing on the swing at the back of the house when she fell off and knocked her head on a stone. She lost consciousness and the nanny ran in to call her mother. Polly rushed out, tripped on the back steps and fell right on her stomach again! In a few hours, she went into labour. It was almost two months early. Dr. Alexander asked the manager to stop the mine stamps and, in the eerie silence, many hours later, Polly was delivered of a tiny baby boy. The baby brother had arrived, and he was alive. They called him Michael John Nairn. He was swaddled in cotton wool to keep him warm, he was so premature. Of course, he was the most precious, spoiled child one could ever imagine.

For two days, Rose was not even allowed to go into the bedroom and see her mother, who had nearly died, and then it was a quick hug and kiss and a tiny look at the baby; a little, ugly, shriveled thing with its eyes shut, not the little doll she had expected. Finally, several days later, mummy was back in the sitting room, propped up with cushions.

Pattie was to the fore. She was eight and she held the baby, but Rose wasn't allowed to, which brought on a dramatic performance and a flood of tears, so she was made to sit well back on the sofa with a pillow on her lap. The baby was placed in a shawl in her arms for a moment. It was enough because she found it quite big and heavy and she couldn't even see it over the wrappings. Really, Michael should have been in an incubator, kept well away from the danger of catching a cold. He had a few weeks to go for his lungs to be fully formed, but little was known about that in those days. What Rose really missed was her big green cot.

She had still been sleeping in it before Michael was born but now she was told she was a big girl and was moved to a proper bed in a little veranda room. She often fell out of bed and was disorientated and nervous. She felt afraid there at night and she started to wet her bed again and have nightmares, vivid ones in colour that she still recalls, eighty-five years later.

One dream was travelling in the car, below a mountainside, in the darkness, with a bright orange sunset lighting the blackness of the mountain top. In black silhouette at the top, was a huge lorry travelling along on the ridge above them when it suddenly began to topple over and was rolling down on top of them. She woke screaming and frightened and her parents rushed in from the sitting room to comfort her and convince her it was only a dream.

Another was also in the car. She and Pattie were in the back and Mommy, Daddy and baby in the front when suddenly they drove into a big pit and the car sank slowly into grey water. Bubbles of air rose to the surface, and she was the only one left, looking out of the back window screaming for help. The water was grey with cyanide and her family was drowning. That stemmed from being warned not to walk on the slimes dam's caked surface in case they fell through and swallowed some of the water as it had poisonous cyanide in it and might kill you.

All her life, she had a fear of someone reversing a car back towards a drop or a river's edge because Bert did just that once and the car sank down in the sand and the wheels spun when he tried to drive out again. Polly panicked, and the children started to scream but he didn't listen and got bogged further down in the sand. They had to take their shoes off, open the card doors and wade out. Polly was frightened enough to go for him instead of assuring the children that it was nothing to worry about. A friend came down with a winch and the car was dragged out of the sand and up on the bank again as they all stood watching.

In another dream, Rose was lying on her back in her bed and she was still awake. She could see the veranda light and lounge beyond her toes. She heard a noise and looked sideways. There, standing still in the doorway, was a huge black man, just staring at her. His eyes glowed in the light of a match he was holding. She knew he had been hiding in the big drawer at the bottom of the large wardrobe in the nursery and he was going to kill her if she moved so she held her breath. She was getting more and more frightened as he moved towards her and she woke screaming again. Both Polly and Bert rushed in, put on the lights and checked the drawer at the bottom of the wardrobe and opened the doors just in case. They checked under the bed and made sure the outside door to the back veranda was locked.

She supposed that dream was linked with the fact that Pattie had opened the drawer and found it was empty, so she had a good idea for it. It could be used as a cot for Rose, so Pattie made her get in and lie in it, and for some reason, she closed it. Rose got claustrophobic in the dark and screamed. Their mother came in and Pattie was once again in trouble. It was forbidden and too dangerous. The wardrobe could tip over on top of them and kill them, she said.

Often, Rose would wake feeling cold and lonely. She would creep into Polly's room in the dark and feel in the cot. If she felt a baby face there, she would creep into bed behind her mother. If the cot was empty, she would climb in it and sleep happily there again. She did it once when she was cold and had wet her pajamas and Polly was cross. Having a large, cold, wet and somewhat smelly frog land against one's back in the middle of the night would have been rather irritating, but her mother never complained. Sometimes she would peel her pajama pants off and climb in buck-naked. Those were some of Rose's memories of being four.

Bert, Polly, Michael, Rose and Patty

Patty, Michael and Rose

THREE

TURBULENCE

Then, suddenly, disaster struck the Mason family and their lives were never the same again. Never again would Pattie race on her tricycle with Rose on the back and never again would she dance on the lawn pretending to be a fairy or climb a tree or run and jump in the river or walk quickly or even stand up gracefully from a chair.

She didn't die. She was suddenly terribly ill, and Rose wasn't allowed to go and see her in her bedroom. Dr. Alexander was in and out a lot. There was a good deal of anxious whispering and Rose was out of all of it, wondering and lonely.

It was the dreaded disease, poliomyelitis. Pattie and another young girl in the vicinity, Evelyn, had been struck down. It was a mystery. No one knew what caused it, but they seemed to link it with horses as both families owned horses. Polly had her mare and Bert had his black gelding. Evelyn had been an accomplished rider, winning cups for dressage and jumping. Both children had to be taken to Salisbury Hospital to be treated by the best specialist in the land, Mr. Huggins soon to inherit the title Lord Malvern and in the future, the Prime Minister of Rhodesia.

Someone drove the car up to the house and Pattie was carried out in blankets and settled on pillows in the back with Sheila Mc Nish, the new companion help. Polly, cradling baby Michael, sat in the front waving goodbye. Rose stood with her father on the lawn and wanted to know why she wasn't going too. She was being left out. It seemed they were all going to Salisbury without her! What had she done wrong to be punished like this? She was frantic. Of course, no one told her that Pattie was almost at death's door and the baby was still breast fed and had to go too.

She screamed "Mummy! Mummy! I want to go with you!" Bert knelt down and held her "Don't you want to stay with your dad? I'm not going either. Won't you stay with daddy?" Rose was torn. Bert carried her to the car to say goodbye and Polly kissed her and said she would be back soon. Rose tried to say goodbye to Pattie, but her eyes were closed. Rose was devastated. She stood with Bert waving goodbye and trying to smile and then she hid behind him, buried her face in his trouser leg and wept as the car swept out of the drive. Bert took her in for sweet tea and a huge chunk of currant cake. That worked – comfort food! Rose began to expand. Of course, he had to go to work and he employed a fat, lazy old woman who seldom talked to Rose and just sat reading or knitting all day, telling her to go and play or go and lie down. Rose was lonely. Nothing was the same. She wandered around each day trying to amuse herself in the garden and with her toys and the animals, waiting for her father to come home.

One afternoon, when the animals were eating their dishes of food together on the back veranda, one of the dogs bit Polly's lovely big blue Persian, Tinkerbell, and broke her back. Bert was still at work, so the woman ordered the servants to finish off the cat, drown it in a bucket. Rose knew nothing about this. She heard a commotion at the back and walked out to witness beloved Tinkerbell being pushed down under the water with a broom by the kitchen boy and fighting to come up for air. She screamed for them to stop it and ran to the woman screaming. Mrs. Summers told her to stop it and sit down because it had to be done. The cat's back was broken. Rose was desperate and crying. Fortunately, Bert arrived that moment.

He sent Rose to her room for a while and swiftly and humanely dispatched the injured cat. Then he called Rose back and the woman had gone for good. Tinkerbell had also gone, but Bert tactfully told Rose she was with the other cats they had had who had gone to catty heaven. They had a long, distracting talk about heaven and what the conditions were there for cats and then it was dinnertime.

It was a difficult time for Bert. Sometimes, Rosemary came with him to the office and sat drawing or reading there, other times she went to stay with friends of theirs for the day, and then he took a week's leave. He took her on picnics, trudging up the surrounding hills so he could prospect for gold. He taught her to crush a little of the rock to powder with a mortar and pestle, and then swirl the sand in water in the pan, pouring out most of the loose mud and swirling it again, then tipping it up carefully, sideways, to leave a trail at the edge which showed traces of gold if there was any, because gold, being heavier, sinks to the bottom. It was fascinating, and Rose was so proud of her little streaks of gold.

After that, they would sit under a tree and eat their sandwiches, drinking cold sweet tea out of a bottle. Sometimes, they spent a Sunday at the river. Bert loved fishing and he made a little rod out of a stick and line with a cork float for Rose and taught her to cast which she found too hard, so he usually did it for her. She would soon get bored, staring at the float and nothing biting, watching for non-appearing crocodiles, so she would amuse herself wandering about but not going out of sight and not going in the river or near it in case a crocodile was lurking there. Then Bert would make a fire with Rose rushing about gathering dry sticks.

He found three large stones, set them in a circle with twigs in between and crisscross on top of dry grass, Rose watched carefully, waiting until he twisted a piece of paper and lit the end. Then he let her light the grass, being careful hold it upwards so the flame didn't come back along the twist and burn her. Then they'd blow under the flame until the twigs caught alight and he'd balance the tin kettle on the stones to boil water for tea. This ritual was very absorbing and satisfying for Rose. She loved the smell of boiling water and the different smell when the tea leaves were put in. She loved the scent of dust and the wonderful scent of the earth when rain fell. It seemed to be as satisfying to the soul as food itself. She loved the wonderful smell of the flowers in the garden, wafting up when dusk fell and the smell of puppies when they were tiny. Even the scent of a candle when it was snuffed and the smoke of a match and cigarettes. The different scents of roses, as each colour had a different smell; how strange that seemed.

In the basket were boiled eggs which smelled funny when you cracked the shell open. They always laughed and said "Poo! Who did that!" There was also bread and cake. They sat on a rug and enjoyed their picnic. Rose had a cushion and she lay there looking at the clouds or dozing while he fished or read his book sitting in a deckchair near her. Then they would pack up and motor home. Of course, she loved her dad and grew closer to him as Pattie grew closer to her mother, and Polly concentrated on her fragile little son Michael, and on Pattie who needed her so desperately.

Then came the great day when mummy, Pattie and baby Michael came back. Rose rushed to her mother and was hugged and kissed and listened to for a while, at least, but then it had to be Pattie's needs and they were real and many. Polly moved into the big bedroom with Pattie. Pattie had been carried into the house by Bert and settled in her bed in the room next to the dining room which led to the sitting room and both back and front verandas. There she could see everyone coming and going and sitting at table, through the open door.

Polly spent a good deal of time with her. She and Mc Nish gave her bed baths and bed pans and changed her into dresses daily. It took a lot of time because Pattie was unable to move her legs or sit up. Her arms were alright, thank God, but she was totally paralyzed from her midriff down. Fortunately, her lungs had not collapsed, or she would have died.

The other girl also survived. Evelyn had calipers on her legs and hadn't been affected as badly, so she was able to walk using a stick. Years later, she qualified as a doctor and continued to wear the calipers all her life.

Rose had to spend a lot of her time in the bedroom with Pattie. Then Polly and Mac Nish could go out for a while, visit friends or go shopping. Pattie was propped up on pillows, so she could look out of the window at the garden, but she couldn't see the drive and gate. She had to rely entirely on Rosemary's company and that became very tedious for both, Rose being four years younger.

Pattie invented a game of make believe, with an ulterior motive, but Rose didn't know this, or she wouldn't have played. Pattie first read Rose a story about knights and gallantry. Then she told Rose "You can be Lady Anne and I will be the queen in the castle."

There was a performance from Rose because she immediately wanted to be the queen. Pattie explained that the queen just sat on the throne and it was Lady Anne who was the important one who did everything interesting. Put tactfully like that, Rose agreed.

"Lady Anne, Lady Anne, fetch me that book and I will read it to you." Rose fetched it.

"Lady Anne, let us have some lemon syrup. There is some syrup in that jug. Get a glass for yourself and the tin of biscuits and pour some syrup in my glass too. We can pretend it is wine. Here, you can choose a biscuit. Have the one in the silver paper if you like." Rose certainly "liked"!

Pattie knew how to charm Rose and keep her fetching and carrying. It was a first-class success.

"Lady Anne, Lady Anne, go to the window and look out. Can you see anyone coming?" Rose got a bit fractious eventually. She said she didn't want to and why should she. Pattie told her that in the story, a handsome prince would come galloping along the road to the castle. Rose obliged, but after the fourth time she felt it was stupid. "Just try once more", said Pattie

"Lady Anne, Lady Anne, what do you see?" Rose stared down the driveway. "There's no Prince, but Mummy and Miss Mc Nish are coming in the gate."

That was what Pattie had been hoping for. She was so bored and so frustrated, at last they were back and perhaps she could be carried into the sitting room. She could have her lunch there, with everyone else at the dining room table visible through the door. She could talk to them as she ate her food and they would join her and have tea in the sitting room with her afterwards.

Pattie had to be propped up on many pillows because her spine was collapsing. Finally, a metal and plastic corset was buckled round her waist and it had two crutch-like props under her arms to hold her up. Already, her spine was S shaped and one shoulder jutted out at the back. Her legs were long, and she was getting quite big and heavy from the inactivity. She would have been a tall woman but for the polio.

The family centered about her. After meals and at tea time Rose usually sat on the carpet and played with Mikey, her little brother, growing bigger every day and now toddling about and getting plenty of attention. Just look at Mikey, look what he can do. Mikey was a great source of irritation for Rose. He bit her and pulled her hair and laughed and she was not allowed to smack him.

Rose, who ate everything with gusto, couldn't stomach the way Mikey was cajoled to eat when he didn't want to which was often. Up at the table in his high chair, she had to endure the sight of Mikey getting the juiciest bits of meat popped in his mouth. He'd chew and chew for ages and then turn his head and spit the meat out on the floor. A ring of dogs and cats sat round his chair, waiting expectantly, snapping and clawing at the food.

Having been so premature, he was a skinny little boy and

they were afraid he might die if he didn't eat enough. They played a game to make him eat. "Look Mikey, see the choo-choo." Darling little Mikey would watch the laden spoon approaching. "Now it's going into the tunnel. Choo, choo, choo, choo, - now open your mouth." Mikey would turn his head away at the last moment and the food would be splattered down his front. Rose wanted to slap him. Just give it to her and she would show him.

Then came the experiment with his crushed quinine quarter-tablet, hidden in a heaped teaspoon of luscious strawberry jam. Rose's mouth watered. She'd only had a glass of water for hers. Michael refused to open his mouth. He squalled and yelled he didn't want it.

Rose was dying to get at that spoon of jam and she had a sudden idea. She said "I'll show him. Just give it to me and I'll show him how nice it is." She looked forward to the big lump of jam. They handed the spoon to her and she acted it out.

"Look Mikey, see how nice it tastes. Yum yum!" Smiling broadly, she opened her mouth and popped the contents in. Then her face changed, and she howled loudly, spitting and choking and purple in the face. Michael's eyes were popping, his mouth hanging open. The experiment was a total failure because the powdered quinine was on the teaspoon under the jam which neatly slid over it, giving Rose the benefit of a mouthful of powdered quinine! She got the full force of the burning, bitter powder which nearly choked her.

The astonished expression on Michael's face sent the others into fits of laughter as Rose choked and spat and howled in fury over it. It was too much for her. She yelled for water and ran into the bathroom to spit and wash out her mouth over and again. It was exceptionally funny to everyone, and she was thoroughly enraged.

They had numerous companion helps, Hughie, then Irene, who married and lived in Umtali, Audrey, then the Irish woman, Sheila Mc Nish. It was she who drank too much at one of their parties and passed out on the sitting room floor. Bert grabbed a vase full of marigolds off the mantelpiece and upturned it, pouring the water over her face. The marigolds had been there for some days and the water stank. Bert didn't miss this opportunity. Dramatically, hand on heart, He exclaimed "Oh my God! She's mortifying already!"

Sheila Mc Nish left and Miss Kish, a French girl took her place, then finally, Emmy Dahl, a young and beautiful German woman. Rose was five and having her hair brushed by Emmy when her father walked through, close behind them. Rose felt Emmy jerk forward against her saying crossly "Herr Gott! Mr. Mason!" and Bert laughing. Rose wondered why. Years later, she thought that he was probably pinching her bottom.

One day, a German Baron Von der Llangen, or some name like that, came to Penhalonga. Bert invited him to dinner and when he was introduced to Polly, he took her hand, clicked his heels, bowed and kissed it. They were astounded. Bert kept doing the same after he left. Polly would laugh in amusement and exasperation, and push him away, saying: "Don't be so silly, Bert!"

The very next day, the Baron called on them again and apologized for speaking to Emmy in German. His manners were impeccable. He and Emmy went out and sat on the veranda together and they were there for the rest of the afternoon.

He came into the sitting room at five and apologized again

for being so rude. He asked them whether they minded if he took Emmy out that evening to Umtali for dinner and a cinema show. Bert and Polly waited up for her, but she didn't come back that night. Bert was about to get out his shotgun next morning when the Baron returned with Emmy.

They were most apologetic. The Baron announced that they were getting married as soon as he could get a special license. He had swept her off her feet and she became the Baroness Von der Llangen and went back to Germany. It was a romantic story fit for a paperback novel.

After that, there were no more companions. Pattie needed some tuition because she couldn't go to school so Polly started helping her with a correspondence course. Parcels of books would arrive, and Rose was dying to join her. All those lovely, new exercise books; the pencils and reading books. She was just busting to read and write as well.

They wouldn't let her and that brought on another dramatic storm, so at the age of five she went to the little school down the road. She was turning six at the end of that year. She completed kindergarten one and two there, all in one year, quickly learning to read and write, counting and writing numbers and she loved every minute of it.

Almost avidly, she added and took away numbers and was thrilled when she got the right answer. To know what two and two made and how to write it down neatly in the little squares in her sums book and to know what a plus and a minus sign meant, satisfied something in her soul.

To be able to read stories like Patty was a delight, so she became a diligent, clever child. At the end of December, Rose turned six and moved into her seventh year, a significant number in her life.

There had been turmoil in the house. Bert and Polly were suffering another disaster. Polly suddenly became enamoured of a young and handsome diamond driller from England and jealousy made Bert unbearable, shouting, brandishing his revolver, threatening to kill her and himself, and motoring off in a rage.

He crashed on the Christmas Pass and ended up in hospital with a bad gash on his eyebrow. The bottom had fallen out of his world. Even though he was flirtatious himself, he adored her and couldn't bear to lose her love.

There was a frightening row one night and Rose saw her mother run off towards the doctor's house. The six-year-old child suddenly panicked and ran out of the back door into the blackness outside. She pushed her way through the bushes in the gully at the side of their house heading in the direction of the doctor's surgery and finally got there. It had been a dangerous thing to do but she guessed that her mother must have gone there, and Dr. Alexander would save her, too, if her daddy decided to start shooting. Dr. Alexander would save them all. Up the steps she stumbled, knocked at the door and kept knocking.

Finally, the door opened, and a surprised doctor brought her into the sitting room. There was her mother looking less than pleased to see her, but Dr. Alexander gathered her in and handed her over to a young nun who was there. She turned out to be his sister who was staying there for a few days. She took Rose and put her to bed on a little sofa in her bedroom. Then she told Rose to turn over and go to sleep. Rose has been staring wide eyed and curiously at her taking off her veil and habit ready to go to bed herself. Rose turned over and soon went to sleep, feeling safe and cared for.

In the morning, they walked back to the house together with the doctor. Pattie and Mike were there but Bert wasn't, so everything seemed just as usual. He came back later, and life went on as if nothing had happened. But it had, really, of course. Plans were being made without Rose knowing anything about it.

Suddenly Polly, Pattie and Mike were off to Durban. Pattie was going to have treatment there, swimming in the saltwater pool to try and strengthen her leg muscles. There was a hope that she could walk after a time. Rose was left with her dad again.

Rose was heart sore. She longed to go to the seaside too, but it wasn't to be. It was a sort of separation. Apparently, years later, Polly found a letter written to Bert by Billy Cartwright about the affair, that 'he' had turned up at the farm when Polly and the children went to stay there. She never quite trusted Billy again although she stayed at farm to be with her best friend, Dolly. Later, she and Dolly fell out and she never went there again apart from one tragic day in their lives.

FOUR

SHERWOOD STARR

Bert and Rosemary were moving too, after seven years at Penhalonga. Everyone was on the go. A Mrs. Berry arrived. She was to be Bert's new housekeeper, taking care of Rose. She was a buxom, dark Afrikaans woman with curly, black hair, brown eyes and an adult son called Leslie who stayed with them frequently. They chatted away in Afrikaans to each other and Rose couldn't understand a word they said. She said Rosemary should call her Auntie Ann.

She wasn't Rose's aunt, so Rose felt odd about it but obliged. Daddy didn't seem to think it mattered. He was busy packing up everything and sending trucks away full of their furniture. Then the three of them bundled into the car with suitcases in the boot and they were off. They were leaving Penhalonga for good. Bert had been transferred to the Sherwood Starr mine in the middle of the country, some five hundred miles away. This was a Lonrho mine set in Sherwood Park, a Lonrho estate. There were many small workings with two or three stamp mills where the owners had found gold. Some of them had been bought by Lonrho for development.

The Cam and Motor was the biggest mine in Rhodesia near

Gatooma, at Eiffel Flats, but the richest yield came from the Globe and Phoenix in QueQue. This mine did not belong to Lonrho. Apparently, there was one section of that mine closed off with heavy bars and padlocks, behind which was an almost solid gold reef. The manager could take a small pick and chip out enough nuggets to increase the yield if necessary.

Next to the Cam and Motor was the Eileen Alannah, once an active mine. Suddenly it filled with water from an underground source and all the water used on the Cam was pumped from there. This colossal mine needed masses of water to wash the gold out of the crushed rock. On huge, shaking tables with thick, matted felt bases where the heavy cyanide and gold amalgam fell to the bottom and was trapped. The stream of mud, weak cyanide and sand was pumped down to the slimes dam for future treatment to extract the gold that remained.

It was a long journey, from the Eastern Districts to the Midlands, and they finally reached a farm near QueQue, in the middle of Rhodesia. They branched out along a dirt road to arrive at Sherwood Park Farm, near the Sherwood Starr mine. This farm took in holiday makers. It belonged to Lonrho and the manager was an old Dutchman with his English wife. The whole place was dry and dusty, and the trees were bare. The spring growth would only begin after October when the rains began.

There, Rose was left with Auntie Ann and didn't know why. Bert had to return and ride his horse to the Cartwrights farm to be stabled there, and then return to Penhalonga, collect the car and settle himself and all the cats and dogs into the new house at Sherwood Starr, where he had been transferred because the Compound Manager had become an alcoholic and was at death's door.

Rose pondered over this. She didn't know death had a door and wondered whether you knocked and if God let you in. And did you climb a long stairway up into the sky to get there? Or was it a ladder? She forgot to ask daddy about it.

Rose wandered round the farm with a couple of boys who were staying there, Dale and Neville Hurrell. It was a dusty, dry place and there wasn't much for her to do but hope her dad would come back soon. She had to share a bedroom with Mrs. Berry and her bed was a large cot-sided one, of all things. It was that night that Rose witnessed Auntie Ann taking off a huge contraption from round her middle. She was intrigued to see her first corset come off and all Auntie Ann's bulges flopping out when the tapes were loosened. Children are extremely observant, and Rose's mother had never worn anything like it. She was slim with small breasts. Auntie Ann had breasts like paw paws! Rose was astounded.

The next morning, Auntie Ann played a trick on the boys who had not yet seen Rose. She told Rose to lie in the cot with her eyes shut and pretend she was a doll. She wasn't to open her eyes or giggle.

Rose lay there trying not to breathe and move her chest and heard the boys come in. "Look at this big doll I bought." said Ann. The boys were not sure. She kept it up and said, "Isn't it a pretty doll?" finally they agreed it was. Then she told Rose to open her eyes and they all laughed.

The adults there ignored her and spoke Afrikaans, so she was bored and lonely. The boys had left but she'd meet them again later at the mine golf club. She wandered about the farm in the thick dust looking at the cattle and farm machinery for a while and then found a book to read. Most of them were written in Afrikaans. At last, next day daddy was back and they were off to the mine, about two miles away from the farm.

The house was a big, square, grey one, made of unpainted Kimberley brick, a large concrete brick. Up four high steps at the side of the veranda and left through a French door was the sitting room. The veranda was wide and the floor a shiny green cement, with a rather high wall at the front and mosquito gauzed opening at the top. The wall was high because the front garden faced the main thoroughfare that ran through the housing area to the mine club and up the next hill to the mine office. There was nothing in the garden at all, just a bit of dry grass, a few straggly geraniums and a low four strand fence of barbed wire.

It certainly didn't have the charm of Penhalonga. The whole area was dusty and hot and there were no mountains around. Finally, they found some measure of beauty in picnics on the river banks and swimming and boating at the Sebakwe Poort, a large, still pool with high, granite cliffs both sides, also on the banks of the rivers, the Sebakwe and the Umfuli. Bert took out a peppercorn lease on five acres of riverside bordered by the main road to Gatooma at the bridge crossing the Umfuli where they could camp and fish at weekends.

There were no neighbours either side of them, just bare grass commonage on one side and bush on the other. Over the road, one of the miners lived, and further down lived a man called Percy who was on the staff. Just up the road was the school Rose was to attend. Of course, Rose was used to the beautiful gardens Polly had created in Penhalonga.

Rose recalled when prisoners came to weed the lawns in front of their house. They were down on their haunches in a row and she was told not to go near them or speak to them. Rose was about four and old enough to want to do what she was told not to. She went out to the garden and talked to them. Of course, none of them understood her. They didn't speak English. One smiled and picked a flower and handed it to her. Then she was called away and scolded for being disobedient. She had to stay inside.

But through the mosquito gauze on the veranda, she could watch the Askari policeman standing there with his gun, overseeing the working prisoners. Then, suddenly, after the usual gabble and laughter of all the blacks there, he called out one prisoner and handed him the rifle which was held with the butt on the ground and he walked off. Apparently, he went to the lavatory and that, for him, entailed going down the hill into the bush behind the house. There were no toilets for the servants. They went to what they called the 'shitteen' - out of sight behind the bushes. God knows what they used for toilet paper, hopefully a leaf, but they usually washed their hands at the garden tap when they came back.

After a while, he came back, took the rifle and sent the prisoner back to work. The prisoner that gave Rose a flower or the one holding the rifle could have been the murderer of his small daughter. Such was Rhodesia when Rose was four - just forty years after the pioneers crossed the Limpopo river.

The sentence for the child killer was probably two years, seeing that his extended family had no bread winner. His extended family meant a couple of wives and possibly twenty offspring, including those of any dead relatives that he automatically inherited, as was the African custom. So, the next African who came looking for work could well be a murderer.

Gardening was Polly's passion and there were green lawns

and beds of roses or mixed flowers on every side, pergolas covered with flowering creepers and massed dahlias or zinnias or larkspur, delphiniums, phlox, violets, poppies, waving about in the breeze and scenting the evening air. She had created beauty in Penhalonga with its soft, misty, almost English climate, and here there was nothing.

Rose felt it quite badly. She was only seven, but it was a loss. However, everything was interesting there because it was strange. Even watching the ant lions leaping out of their cylindrical hole in the dust when an unfortunate ant slipped down the slope was interesting and different. As everything ended in her mouth for sampling, she broke bits of the dusty euphorbia hedging at the back and, seeing the white milk dripping out, sipped it to see if it tasted nice. Immediately, it turned into a lump of gum that could be chewed.

Fortunately for her, it had a bad taste, so she left it alone because it stuck on her fingers and turned brown with dirt. Apparently, it was a carcinogen! The poinsettias made a show of bright red on the side fence and there were a few bushes at the back covered in bunches of yellow trumpet flowers. Two other bushes were the highly poisonous oleander covered in bunches of pink flowers. It was said that some natives had died after they used dry sticks of oleander to stir the maize meal in water over a fire to make their staple food; a solid lump of thick porridge they called sadza. Using oleander sticks poisoned the sadza.

The piano was in the sitting room with the big chesterfield suite re-covered by Polly in a pretty, flowered chintz, so all was homely enough. Rose was used to Auntie Ann by now and rather liked her. She was very motherly and kind to Rose who enjoyed the hitherto rare singular attention, and they soon spent a good deal of time at the mine club. What Rose did not know was that Auntie Ann was going to run the club and move into the flat attached to it when Polly returned. The months passed, and Christmas came before there was any sign of that.

Rose asked Father Christmas for a new doll. She had to write a little letter to him because he would come to the club a week before Christmas Day and hand out gifts. This was fun. Her mother was hardly missed. Auntie Ann could cook lovely Dutch things like melktert, a puff pastry tart filled with thick cinnamon flavoured custard, and koeksusters, deep fried and soaked in syrup, delicious and very fattening. Rose soon grew quite podgy.

Three days after Christmas, Rose woke on her eighth birthday expecting a parcel on her bed – nothing! - Floor? – Nothing! She washed and dressed quickly, went into the dining room and looked at the table, set for breakfast – nothing. She waited for Bert and Auntie Anne to sit down, bearing parcels, perhaps? Nothing! Seeing a slight purpling of the face, Bert asked her what was the matter? "Nothing", she said. Anne Berry persisted. "It's my birthday!" There was a stricken silence for a second, then Bert said. "I have a surprise for you, we hadn't forgotten. Let's have breakfast first. I must go and fetch it.

He kissed her and said happy birthday and hurried off in the car somewhere. Auntie Anne disappeared into her bedroom and returned with a little brown paper parcel. On it she had written "For Rosemary, with love". It had a little bottle of scent in it and a pretty handkerchief with flowers in the corner. There was an A embroidered on it and she said it was to remember her by. She chose it especially for that. Rose believed her.

Daddy returned with a paper bag containing sixty little oblong, wrapped, Cadbury's chocolates in a box with a special book.

It was the best he could find in the mine store which didn't sell toys. In each packet was a card with an animal on and the book contained pages with blank spaces in the forest where the animals were to be stuck. Rose had to cut out each animal and stick it in the right space. Like a stamp, the cards had glue at the back. Rose was delighted. Told to eat one chocolate a day, she started well, but soon she felt she just had to eat another, then another and soon they were all gone. She felt a bit sick but was totally absorbed in cutting out the animals. There was to be a prize for the best book returned and she soon gave it to Bert who promised to post it. She had cut and glued them so carefully she was quite sure it would be the best. That was that. She never heard anything more about it or got the book back.

Then one day, Bert knelt and held Rose, he seemed upset. "You love mummy, don't you? Don't you want her to come back? I think you should write a letter to her asking her to come back." Rose agreed and laboriously wrote a shaky little line or two. Bert took it to post.

And a couple of weeks later suddenly they were back. Daddy went to QueQue and came back with all of them. What a lovely surprise! What joy! Rose was kissed and fussed over, and Bert carried Pattie into the house and settled her on the settee with lots of cushions. She was Pat now, she said, call her Pat. Rose saw how big Mike had grown, He was a little boy suddenly, not a little baby; a skinny, cheeky little brother and very naughty too.

Rose clung to her mother, sat close and couldn't get enough of being cuddled and mummy listening to everything she had to tell her. The sad story of Tinkerbell upset her and then she was questioned by Polly about calling Mrs. Berry Auntie Ann? Her mother had that look of complete distaste and Rose felt offended.

She was indignant and tearful. "What must I call her, then? SHE said I must call her Auntie!" Polly couldn't think of anything else herself, so she reluctantly agreed that Rose had no alternative. In the Afrikaans culture, this was considered polite, Bert told Polly. Her mother and Pat were calling daddy Pa, so Rose said Pa to them and Dad to him.

Pat and Polly were very close, more like sisters. They shared the big bedroom. Bert had his little back veranda room leading off the sitting room and into the bathroom. He chose that one because Ann Berry slept in the big main one and Rose had the second room to herself on the other side of the dining room. It had French doors to a front veranda room. Michael shared Rose's bedroom for a while, until he became accustomed to the new surroundings and move into the little veranda room on his own.

Pattie, or rather, Pat had something to show Rose and her father. She was helped up on her feet, and she could stand on her own! They were all delighted. With an arm to lean on, she could take a few steps too, before she needed to be helped down again. Her main difficulty was that her knees were unstable. The muscles were useless because the nerves had been destroyed by the polio and, unless she balanced herself carefully on them, they bent back instead of forward and she fell over. She really should have been in calipers like Evelyn Forbes. She refused to wear them. She was a very stubborn, determined girl, a typical Arian, born in March – the ram that keeps butting the dam, they say. Mr. Huggins, the orthopedic specialist who treated Pattie in Salisbury hospital, said he never thought she would walk again and here she was, standing and even taking a step or two.

Polly had brought Rose lovely gifts, and all was fine again. Being closely questioned one day, Rose related how Daddy and Auntie Ann were rolling around on the carpet and she was laughing because he was tickling her.

Her mother looked at Pat and there was a silence.

"Oh Yes! Were they? What did they do then?"

"Nothing, they just got up and went into Dad's bedroom and shut the door."

"Is that so, and when did they come out? What did you do?" "They didn't come back so I just went to bed." said Rose, wondering why her mother and sister were looking at each other like that.

Bert spent quite a lot of his time at the club with Auntie Ann but so did Polly. Often, the whole family would go and have a meal there, or tea in her flat. They became close friends.

Mrs. Frank was often there. She had run the club before Anne Berry. She left to look after her husband who was depressed and out of work. Mr. Frank had taken to drink, they said. Rose couldn't take her eyes off Mrs. Frank, an otherwise ordinary, squat little blonde Jewish woman with a bent back and thin little legs. She had the longest pointy nose Rose had ever seen. It jutted out forward and stuck right out of her face.

She had a story to tell about her job before she came to the Starr. She worked in a "lunatic" Asylum and one night she was alone in the padded cell section with the most dangerous patients. As with the patients in the film 'The Nun's Story,' they

84

were warned. Not on any account were they to open the doors in case of an attack when they had no back up of a strong warden. There was the little window in the door they could open and see all was well inside and that was all.

This, Mrs. Frank did religiously but she couldn't see one of the patients anywhere, so she put her face close to the little opening to see the side next to the door. The man had been waiting right against the wall and he grabbed her nose and held on, trying to pull her in. She could hardly breathe, or shout, and it was ages before help came. She nearly lost her nose, she said. Rose could just imagine how tempting it had been to see that long proboscis poking through the little window.

A Jewish man called Solly managed the mine store. Isaac, Solly's brother, lived there but he wasn't often seen. No one knew he was an epileptic. Down the road lived old Percy. He was a garden lover too and often stopped to admire the garden Polly was creating. They were close friends. Percy had apoplexy and was very red faced. He seemed quite well but, to their dismay, he suddenly had an apoplectic fit and died. Bert and Polly were shocked and sad.

A week later, suddenly Isaac died during an epileptic fit. He was only in his thirties and that shocked all of them. Everyone was talking gravely about it. Who would be the third? Death always came in threes, was the superstition.

Sure enough, then Mrs. Frank's husband committed suicide! Apparently, he had been borrowing money from other Jewish friends and drinking so heavily that nobody would lend him more. That was the end for him, and he drank some cyanide water. So, three deaths within a matter of weeks was indeed extraordinary in such a small community.

Pat had a new teacher. Her name was Dido Appledore and she looked like it. She was fat and blonde with a pouting mouth and piled up yellow curls. She decorated her little bedroom with large silk cushions thrown on the carpet, on which she lounged in her harem pants and bra, smoking a cigarette in a long, black holder and drinking wine when she was off duty. She propped Pat on her bed and tried to teach her the value of being a free spirit.

Pat began to smoke and drink with her. Dido fascinated Rose who thought she was funny and odd. Unfortunately, Pat shut Rose out of the room and kept Dido to herself as she had jealously claimed Hughie years before. Dido didn't last long as both parents felt she was corrupting their daughter, but she was unforgettable.

FIVE

SCHOOL AND OTHER SOURCES OF EDUCATION

Rose, meanwhile, started standard one at the little school up the road. It was a corrugated iron, one roomed structure with a covered veranda in front and a little tin lavatory up at the back. They all used it but there was no water basin, so they had to use the tap outside to wash their hands afterwards and air dry them. There was an acre or two of bare playground. It was sparsely covered with grass but there wasn't a single tree on it. The whole of Sherwood Starr was devoid of trees and many of the hedges were made of the dull green, milky, dusty, euphorbia. It was a hot, dry part of the country, nothing like Penhalonga in the Eastern Districts.

The children ranged in age from six to fourteen and were all miner's children except Rosemary. Little ones sat in the front and big ones right at the back. At the back was a very pretty girl of fourteen named Dot. At break, when they all went out on the veranda to eat their sandwiches and play, Dot stood leaning against a pillar staring out and not talking to anyone. Rose and the others stared at her admiringly because she had bosoms! Big bosoms that stuck straight out ahead of her. All the boys stared at her too.

Rose was in the second row of desks and somewhere in the middle was a total extrovert called Ginger and he was Dot's brother. This was a good-looking boy of about eleven, with a mop of auburn, curly hair and freckles. One morning, the teacher, Miss Maree, ordered the class to read their lesson books and behave. Off she went, and they could see her head bobbing through the window until she was out of sight, on her way to the outdoor toilet.

Suddenly, Ginger climbed up on the top of his desk, curled his arms under his armpits and began jumping up and down like a monkey, chanting:

"Pounds, shillings and pence,
The donkey jumped over the fence
And killed the baby, inside the lady.
Pounds, shillings and pence."

Then he saw Miss Maree's head bobbing back so he leapt down again and picked up his book, looking innocent.

Rose was shocked. What a rude boy! What had he said! How terrible! Babies came with the stork, they ended up under gooseberry bushes. She couldn't wait to get home! She had to tell Pat. The bell finally rang, and she ran home quickly. She couldn't say anything to her mother. It was too dreadful! She'd tell Pattie. She did, with lots of whispers and oohs and aahs about Ginger's shocking, rude poem.

Pat had a private conversation with Polly. Pat then spoke to Rose and that was when Rose learned the facts of life – or some of them. Parents loved each other. They kissed and slept together in the same bed and they made a baby which grew like a seed in mummy's tummy. Then, when it was big enough, it came out. The rest was left to her imagination. How it got out was not disclosed.

Hours and hours of thought went into it and, finally, she worked it out. She decided it was what a belly button was for. Dads and Mums lay together facing each other, kissed, with their belly button holes pressed together and - voila! A little, tiny baby floated through. She even wondered if a tiny stork was carrying it, but she abandoned that idea. It was too unlikely.

She told Pat and Pat said "Don't be silly! You don't know so don't make up stories!" There was the usual heated debate and Rose went off in a huff. Pattie just didn't know anything! And how DOES the baby get out? Of course, it MUST be out of the belly button!

Polly grew a 'mile-a-minute' Zimbabwe creeper all over the iron roof of the house. It cooled the whole house and covered it in beautiful bunches of pink bell-shaped blooms for most of the year. The whole garden was transformed, and the wire fences dripped with vivid orange of the golden shower creeper which covered them rapidly. There were beds everywhere, full of lovely flowers again. At the side, she got Bert to have four long poles planted with wire fencing in between and there she planted sweet peas, masses of them in all their lovely colours. The house was scented deeply by the large bowls of sweet peas everywhere. The place was transformed. She had several highly polished brass bowls and large brass trays glimmering in the sitting room and a pair of brass candlesticks on the mantelpiece. On the floor was a large Persian carpet. The result was beautiful.

Suddenly, when spring came, the poles planted for the sweet pea fence took root and started to sprout. They became trees along the west side of the garden, straight out of the bushveld, shading the house from the hot setting sun and really transforming the whole garden.

It was decided that Rose wasn't getting the best schooling at the Starr, so by the time she reached standard three she was a boarder at the Gatooma School. Bert and Polly played golf at the Gatooma club and they knew everyone there. Their friend Dr. Warne, the mine doctor, lived there and that decided them. School clothes had to be bought, packed in a new trunk after name tapes were laboriously stitched on and Rose felt excited at first. She turned nine that Christmas and two weeks later they were off to the school hostel and she was left there feeling rather nervous and abandoned. All the other children in her dormitory spoke a language she didn't understand. They were mostly Afrikaans and mainly the children of farmers in the district.

She was one of the few English children there. Some of the girls were fourteen with big bosoms. The school was co-educational and some of the boys were like young men. The Afrikaans farmers didn't send their children to school until they were at least eight or nine. Out in the playground, where the boys and girls got together, she was particularly plagued by a fat, Germanic looking boy with piggy eyes and short, bristly yellow hair, called Dan.

He had made a farm whip, a long stick with a cowhide strip attached for flicking the bullocks when pulling a wagon or plow. He was clever at cracking the whip and delighted in lurking behind corners and stalking Rose. Then he'd flick the whip and catch her on the top of her legs where it stung and raised a welt.

It seemed to her that some of the Afrikaans children ganged up against her because she was English.

Rose didn't realize that it was only 34 years since the end of the Boer war when the British fought the Boers in South Africa and defeated them. The Afrikaans families in Rhodesia were of Boer descent and hated the English so the children at the school looked upon Rose as an enemy. To them, she was a 'verdomde rooinek', a damned red neck, as their parents called the English.

There were two big girls, the twins, Lettie and Vollie, who pretended to be friendly and Rose believed they were at first. They said, "Come and we'll play with you on the see saw." This was a massive wooden plank, the centre standing head height to Rose. Each side was so long that it rose about eight feet from the ground.

"Sit right at that end and we'll sit the other side and start seesawing." they promised. "It's good fun."

They sat half way along their side and gradually wriggled back so that Rose went higher and higher. When she was right in the air, they suddenly jumped off and ran away laughing.

Rose crashed down and fell off. It was frightening and confusing. A few days later they asked her to play on the see saw again. They linked arms with her and put an arm round her waist and promised faithfully not to get off again. Finally, she was persuaded once more. She hung on tight this time and they did the same thing. Down she came with a bang and didn't fall off, but her foot was caught under the wood, twisted and grazed and very painful. She had learnt a bitter lesson. This was true bullying. Rose suffered and wished she was back at home.

Sitting at the long refectory table one morning, the children were all talking about having to speak English. They all thought they should be speaking Afrikaans because it was the best language. Rose recalled her father's words and suddenly thought she could show them that English was part of their own language. She remembered what her father had said and piped up her contribution:

"My dad says that Afrikaans is just a mixture of English and Kaffir."

The children all leaped up and shouted at her. She thought they were going to pounce on her. Mrs. Reeves, the boarder's mother sitting at the top of the table, ordered them to sit down. "Leave her alone, she doesn't know what she is saying!" The mob glared at her malevolently and she worried about what they would do later when Mrs. Reeves wasn't there. She had at least made friends with one or two girls by now who spoke English and she made sure she stayed with them outside and avoided the others, but she wasn't happy there.

She did well at school and came first in class that term. She went back for the second term and the third, despite feeling rather reluctant. She had made one close friend who had an English mother, so it wasn't so lonely. There was a wooden hut in the grounds which all of them could use at first, but the big teenagers soon commandeered it as their own. The younger ones were barred.

It seemed to Rose that only one or two big boys and girls would shut themselves in and the others would stand guard outside. Then they would come out and others would take their place. She wondered what secret things they did in there. It was like a secret society. She wished she was a big girl!

Just before the end of term, she saw a large group gathered round the water tap so she went over and peered through to see what was happening. The biggest and most popular boy in the school, Cecil, was holding something over the tap which was turned on. She was amazed to see a long, white balloon getting fuller and fuller and longer and longer until it was several feet long and they were all laughing. How she wished she had a balloon like that! It didn't even burst. What a treasure!

Polly and Bert came to pick her up for the midterm holiday and she could hardly wait to tell them about it. Could they buy her one?

"WHAT was it like? It had a funny, long little balloon at the end? "No! They couldn't buy her one!" Her parents looked at each other and it was that particular look Rose knew so well. There was a murmured altercation between them that Rose couldn't understand and then they told to go and pack her clothes in her trunk because, to her joy, she was leaving the school for good. Polly and Bert went into the headmaster's office alone.

So, Rose had the pleasure of being at home for half the last term of the year. She still yearned for one of those balloons. She nagged them about it. Finally, both parents became annoyed and she gave up. Obviously, she thought, they were stupidly thinking it was just an ordinary balloon. She said she would ask in the toy shop when they went to town and she was told not to or else she would be in trouble. They said they were special medical things and the boy shouldn't have had one. When she asked what they were for, she was told rather abruptly to stop asking about them, so she did.

They went to Gwelo for an interview at the Chaplin Junior

School and Rose saw the place she would be going to for standards 4 and 5. It was a lovely school, just down the road from the Chaplin High, which she hoped to continue in. That was the senior school where the head boy, then, was Ian Smith, later to become Prime Minister of Rhodesia.

A complete set of new clothes had to be bought, six of everything, with green gym slips over white shirts and a striped green and gold blazer. Wide brimmed grey hat with a green and gold band. By Christmas time all was ready and packed.

Durban - Dora, Michael, Auntie Ann, Rose, Pat

On the road in Rhodersia; Michael, Rose, friend, Bert

There was just enough time to get down to Durban for a Christmas holiday at the seaside. This time, they stayed at the Esplanade hotel on the Esplanade. There Rose met a boy called Ian. He was about two years older than Rose and his parents ran the hotel. They had Christmas dinner at the hotel with the Beatties. Rose was given a big baby doll, beautifully dressed by Polly, for her tenth birthday. When Ian asked her if she'd like to come to the matinee at the cinema that Saturday, she was allowed to go with him and she decided to take her doll.

This was a treat for Rose. She had never been asked out by a boy. This young man went to school in the city. Obviously a very popular boy because at interval, there were calls of "Hey, Ian, is that your wife?" and wolf whistles which embarrassed her, but Ian said, "Take no notice of them!" He bought her an ice cream and some popcorn, and she was really enjoying being there.

At interval, her new doll was noticed. Then there were calls of "Ian! Is that your baby?" Rose blushed, and Ian called back loftily: "Don't be stupid!"

She thought it over later, back at the hotel and decided that she really liked Ian and would like to marry him one day when they grew up. But then, on further thought, she regretfully decided that she could never marry a boy who had the name Beattie. They called their bottoms their B.Ts. She couldn't be a Mrs. B.T. It was too rude. Imagine being a Mrs. Bottom!

On the last night of their holiday, they were invited to dinner by Ian's family. After dinner, Ian asked her if she would like to see what he had been given for Xmas? It was a Chinese lantern. Rose didn't know what that was, so he told her it showed slides.

She was no wiser, so he said come up to my room and you can see the slides.

He set the lantern on the end of his bed facing the wall and they lay behind it on their stomachs as he worked the slides and shutter. First, he put out the light. The scenes were brilliant and there were lots of slides.

Suddenly the door burst open and the light was switched on. "Rosemary! Ian! What are you doing in here with the light off?" All four parents were in the room. Ian explained, but Rose was told to come along, it was time for bed! She was furious! Why? They had not finished the slides.

She was bundled out and away. It was late, and they were leaving early next morning. Rose heard her father say something about etchings and the grownups laughed.

So, it was packing of cases, to bed and up early and away before she saw Ian at breakfast. She craned around hoping to wave goodbye. She asked if she could run in and say goodbye, but they just set off. Rose was heartsick about it and she craned her head through the back window hoping to wave goodbye.

Once home, there were a few last-minute purchases to make, plus bigger shoes, and then she was off to the new school. Gwelo was only about fifty miles from the Starr but she didn't get home for more than long weekends and holidays. There were mostly English children there and the Afrikaans ones spoke English, so she was much happier there.

There was one boy from the Sherwood Starr mine in her class, called George. He was a year older than Rose and she saw little of him at his home. She used to go there to play with his smaller sister, Esme. One evening, sitting on the carpet at home painting a picture, she heard her father say that Esme's mother hung a red light over her front door. Mrs. Y. was a tarty blonde woman with bottle blonde hair done up in curls high on her head. Apparently, she had been caught behind the woodpile at the bottom of the hill, 'in flagrante' with one of the single quarter men. She had a reputation. Rose heard this and couldn't decide what 'in flagrante' was so she decided they must have been stealing wood. Why, she didn't know. Daddy used as much wood as he needed for the boiler and the stove or anything.

Hard as Rose thought about it, she couldn't recall a red light on that veranda so, next day she went off to investigate. Esme asked her why she was looking up at the veranda roof and on the walls. "My dad says your mother hangs a red light outside the door." Esme went to ask her mother about it and she didn't come back. Finally, Rose knocked on the door and out came Mrs. Y. looking like thunder. Rose was told to go home and not come back! She couldn't think why.

She told her parents about it and they looked at each other in silence. It was that certain look that Rose knew meant trouble. However, after a murmured consultation she couldn't quite understand, they just said that definitely, they were not friends any longer and she mustn't go there again.

The look was the same when she heard her father saying two men they knew were brown hatters. "What's a brown hatter Daddy?" asked Rose. There was a strangled noise from Polly and she said, "Now you've done it!" There was that look and a silence.

Bert struck a match to light his pipe and as she didn't get an answer, Rose had to guess. "Does that mean they wear brown hats?" Her father looked as if he might laugh but he said thoughtfully "Yes, I suppose you could say that." Polly said "Shush Bert! Don't make it worse. Rosemary! You shouldn't be listening to grownup's conversation. Go on with what you are doing or go to bed."

George was a clever boy and he and Rose seemed to take it in turns to come first in their class. She came top at the end of the year. That Christmas, Rose was given a lovely black tin box of water colour paints and some books of special paper to paint on. For her birthday, she was given a ukulele. She learnt the chords quickly and enjoyed strumming on it and singing. She turned eleven after Christmas and moved into standard five. She still excelled at school except for physical therapy. and she wasn't good at sports.

That was the year that she was chosen to play the part of the Princess Juju in the end of year musical called 'The Princess Juju'. Rose was so proud of being chosen. She could hardly wait to tell her mother and father. Here she was, doing just what mummy had done – taking the lead in a musical.

That year a big, shy boy called Tom asked another girl to ask Rose if he could be her boyfriend. He was too shy to ask her himself. She was moderately flattered but only said yes because he agreed to let her use his football boots. That was all there was to the romance and it faded away when she decided she didn't like playing football after all.

Anyhow, Rose was far too busy with her rehearsals and singing lessons. Mrs. Burr was the music teacher and she said she hoped she could teach her in Chaplain senior school as well. She made sure to book seats for her parents, Patty and Michael in the front row of the school hall for the performance at the end of the year.

Just before the end of term and the Christmas holidays she was surprised and puzzled when her parents turned up in the car to take her out. It was the day of the dress rehearsal before the show and they took her to the restaurant in town and treated her to a long glass full of ice cream, fruit and whipped cream! That, itself, was such a surprise. She noticed that they didn't have much themselves, it seemed to be her treat only.

When they got back to the hostel she asked where they were going to spend the night, were they going to the hotel and would they see her next day, because she had to go to the dress rehearsal later and the show was the next night. Then they could all go home together as it was the last day of term.

Then the blow fell! They said they had to go right then. They were on the way to Durban. Rose was aghast! Weren't they going to come and see the show? What about the holiday and Christmas? They said she would be picked up by Paddy, her half-brother who lived in Bulawayo and she could stay with him and his wife until they returned from Durban. Rose was devastated. Pat and Michael were going to Durban with them.

She made one last try. "Can't you stay one more day and see the show?" Bert and Polly looked uncomfortable and said they couldn't. Rose stood there trying to wave goodbye and to smile when her lips were wobbling, and the tears were beginning to run down her cheeks. Her heart was thumping painfully in her chest as the car disappeared down the road. The pain was unbearable. She couldn't believe this had happened.

Some of her friends gathered round asking her what was wrong, and she could hardly speak. Then she went to the dormitory and buried her face in her pillow to hide her sobs. She cried herself to sleep and didn't get up for supper. She was numb with disappointment and felt she was living in a dead world. The boarder's mother took her to the infirmary and gave her an aspirin and some soup. They said she had to go to the dress rehearsal.

She still went through the motions, sang her songs and didn't forget her words. One began "A little Jap's heart is breaking." She really felt that was true. Her heart felt as if it would too. The teachers were worried about her.

The Headmaster, Tony Tanser took care to comfort her. After the rehearsal, at ten that night, he took her home with him. He and his wife chatted to her, asking whether her parents would be there to see the show. When she told them the reason they couldn't, they said she must look in the front row next night where they would be sitting enjoying it. They gave her a lovely mug of sweet, milky cocoa and some ginger biscuits and then took her back to the hostel. Tony Tanser was so fatherly and understanding that Rose began to heal a little.

The performance went over well, and in the morning, she made sure the trunk and all her personal things were packed and ready for Paddy to collect. She then said goodbye to everyone in the junior hostel and school because next year it would be the Dominican Convent for her. Her father thought she should go to a girl's school and not a co-ed. Rose made a special point of going to the headmaster's house to thank them and say goodbye. Their small boy was there. His name was Tim and Rose wasn't to know that he would become the expert lawyer who handled her legal affairs years later.

Paddy arrived on time and off she went, waving goodbye to all her friends. Paddy was quite a stranger really. She hadn't often seen him.

She eyed him sideways, thinking how fat and how sweaty and pink he was. He chain-smoked and asked her questions about school and the family.

Then he began to tell her silly jokes and pinching her on her leg and side. She laughed, but it was making her uncomfortable inside somehow.

She was surprised when he suddenly slowed down and drove down a small side road and stopped the car off the road amongst some bushes. "If you want to go, just go into the bush that side. I'm going here." He got out, leaving the door open and staying in full view of her. When he started to undo his trousers, Rose turned away and looked out of her window. Paddy got back in the car, turned and slid his hand up her leg to her knickers. He began to feel her and push his fingers under the elastic, rubbing her private parts.

Rose was frozen with shock and afraid suddenly. What was he doing? Her whole body stiffened, and she pressed her legs together tightly. This was something she couldn't believe was happening. How could she get away? There was nobody to run to. What could she do? She began to cry which stopped him.

"What's the matter? Why are you crying? Girls like this." Rose resorted to sobbing loudly and his hand moved away from her body. She felt a glimmer of hope and had a sudden inspiration.

"I'm homesick. I just want to go home," she said. She pulled her clothes tightly round her legs. Paddy lit a cigarette and puffed deeply and silently, staring out of his side window.

"I won't ever touch you again, don't worry. I thought you'd like it. Don't say anything about it to anyone and forget it ever happened." He started the car and reversed out of the bushes. To Rose's relief, they were on their way again, in silence.

He was so silent that Rose began to feel guilty, as if she had failed him in some way. They arrived at the house in time for tea and Rose was welcomed by Dot and her sister Margaret. Paddy disappeared somewhere and didn't emerge until dinner time. Rose liked Dot and as they talked and ate the lovely tea cake they had made for her, she began to feel more comfortable.

Margaret was very young and immediately they became friends. Rose went to bed early and was soon asleep. The day's events had exhausted her, and she kept thinking about Paddy's behavior. She decided to stay away from him as much as possible.

Fortunately, as they all went to work, she was left free to roam around the streets and avenues of the city and there was much to see there. Dot came back from her office at lunchtime and Paddy stayed away all day, returning just before dinner. All in all, the days passed uneventfully, and Rose made a few friends among the children living near. They were all on holiday from school too. She counted the days waiting to go home again.

When it stormed, Rose loved it. The more it thundered and lightening flashed, the harder the rain sheeted down, the happier she was, out in the thick of it getting soaked and wading along the wide roads of the city, knee deep in rushing water. It was fun for an eleven-year-old, but far more dangerous than she knew.

There was no one else out in the avenues to see her if she got into trouble and was dragged down into the drains. The water was up to her knees as she waded closer and closer, feeling the pull of it, like the backwash at the seaside dragging her down. It was exciting, and she felt like swimming against the drag as if she was in the sea like the rest of her family.

Her clothes were wet already, so why not? Fortunately, she heard Dorothy calling out for her and realized it must be lunchtime, so she ran in and confronted an astonished Dot. She was warned of the danger and promised not to try it again. There had been more than one drowning down the drains there, let alone people being struck by lightning.

Bulawayo's city streets were famous for the way they had been planned after 1890. They were wide enough to allow an ox-wagon with a full in-span of fourteen oxen to turn and face the other way. Originally, they were dirt roads but now they were tarred, with deep dips at the sides to allow the rain water to run away. In heavy storms there was a torrent almost sweeping one off one's feet as the water rushed down the drains at the crossroads. Paddy's house was two blocks from the city centre.

Christmas came, and it was vastly different but so much so that Rose didn't feel too unhappy about being without her parents. She was given some nice presents including a brush and comb set from Margaret. On her twelfth birthday, they went to the cinema and treated her to ice cream and popcorn. Nothing like that happened on the mine. They had no refrigerators on the mine and kept food cool in a safe with sides packed with charcoal behind chicken wire covered with hessian. Down the sides dripped water out of a pierced tin. That cooled the interior as it evaporated. All the cold meats, butter, milk and vegetables were kept on wire racks inside.

Rose had been counting the days for the return of her family and at last the Armstrong rolled down the driveway, and they were back. Probably feeling guilty, Bert and Polly made a great fuss of her and unpacked several parcels for her to open as they had tea and talked about the holiday. Rose told them all about the Princess Juju and they were careful to give her full attention.

Polly encouraged her to stand up, sing the songs and tell the story. She was in her element and all her troubles were wiped out of her mind. She had been given a set of postcards by Tony Tanser with photos of her on stage as Princess Juju. These she had written on and posted in Bulawayo to her parents addressed to the Sherwood Starr as a surprise for her family.

She said nothing at all about Paddy's behavior, not even to Pat. Somehow, children bear these burdens themselves. They were both in their twenties before Pat told her that the same had happened to her when she stayed with Paddy for a holiday once. Strange it is that children seem to protect their parents from the weight of knowing these things. They feel a huge guilt and shame and have no idea of how to deal with it. They fear upsetting them or even angering them and not being believed.

Home at last, Rose was getting ready to go to Gwelo Convent School. So was Michael who would be over the road at the Kindergarten hostel next to the Catholic Church. Pat was fifteen and no longer needed a governess. She was doing a correspondence course in shorthand and typing, and she had a lovely little typewriter of her own. She was blossoming into a beautiful young lady, looking very much like Judy Garland and she wore makeup, which made Rose very envious. Pat turned sixteen in March.

Polly was busy making blue cotton knickers and buying all the blue and beige uniforms etc. Then came the tedious business of stitching name tapes on everything. Rose had to try a suspender belt and attach long black stockings. Rose was hot, furious and tearful before she finally mastered it. She was podgy and the contortion round her posterior, holding a slippery stocking up and trying to get a metal loop over a button base without being able to see it, at the same time making sure the stocking top was over the button, seemed impossible at first. Polly and Pat were careful not to laugh.

The day came when they were off to Gwelo. It was strange being met by nuns and having nuns teaching them. Rose enjoyed the classes and set herself to get to the top if she could. Naughty little Michael was taken over the road to the little boy's hostel next to the Catholic Church. He led the pack into as much mischief as he could and was always getting the ruler from the old boarder's mother. The old nun was unaware of the way he crossed the road when he wasn't supposed to – creeping under her long habit as it billowed out behind her.

Before they travelled to school, Michael also had to try on clothes and be praised in his new uniform, big hat and tie. Finally, getting so much attention, he rebelled and started throwing things and shouting. His tantrum resolved itself in a firm declaration that he was not going! He would run away! They laughed at him for crying and he shouted, "Shup UT!" instead of shut-up, which made them laugh more.

So, he ran away into the bush and the piccanin had to rush after him and bring him back. It was dark, and they were getting worried before the piccanin returned with him. Only the gift of his little school suitcase for books and his lunch box pacified him

He excelled in naughtiness one afternoon when the old

parson from town came to tea. He had a totally bald head which Michael couldn't take his eyes off. After his tea was finished, he was sent to play on the veranda. Just when the parson raised his cup to his lips, a golf ball travelling at full speed hit him fair and square on the shiny pink target. He jumped and nearly fell off the chair and spilt the tea all down his front. Polly had a busy time apologizing and mopping him up. Mikey was in disgrace and the dear old man said don't punish him, I'm sure he didn't mean to hit me. Like Hell, he didn't, thought Rose.

She had a bitter memory of his deadly aim the previous year, when she had passed his bed one evening and received the hard corner of a book on the back of her neck. It had been flung from across the room. It really stung, and she was so furious that she picked it up and threw it back at him, aiming to just miss him by throwing it at the bed. Unfortunately, she miscalculated. "My wee!" bellowed her little brother, screaming at the top of his voice. Rose was afraid she had done more than she intended.

Parents came rushing in and examined the damaged article and her father lost his temper and dragged her off to the bathroom. "Sorry Daddy! I didn't mean it. He threw it at me first!" Bert was in a rage, unbuckling his belt. "Bend over that chair! Take your knickers down. Now, over that chair!"

After a couple of heavy beltings, she began to scream, and he didn't stop until she had had several of them. "Now go to bed!" he disappeared.

Rose hobbled off, pulling up her pants, sobbing, and lay on her bed with her face to the wall; She felt totally wronged and embarrassed and she couldn't believe her father could have done it to her if he loved her, which she had been so sure of up to then. Nobody came to sympathize and listen to her side of things. She never quite felt so close to her father after that. There was a rift between them.

Polly and Pat came in eventually when they thought she was asleep. Polly, pulled down the bedclothes and exclaimed in a whisper to Pat about some blood. She sounded appalled and said to Pat that he shouldn't have done it. Pat said, "She deserved it, anyway." Rose thought bitterly that she would say that. Anything to show Rose in a bad light.

A day later, it was time go to Gwelo and drop Rose at the Chaplain Junior School. Bert and Polly thought it wise to tell the Headmistress about the incident to explain why Rose had red welts and bruises on the back of her legs. Apparently, this was frowned upon heavily and Bert was frostily warned never to touch her again or it would be reported. Bert hadn't expected that reception. Rose was quietly delighted and felt vindicated. Finally, someone had stood up for her.

Now, two years later, it was up to the old nuns to battle with the seven-year-old little devil. Michael climbed on the roof of the toilet block, he claimed, dislodging the vent pipe because it came out when he tried to climb down holding it. The little girls inside made haste to inform the nuns that he had been spying on them. Down came a belt on his behind this time, wielded by the Mother Superior herself!

He said he was often sent to her for a whipping. Not surprising as another thing the little boys thought of doing was creeping round the back of the antiquated bucket lavatory the nuns used, peering in and poking them in the rear with a stick.

Rose had her finer moments too. At her first lesson in science class, they were given a small amount of the liquid metal mercury on a plate to study and see how it separated and then rolled into a single lump because it was magnetic. Rose hid a little in her hand and took it out to play with. Fortunately, she finally lost it in the playground when it slid off her palm. The third science lesson was about the unstable qualities of phosphorous. The small pieces were kept in a wax base. The nun demonstrated how it would explode if rubbed on the table. It was fascinating!

Of course, they all secreted a bit in anything they could think of when the teacher wasn't looking, but it was Rosemary who tried it out on the refectory tablecloth at breakfast next morning. It exploded, bounced around and set the tablecloth alight. The two nuns were running about frantically dabbing it with napkins and burning holes in those as well. Rose was made to give up science class and study Hygiene and Physiology instead. How dull that was!

Some of the teachers were good but, although it was an expensive private school, the nuns were German Dominicans and some of them could hardly speak English. The English teacher was very old and fat with a round, rosy face and she couldn't speak English properly, let alone teach it. Rose never forgot the first poem she had to learn.

Sister Joanna made somebody read it aloud. Then she demonstrated how one should read - with expression:

"Grreat beeg dorg, 'ead upon 'iss toes.
Tiny leetle bee, settles on 'iss nose.

Grreat beeg dorg, tinks it iss a fly.
Never says a vorrd but vinks verry sly!

Den 'e makes a snap! Qvick as qvick could be!
Does 'iss level best but doesn't get dat fly.
Tiny leetle bee, alive and looking vell.
Grreat beeg dorg, mostly gorn to svell!

And this was English tuition! The whole bunch of twelve-year-old philistines were agog! Never had they had such a chance to feel superior to a teacher. They began to giggle and mock the poor old nun unmercifully. She was over seventy and fragile for all her bulk and she wasn't much taller than they. She banged on her table

"Gurrls! Gurrls! Be qviet! Stop it now or I vill send you to ze Mudder Superior!"

That made them were worse, laughing at her and mocking her when suddenly she started to cry. Turning purple, she hurried out of the door. It was Rose who suddenly began to feel sorry for her. Also, she had a feeling that Mother Superior would come down on them like an avenging angel. After all, she was also a German.

She said they should all go and fetch her in and say sorry. That convinced the others and they hurried out and found her just outside, dabbing her face and blowing her nose. They put their arms around old Sister Joanna and promised they wouldn't do it again if she would please come back.

After form two, Rose had to give up geography to study art for her Senior Cambridge Certificate. This entailed going to the art room alone for an hour every week. Sister Veronica was tiny and quite sweet, but she spent the whole hour sitting at a table painting dainty little flowers and leaves on doilies and decorating them round the edge with glue and glitter. These sets of three or six were being prepared for the end of year fete and the nuns sold them to the public to raise funds for the school.

She sat Rose at a table and gave her a pencil and drawing paper. Then she brought a jar of water with one nasturtium and a leaf in it and put it down in front of her. "Draw dat," she said. That was all. She went back to her side of the room and they got on with it in silence. Rose did her best and fortunately she had a God given talent. The nun returned when the hour was nearly over, and she had just finished drawing the flower. "Dat's goot," said Sister Virginia. That was her drawing lesson! No tuition about perspective or positioning – nothing about pencils, paper or style. That was the way of it for her next two years.

There was an extra charge for art lessons of course. Rose gained a credit for art in her final year but with proper tuition it would have been a distinction as she gained in mathematics. Only years later she was to see what real art tuition was. She spent so much of her two hours final exam time trying to get a facial likeness when she had to draw a complete figure that it ended up unfinished and out of proportion. She knew it but there wasn't time to start again. There had been no tuition over the year from the nun. She sat outside on her own and drew a tree. She was given books with pictures in them by famous artists and the nun carried on doing her private work.

One teacher was very good. That year, Rose took music as a subject as well. She had Sister Margaret teaching her and she was excellent. Rose had heard her mother playing Rachmaninov and Chopin's music and knew all of it by heart, so she chose pieces that her mother played. It was relatively easy to achieve some proficiency very quickly so Sister Margaret prepared her to take the Cape intermediate exam. This she passed at the end of one year. Unfortunately, she had to stop music lessons because circumstances changed suddenly at home.

SIX

LOSS

A week before Christmas and her fourteenth birthday, on the night of the nineteenth of December,1940, the grim reaper passed over their house and their father was taken from them. Bert suddenly felt the dreadful pain of a heart attack and at two in the morning he was rushed by car to Gatooma Hospital.

Rose woke because she heard people talking and lights were on. She stood in the doorway of the dining room asking why her father was being helped by a neighbour to walk out to the car. He saw Rose and stopped.

"Aren't you going to say goodbye to your old dad?" said Bert.

"Of course, Daddy," said Rose, wanting to run to him and hold on to him. He came to her, put his arms around her and kissed her on the forehead several times. "Goodbye." Rose felt a wave of relief and smiled at him. She kissed him saying "Goodbye Daddy," and he was gone. It must be alright, she thought, it's nothing bad after all; just a checkup to see what is wrong. Relieved, she went back to bed.

In the morning, she woke to find Ann Berry there to fetch them all for breakfast down at the club. She confirmed that

Polly would be back later, and Bert was in the hospital for investigation. Perhaps they both would be back soon.

Rose kept going out of the sitting room to check and just after morning tea she saw the car draw up at the top gate. She ran up the path as her mother came towards her. "How's Daddy, Mom?" Her mother looked tired and drawn. "What is it, Mom?"

"He's dead!" Rose was stunned. It was a terrible blow. Then she had a sudden wave of what seemed like relief. She rushed ahead and burst into the flat shouting "Daddy's dead!" She felt a wide grimace on her face and thought she was smiling but didn't know why. She felt like screaming "No! No! It can't be. Daddy! Daddy!"

Ann Berry rushed out to Polly and brought her into the room, sitting her down and talking in hushed tones, holding Polly's hand and questioning her. Pat was with them and Rose was excluded somehow. She walked away into the garden and paced up and down. She couldn't think properly and wondered why she was moaning. "What now? What would they do?" She wanted to go and wake her father and bring him back. She fought to accept the fact that she couldn't.

Her mother had often spoken about the things she wished she could do if he 'popped off'. She suddenly felt bitter towards her mother and blamed her. She went back and stood in the doorway. They took no notice of her and talked in whispers and bitterness welled up.

She glared at her mother and said: "Well? Aren't you glad? Now you can do all the things you said you would do if daddy died!" There was a silence. Her mother looked stricken. Rose suddenly felt sorry for her mother and wished she hadn't said that. She was crying as she turned and marched off alone again into the garden. There, she just kicked stones and felt as if her world had collapsed about her. She was totally miserable. What a spoilt Christmas – without Daddy! Why had she said that? Her mother's face haunted her.

Ann Berry came to the rescue eventually. She walked out and said Rose had said things that were not right. Why? Rose explained that it was the truth and Ann said perhaps, but you should apologise because Polly was upset and didn't mean what she had said. Finally, she brought Rose in and she awkwardly said sorry, feeling that her mother should also say she was sorry for saying things like that.

As the reality of their situation dawned, the main problem at that time was Bert's life policy and where it was. Rose, wanting to make amends, said she could cycle up and fetch the box of papers for her mother. She took the house key and cycled as fast as she could up the hill. All the way, she was groaning aloud, and tears were running down her cheeks. She didn't realise that this was mourning for her father.

With a pain in her chest, she rushed into the house as if the hounds of hell were chasing her. Clutching the box, she rushed back and gave it to her mother. There began a hunt for receipts. Polly had telephoned the lawyer, the Jewish father of a girl who went to the convent, theoretically a friend of theirs. Apparently, he held the life policy as security for a large sum Bert had borrowed to purchase the Armstrong. He said that the last instalment hadn't been paid on due date, so he was within the rule of law to cash in the policy himself as Bert had ceded it to him. This was a terrible blow.

Polly needed the money desperately. There were all the

household bills to pay and there would be no pension or gratuity from Lonrho. There were Convent fees outstanding for the last term and more to pay for the following year and funeral fees to pay. They would have to move from the Sherwood Starr house and find somewhere to live – where, she hadn't the faintest idea. What the mine manager managed to do was allow them to remain in the house for an extra month, until the end of January. Rose had never seen her mother looking so haggard and frightened.

After two days of hunting through every piece of paper available, just when Polly was about to give up, Rose found it! How glad she was that she had been the one to find it. It was the receipt for the last instalment. Immediately, they went to QueQue and claimed the insurance policy.

The next shock was to be informed by the insurance company that they would only pay back five hundred pounds, the amount Bert had paid in instalments, because he had failed to tell them that he had ear trouble and a mastoid operation at the age of fourteen. The fact that thirty-three years later he died of a heart complaint didn't stop them from using it to their advantage. The plight of a widow and her three children was obviously very secondary to hanging on to cash by fair means or foul.

Bert's son Dick, from his first marriage, had tragically died suddenly of a burst appendix and gangrene two months before. His possessions, the sum of five hundred pounds, a gramophone and records had been sent to his father. That money at least assisted Polly and her family to survive financially for a short while.

Friends rallied round. The magistrate in Gatooma kindly

offered her a position in the court as his personal secretary, starting at the princely sum of eight pounds a month! She had never worked in her life, but he said he was sure she would soon be good at what she was doing, and the salary would rise substantially.

Another friend was the town clerk. Pat had qualified as a shorthand typist and at the age of seventeen and a half, Mrs. Blackburn took her on as Assistant Town Clerk. Her salary would be twenty-two pounds a month. Pat's adversity had finally meant that she was the one who was the bread winner.

Then the beautiful Armstrong developed some trouble with the Wilson gearbox. There was no money for a repair and it had to be sold. They hated to part with it but the money helped. They were moving into the residential Grand Hotel in Gatooma and there wouldn't be a garage for it in any case. Also, the Town House where Pat would be working was only a couple of blocks away from the hotel and the Court House where Polly would work was not much further. On her way to work. Polly could help Pat walk to work and back. Their close friends, Dr. Warne and his wife and family were there as were many others Polly knew well. She could join the Dramatic Society and play golf at weekends. They had just enough in the bank to keep Rosemary at boarding school for her final year.

Rose was able to finish her schooling at the convent. She would be catching the train to Gwelo and back for holidays as many others did and that seemed quite exciting. Michael was to be a weekly boarder at Gatooma School. That suited him, too. His mother would be just a few blocks down the road and he could spend weekends at the hotel with her and Pat. Of course, wherever he went, sooner or later there'd be trouble. Mike was a loose cannon; he couldn't help it.

That Christmas was the saddest and dreariest they ever had. It was just five days after Bert's death. They didn't go with their mother to the funeral in Gatooma. Now almost eighteen, Pat stayed with the younger ones. They had to wait several hours for Polly's return, feeling bereft and as though the hours were dragging. At last she was back, and life seemed to have some focus again.

They could no longer afford to keep their faithful servants, but Polly wrote them all good references and managed to find work for them with friends on the mine. Their dear cook, Nest, was the hardest to say goodbye to. Polly had found him an excellent place as head Chef in the household of the High Commissioner in Salisbury.

He had been with them since Rose was born and as he shook their hands, he held hers in both of his, saying "Goodbye Miss Gooseberry, be a good girl and look after the N'kosikaas. Don't you fight with her!" They all laughed, and it broke the tension. Before he left, there was a knock at the back door and Nest called Polly. There, standing outside, was an ancient African man from the Compound holding a bulging cotton bag. This, he held out to her saying he was the spokesman for all the Africans on the mine. They wished to say how sorry they were about the N'kosi. This was for the family from them.

Polly looked in the bag and it was full of coins – a collection of pennies, tickeys, sixpences and shillings. Little that the Africans were paid, they had done this. Polly was in tears over it. They all went out to shake the old man's hand and send their thanks to all the men who had contributed. Polly asked the mine manager to give each of them an extra bag of maize meal and a double ration of meat at the end of the week. They could then have a wake.

Rose's birthday was even gloomier because there was only one small gift – an oblong eraser to use for her drawing. Rose, who had expected something better than that trivial article, couldn't believe it. She lost her young teenage temper, cried and found something cutting to say about how she wished dad was still alive and that everything was terrible without him.

Once again, she had to witness her mother breaking down and crying and immediately, she felt guilty. Pat glared at her and said she must apologise. She felt sick inside, worrying about upsetting her mother again and realized that her birthday present didn't matter at all. She grew up a little.

Polly said she hadn't had time to get anything else and Rose put her arms around her and said that she needed a new petticoat and she'd love a pretty lace topped one for her birthday.

Back at school, her friends were very kind and sympathetic. Strangely, not one of the nuns mentioned it. They were all German Dominicans and World War Two was being waged. The children were not above insinuating that they were the enemy and probably this attitude had put their backs up. Rose was often on her knees for some fall from grace, particularly in the dormitory where the chief boarder's mother reigned. This was Sister Ludovica, old Ludy as they called her, and she was stern and quite poisonous.

On one occasion, Rose hadn't washed her face because the water was frozen and Sister Ludovica ordered her down on her knees for half an hour. She answered back that she could hardly wash when they weren't allowed to have hot water and there was ice on top of the water in her basin.

Old Ludy, lost her temper and began a torrent of abuse. Spittle rained down on Rose, in her vulnerable position on the floor, one spot fell on her cheek, so she made a deliberate performance of wiping it off. This infuriated the nun totally and she passed a remark she immediately regretted. "Your father didn't pay for your tuition last year either!"

Rose was stunned and there was a deathly hush for a second or two. Then she said icily "Well, it's been paid now, hasn't it?" Sister Ludovica apologized saying she shouldn't have said that. It was Ludy who paraded about the veranda out of sight in the dark telling her beads, in the evening when the seniors were allowed in the garden on the grassy patch where they could lie about looking at the stars and chatting. It was amusing to glance sideways and watch the corner. They were sure that sooner or later her nose would appear and then an eye goggling round to see what they were doing. Only years later did Rose realise what she suspected the girls were doing.

One other mystery for Rose was a statement Ludy made to her when they were all watching a film in the hall. The nuns had a projector and hired suitable films to show them occasionally for a small charge. She was standing at the back helping run the projector with the nun. There happened to be the hero kissing the heroine passionately just before the end. The lights were turned on and the children were filing out. Ludy turned to her and hissed "Did you see Elaine when they were kissing? She wasn't looking at their faces!" This puzzled Rose. She wondered what Elaine had been looking at anyhow. She just shrugged and said she hadn't been watching Elaine and Ludy didn't elaborate. It was years before she realized what the nun meant. Elaine, by the way, bunked out one night and was found somewhere in the arms of an airman from the Training Camp. She was not seen again at school as she was expelled.

One of the airmen was caught exposing himself through a gap in the hedge early evening, flashing for the benefit of the girls walking around inside. Why any male thinks it is an inviting sight, is hard to fathom. One only needs to look at the bare base of a baboon to know that it is hardly an oil painting!

Rose didn't see him but other girls, particularly the smaller ones had been shocked and upset. Elaine wasn't, apparently. Most of the ground crew at Thornhill airfield were British and they were a mixed, unruly bunch. The nuns hit on a cunning plan to save the virtue of the juniors. The police were called in for surveillance and they hid upstairs in the little boy's dormitory over the road. The nuns kept the smaller girls in the recreation room and let a group of big girls roam in the grounds near the gap. Sure enough, the following evening there he was, and he was arrested.

It was probably tempting to pass a Convent school full of nubile young females and they tried their luck at getting them to break the rules and come and enjoy what was being offered! There were also Australians amongst them and they were a pretty wild bunch.

That Christmas holiday, when Rose turned fifteen, she spent the time at the Cartwright's farm near Marandellas. Dolly and Billie had a daughter, Joan, who was almost Rose's age. They hadn't been very close friends because Joan went to a boarding school in South Africa and Rose seldom saw her, but

Dolly and Dora were at school together in Durban and they were very close.

Both had ended up in Rhodesia married to Englishmen who had emigrated. Bert had joined Lonrho and Billy had settled on farming. The farmhouse was a converted tobacco barn with a huge veranda added on one side on which a wooden staircase led up to two big bedrooms, the floors of which were the wooden ceilings of the rooms below. Gradually, over the years, they had added a kitchen and a proper bathroom and built thatched huts nearby to accommodate visitors.

Rose felt almost related to the Cartwrights. All her life, they had spent weekends and long holidays at the farm, mostly without Bert as he had to work, but Dolly and Dora had been bosom companions since kindergarten in Durban. They loved each other's company, and both had three children. Dolly had Joan first and then Guy and David, Dora had Pat and Rosemary and then Michael. Dolly didn't have her first child until Rose was a year old and by the time she remembered spending a holiday at the farm her first recollection of all of them together was when she was about six.

She remembered a toddler called Guy and small girl of five called Joan and her vivid memory was having breakfast and the children given a bowl of porridge with something scattered on top of it that she found bitter and oily. Joan was trying to eat it because her mother said it was good for her, but Rose took one mouthful and it was horrible. She pushed her plate away and said so.

Her mother was cross because Dolly had bought it especially

for them and the battle was on! "Be quiet, Rose, there's nothing wrong with it! Shush! You'll sit there until you finish it."

"But it tastes horrible, mummy!" whined Rose. She stared at the rancid tasting wheat germ and saw something wriggling. She looked harder and longer and saw tiny wriggling worms. "There are WORMS in it!" she yelled. "Don't be silly, of course there aren't! Behave yourself and eat up." Her mother was ashamed of her child's behavior compared with Dolly's little girl. Here they were, welcome visitors and her child was letting her down.

"There ARE!" yelled Rose "Look!" Dora and Dolly peered at it "There's nothing." "There IS! Can't you see them? I can see HUNDREDS!" All over the top of my porridge!

Dora picked up the plate and the two mothers went over to the window. They put on their spectacles. There was a murmuring and then Rose saw their shoulders shaking. They were laughing. She was prepared to have a tantrum when they turned around and agreed that there were tiny worms. The plates were cleared away quickly, and they waited a while for boiled eggs and soldiers.

It wasn't the only food war Rose recalled. There was the boiled egg battle on another occasion. There were eggs and soldiers for supper on that occasion as well and Rose was delighted. Her egg had its top sliced off but to her horror the white was hardly cooked, in fact, it was not far from raw. Once again, Rose swore she wouldn't eat it. "It's BIBBLY mummy!"

There was about to be the usual storm when Pattie saved the day very diplomatically. "Umm, I'll have it! Give it to me. I'll eat it!" Rose was uncertain. This was, after all, all there was, except toast soldiers and Rose loved her food. Why did Pattie like it? She wondered, and Pattie told her "Look, mine's also bibbly and I do this," she dipped the toast into it and ate the end, smacking her lips "Ummm. Lovely! Pass me yours."

"No! I want it!" Rose started dipping her soldier into the egg and was pleasantly surprised. It was a bibbly egg demand every night after that. It was Patty who had said, when she was bed ridden "I know how to make Rose put the light off when I want it. I just say I want it on. What a little darling Rose must have been!

The next time Joan was at home from Durban, she was about eleven, but she had brought a school friend to the farm and they excluded Rose and concentrated on each other because they were best friends. Rose decided she didn't like Joan much.

So, now Joan was thirteen and on her own. She told Rose that she hadn't liked her before but now she did, and they could be best friends. They played tennis together and rode the horses every morning. In the afternoons they went visiting other farms or went to the village and had tea in the hotel or the tearoom after shopping with the two mothers. In the evening they all sat on the lawn or veranda watching Joan giving a display of her acrobatics and ballet dancing.

She was double jointed and able to fold herself into a tiny parcel of body, with her head tucked under her back bone. Dancing was her chosen future and she going to London to the Royal School of Ballet when she left school the next year. They parted that holiday vowing to be together at Christmas time when Rose would have finished her schooling.

Rose's final year passed rapidly and was only marred by Rose putting on a lot of weight and feeling self-conscious about it. For the first time, she wanted to be thinner and she vowed that she would try to lose some of it. It was difficult because the German nuns in the kitchen cooked meat balls swimming in fat, stews with huge dumplings and heavily crusted pies predominating. Every break time in winter, tea was served accompanied by foot-long, thick slices of bread dipped in dripping and baked crisp. It was too tempting for Rose to resist. The pounds piled on.

Then, suddenly boarding school was over. Back she went to Gatooma and the hunt for work began. She had been asked what she wanted to do before she left the Convent as there was a government assessment of the school leaver's capabilities. As she achieved five credits and a distinction in her Senior Cambridge Examination they recommended higher education at University, but she knew that her mother could not afford it.

The alternatives listed were nursing, telephone operator, machine operator or shop assistant and things like that. She really wanted to be a student nurse, but she was only fifteen and had to wait until she was seventeen. She chose to try and train as a photographer. Polly tried to find a photographer who would employ and train her. Nobody in Gatooma could oblige so Rose had to think again. Perhaps she could be a telephone operator. In the meantime, they had all been invited to the farm for Christmas and they decided Rose should holiday there and Polly would continue trying to get her employed somewhere in Salisbury.

For Christmas, she bought Rose a lovely green floral dress in a silky material and made her a long evening dress with a pink lace top, a gathered pink net skirt and a velvet ribbon sash.

They were invited to the Cartwrights farm for two weeks holiday and would be there for New Year too.

Dolly had invited the usual additional bunch of servicemen to stay for Christmas and New Year. This time there were six British Airforce officers. One was Pilot Officer Meaker and another was Flight Lieutenant John Pemberton. Another was a handsome young officer that Rose immediately rather fancied but was too shy to even talk to. Her mother and Dolly both gravitated towards John Pemberton, a very sophisticated and charming man, unfortunately married.

Pat found herself singled out by Mickey, as he was called. His name was Edward Pritchard Meaker.

Joan and Rosemary spent most of their time together, riding the horses around the farm and over to a neighbour's place to have tea with them and see their sons Tony and Francis. In the afternoons, they played tennis or went off to the river with Guy and Michael to swim.

Once, they went off to climb the surrounding hills. There, they came across an odd collection of clay pots. They brought one unbroken one back to show the others. Billy and Dolly were not impressed. They said it was probably an ancient burial ground. The superstition was that it was a bad omen and brought bad luck and disaster to anyone removing them. Billy took it and gave it to the cook to return to site if he could find it.

Pat and Mickey found that they had a great deal in common and the friendship seemed to be developing into something much closer. Mickey said he was about to return to England as he had failed to qualify as a pilot and was going to train as a navigator in Lancaster bombers. He asked Pat to correspond with him as he wanted to return to Rhodesia after the war ended. They were unofficially engaged by this time, but they didn't announce it to anyone.

On Christmas morning Rose was given a lovely big cut glass bottle of Cologne. This had cost her mother more than she could really afford but she felt that Rose needed a special gift for doing so well in her exams. Dolly gave her Mitcham's lavender bath powder and Pat gave her a writing set in a special box.

It was a festive crowd, somewhat drunken and Rose was allowed a small glass of wine. The only disaster was Dolly's huge Christmas cake that afternoon. It looked so fabulous and large slices were handed round to everyone sitting in the garden. One bite and they all gagged and had to dispose of the mouthful in as dignified a way as they could. What Dolly had thought was sugar had been salt! Finally, they laughed about it.

The Cartwrights had invited all the surrounding farmers and their families to a barn dance on the 28th. They held these in a tobacco barn, suitably decked out with bunting and tables for food at one end with chairs all around the sides. Plates, glasses and chairs were hired in the village and the smooth, slippery cement floor in the middle was strewn with maize meal on the morning. Apparently, this helped to keep the dancers from suddenly landing on their backsides.

Rose and Joan decided to perform for the crowd at intervals through the evening. They had the gramophone and records for Joan's ballet numbers. She wore her lovely tutu and danced on points and looked very beautiful. For other numbers, she ran in and did a gymnastic display. Rose wound the gramophone and started the music when Joan was ready at the door. On the night she brought the crowd to its feet.

Rose, too, got a lot of applause. She had practiced her songs, sitting on a chair with her pretty green frock flowing down to the floor around her, accompanying herself on her ukulele. She knew 'Isle of Capri' and 'Indian Love Song', 'The Umbrella Man' and 'Danny Boy'. She was able to play one or two others if there was an encore.

But it was the night for Joan to shine like a star. Dolly looked so proud of her and it was a night to remember for her and Billy. To see their lovely daughter dance on a stage for the first time was something they had not expected. Dolly loved the ballet and she had never had the training she had yearned for. Her parents were struggling when she was young, and they could not afford the lessons. Later, they became wealthy hotel owners, but by then Dolly was too old to begin.

They all saw the New Year in together and had lunch before Pat, Michael and Dora had to return to Gatooma. Rose stayed at the Cartwrights. She was going to return to Gatooma by train when Joan went back to school in South Africa.

The officers had returned to Cranborne airfield and Dolly prepared to welcome six Australian ground crewmen. This was their war effort, giving some of the forces a home from home at Christmas time. They were strange characters that enjoyed teasing the Rhodesians by making up stories about Australian animals and birds and swearing they were true.

One day, they told them about a vine with huge leaves full of holes that bore fruit like a pineapple, but the fruit ripened in sections from the top and tasted like a fruit salad. One layer tasted like banana, the next like peach or pineapple. It was called the delicious monster. Nobody believed it and they insisted that was true. Nothing could convince everybody that such a vine existed or had such a stupid name. Years later, Rose found out that it was true after all. The vine was a Monstero Deliciosa. Well they had told so many stories it served them right.

A couple of days later, Joan suddenly complained of feeling ill. She had a bad headache and Rose said she also felt a bit sick. They both went to bed straight after dinner and Dolly gave them both aspirin and a glass of water. Rose tried to chat as they undressed but Joan was silent. She just turned her back and seemed to go to sleep so Rose did the same.

In the morning, Rose was up early and quite well but Joan had a raging temperature and her headache was worse. Billy and Dolly moved her into their room and darkened it because she said she couldn't bear the light. The doctor came and examined her. There was a consultation and it was decided to wait a day or two and if she didn't improve, drive her up to Salisbury to see Godfrey Huggins. The doctor thought it was possibly meningitis. He wanted a second opinion.

Rose asked if she could go in and see Joan, but they said she was sleeping. She wondered what she could do to help and suddenly she remembered her bottle of Eau de Cologne. She asked Dolly to take it and wet a cloth with it to put on Joan's brow. Dolly looked dazed and said that was an idea.

The following day, Joan was carried to the car and Dolly and Billy drove away leaving Rose in the care of a Mrs. Pemberley, a friend staying at the farm. She was an alcoholic and living permanently in the guest rondavel in the side garden. She was on the wagon theoretically, but Dolly kept a close watch for signs that she had fallen off.

The Australians were still there, and Dolly moved Rose into Mrs. Pemberley's room which contained two single beds. She didn't quite trust the men alone in the house at night with a fifteen-year-old girl. They were rough diamonds indeed. On one occasion, she was sitting on the sofa laughing and joking with them when a hard-faced man next to her suddenly grabbed her and tickled her hard on her ribs and breast and he didn't stop. That made her laugh so hard in embarrassment that it took her breath away. It seemed to spur him on.

She struggled and laughed, trying to get away but he carried on. The others laughed and watched as he pushed his tongue into her ear and started biting it. He grabbed her breasts and she wriggled as hard as she could. "Stop it!" she called. He was biting so hard and it was hurting so much that she didn't know what to do. She was hysterical and screamed "Stop it, you're hurting me!' Dolly and Billy were nowhere to be seen. Finally, the others intervened and made him let her go.

She was purple in the face and her clothes had ridden up, so she was almost bare to the waist except for her pants. He released her, and she leapt up pulling her clothes down and ran out without looking at them to wash her face in the bathroom then went straight to her bedroom where Mrs. Pemberley was resting. This was a punishable offence, but she didn't know that. She avoided them after that and she was glad when they left.

In three days Dolly and Billy were back at the farm to tell them that their beloved daughter was dead. She had poliomyelitis and it had destroyed the part of her brain that controlled her breathing. Dolly disappeared upstairs and didn't come down for two days. Rose didn't know what to do. She asked Billy whether he had told her mother and whether she should go home but he said she must stay. She noticed that all the photos of Joan had been removed from the tables and walls. Dolly was busy upstairs packing away Joan's clothing in trunks. Mrs. Pemberley and Billy asked her not to speak to Dolly about Joan as she couldn't bear it.

Rose felt unhappy about this. It seemed as if she had never existed there. They had wiped out all trace of her friend. Rose missed her terribly. However, only a few days before she left them forever, she had her evening of being the shining light and Dolly and Billie had that, at least, to remember. All the farm Africans were motored up for her funeral and burial in Salisbury. They were given a bull calf for their wake at the farm at the weekend. They were not forgotten.

Rose stayed on at the farm. Dolly and Billy were numbed and silent. They walked around like sleepwalkers and it was hard to think what to say. Billy told Rose not to mention Joan to Dolly, he said she couldn't stand it. The Australian Airmen were still at the farm and Dolly tried to be the hostess she always had been, presiding at meals and having tea in the garden where the ghost of Joan haunted Rose. She kept feeling that she'd suddenly see Joan doing acrobatics on the grass.

Rose remained in the guest cottage with Mrs. Pemberley. In the night Rose heard the clinking of bottles and told Dolly. She came over when the coast was clear to seek for the evidence while Rose kept a lookout at the door.

Sure enough, Dolly found empties stashed away in cases and had it out with her. She had to move on! Her ex-husband was an army major who could make old Cinders, the fat, grey horse, perk up and look like a Lipizzaner. For Rose, that horse emulated the 'old, grey nag' – dragging along and eating grass; not even putting his head up if she tried pulling on the reins. Yet, he could gallop faster than Joan's old horse Mary. Occasionally, when Rose managed to spur him on for a race, he would pull ahead of Mary. As soon as he almost passed her, Mary would bite him on the rump. On one occasion, he took off at right angles with Rose hanging down the side, trying to get up and hanging on for dear life. He just bolted. Once, as her girth was being tightened by the groom, Mary turned her head and tried to bite off Rose's knee cap. She managed to step back quickly but she had purple bruises all round her knee.

Dora thought Rose should stay at the farm and give Dolly some much needed support until a week before they went back to Gatooma, but Rose found it difficult. Joan couldn't be mentioned. Perhaps Rose was wanted there, she didn't know but she hoped so. She was always welcomed at the farm in the years to come and spent many weekends there as if she were a loved member of the family. It was just so difficult to act as if Joan had never existed.

SEVEN

SALISBURY AND UMTALI

Rose now needed to get a job quickly. Dora remembered E.T. in Umtali so she contacted him, and he agreed to take Rose on at a minimal wage. Irene Arter was still living there with her husband and she said Rose could stay with them.

Rose enjoyed working for E T and it was pleasant staying with Irene and her husband. Irene cooked plain meals, nourishing enough and not over rich and Rose had to rise early, make her bed and help with the washing up and tidying before she walked the mile or more from the house to E. T's, in the centre of town, then back after work. She began to lose the puppy fat she had gained at the Convent. She didn't know anyone there but Irene, so at lunchtime, she wandered around the town, window shopping to pass the time.

Seeing a piano for sale in a furniture shop called Harmony House, she went in and sat on the stool in front of a baby grand. She thought it was the most beautiful piano she could ever have seen. Tentatively, she played a chord and tried a piece she knew. Suddenly, someone said, "Hello, can I help you?" Rose was flustered and felt her face going red. She jumped up, feeling guilty. "Sorry! I didn't see anyone here. Is this piano for sale?" It was the owner of the shop, Meyer Bloom. "Carry on, play some more, I enjoyed listen to you. Do you want to buy a piano?" Rose said no, she just loved it and wanted to hear how it sounded. She said she couldn't play very well but her mother did, and did he play?

Meyer told her he played and wrote music himself and Rose asked him if he would play for her. He sat and played, and they talked. Rose told him all about herself and he told her he was married and had three children and the lunch hour went far too soon. Rose said she would come back next day. She had made a friend. She haunted his shop every lunch hour and Meyer Bloom must have realized how lonely she was. He was very kind and probably appreciated her adulation. She was a fan. She couldn't get enough of his playing and singing, and he asked her to sing for him. Rose fell in love!

It wasn't a sexual attraction really, she fell in love with the music, the talent, the playing, his looks, his sweetness to her, everything about Meyer and she haunted the place, oblivious of the fact that to him, it must have been obvious that she had a crush on him. Gradually, she began to wish she were married to him and regretting the fact that he was married. Finally, it came as a shock to her when he told her he was leaving Umtali and going to England. He wanted to further his musical career there and had sold Harmony House. He gave her his address in England and hoped they would meet again there one day. That was the end of that short but pleasant liaison.

Rose was invited to a party by a girl she had met at a house down Carrington Road that she passed when she went for a walk in the evenings. She had nothing to wear so she bought three yards of pretty, blue flowered material and cut out a sleeveless dress with a full length paneled skirt, stitched it up on Irene's sewing machine and bound the neck and armholes. All this was done rapidly on Saturday afternoon and she had to bath and dress and walk there at seven p.m. She squeezed into it with five minutes to spare and had to leave four inches of waist unstitched to get it over her well-developed bust. She pinned this gap together with huge safety pins and hoped that would do.

Irene had gone to the cinema and it was a miracle of contortion to get the pins done up on the inside without it showing on the outside. Finally, she ran down the hill and arrived half an hour late. Nobody really noticed her, and the dancing had begun. She sat at the side wondering whether she should slip out again when a tall, good-looking Greek man suddenly asked her to dance. His name was Costa and the record they were playing was a tango. Rose was delighted to have been singled out to dance, but she had absolutely no idea how to dance a tango. That didn't worry Costa, however. He wanted to show off his expertise and he simply put his arm round her waist, firmly clutched her hand and they were off.

Rose felt that she was pressed to his body all the way down, almost embarrassingly. He gazed into her eyes and she was mesmerized. Each step he made, she followed and suddenly he bent her back, almost to the floor and then pulled her up and whirled her round, walked her backward with her cheek against his, then with a flick of his wrist, maneuvered her so that she had changed cheeks and they were stepping back and with a sudden bend back to the floor, the dance was over. She found that everyone else had been sitting it out and watching the performance. They all clapped and whistled, and

Costa thanked her and led her back to her seat. When she went home, she felt wonderful and couldn't sleep for a long time thinking what a success the dance had been. She loved the tango, it was such a fantastic dance.

She learnt quite a lot at E.T. Brown's in the short time she was there and, at first, E T kept his distance. She worked there for about three months. One morning, E T was showing her how to glue a photograph to a backing sheet for framing, using a ruler and lightly penciling on the position, then rolling on a 'gloy' made of boiled water, flour and clove essence, scraping most of that off and carefully pressing the photo in position. Then using a damp cloth to press it down firmly and wipe off the excess glue. It was an absorbing, difficult job which required care and concentration and Rose was leaning over the table wiping the glue off, when E T put his hand under her arm and groped her breast. She was shocked! She dropped the brush and backed away from him. All she could think of doing about it was to rear up and say loftily, "Please don't do that E T!" He smirked and carried on talking about the photo framing, but everything was over for Rose.

She phoned her mother and Dora came down by train immediately. She had a word with E T and demanded Rose's pay and three month's leave pay and they returned to Gatooma together. Rose had to get a job as soon as possible. Dora saw that the Government advertised vacancies in various departments and Rose thought she would like to try working in the Telephone Exchange for a while. She intended to go nursing but she had to be seventeen for that. She was accepted into the Exchange on condition that her mother moved to Salisbury with her. They thought she was too young to be on her own in the city.

Dora had been wanting to leave Gatooma. She felt that Pat was alright alone there. Pat had a small car that Dora had bought her, and a good job and Mrs. Blackburn promised to assist her at work. Also, she had made a lot of friends there and was going to be her friend Gwen's bridesmaid in a couple of months. Her dress had already been made. Gwen had chosen white organdie with tiny black dots on it and red sashes and Pat had already been photographed in it and framed enlargements done as gifts from the bride. She didn't want to move, at least until the end of the year.

Dora and Rose booked into a residential hotel called the New Manor, just three streets away from the Telephone Exchange, also Lonrho Head Office and the city centre. Dora had been taken on as the General Manager Sir Digby Burnett's secretary. This position had been arranged for her by a friend of hers, the manager of Cam and Motor Mine, near Gatooma, Charles Dillon. Charles acted as General Manager when Sir Digby went on leave.

All went well with the new job as Rose was being trained and they considered that she was good at it. After two weeks, they decided that she knew enough to do shift work. The shifts were from six a.m. to two p.m. and two p.m. to ten. They didn't expect her to do the night shift, from ten p.m. to six a.m.

Dora agreed to walk home with her at ten. There were street lights and, although there was one right outside the door, Dora had to wait on the pavement until Rose came out of the door, which was locked at five. There was no waiting room inside and the Exchange was straight upstairs. Dora tried it for a week and that was that! She said she was not prepared to stand under the street lamp like a tart, so the authorities decided that as Rose had achieved honours in math, they would train her to be an accounting machine operator. The pay would be the same and she moved to another department. This was far easier for her and she was off at four every afternoon too. They taught her to use a comptometer as well, because they needed someone to work on one at the Army Supply Depot.

She had to cycle two miles to work and sit in an office with about thirty typists and clerks, all of them in army uniform except her. Large sheets of figures were given to her by the accountant and she spent all day seeing if their figures were correct. She almost died of boredom after the first week, so she livened things up a bit by deliberately ignoring errors. She had heard that heads were about to roll over the massive shortages of stock discovered by the auditors. At sixteen, her logic was somewhat misplaced. She wanted to be fired to show that she wouldn't work for thieves. She lasted two months before she was given a month's notice.

She left a week early in the end. One morning, she found to her dismay, that her period had started, and she hadn't brought any protection. She went to the woman in charge and explained the problem. The woman dug in her purse and handed her a tampon. Rose hurried to the restroom and unwrapped the small cardboard cylinder, it was something she had never seen before, and she hadn't the foggiest idea how to use it. Finally, she lodged it in limbo somewhere and hoped for the best. It was extremely painful riding the two miles home, suffering all the way. What she found out when she told her mother, was that you push the cotton wool tampon out of the cardboard holder. Only the soft cotton tampon stayed there.

Dora phoned the office and told them Rose was unwell and wouldn't be returning. Back she went to the training centre and she was put back on the accounting machines to be trained up to speed, and the following month she told the instructor that she was leaving to go nursing.

In December, Pat, Rose, Michael and Dora spent three weeks at the Cartwright's farm and that saved them the cost of hotel accommodation. Pat was moving up to Salisbury and would be living with her mother, sharing a cottage with two other girls. They had one front bedroom and Pat and Dora had the other and they shared the lounge, kitchen bathroom and veranda. Rose would live in the nurse's home at Salisbury Hospital but if she stayed with them, there was a small room at the back she slept in. With the money she had saved, Rose had to buy her uniforms and white shoes and stockings. The money didn't stretch to special shoes and Rose found some cheap ones that were just suitable. They had hard, uncomfortable soles but she thought they would soften up with use.

For three months, the trainee nurses were schooled and had to sit for oral and written examinations. Rose, who had a credit in hygiene and physiology, did well and passed with flying colours. Some of the girls left and the rest moved onto the wards. The long day on her feet in the cheap shoes meant that when she finally got to bed, she couldn't sleep for pain. Finally, they hardened, and it became bearable. Rose was always the one who fetched bed pans while the others walked past pretending not to have heard desperate calls from the patients. That made her late for what she was supposed to have finished doing. She lasted the first year and then had to go. The matron asked her why she didn't pass the practical assessment, and she had no answer.

Later, thinking it over, she realized that it was partly her vanity. She didn't wear her glasses because she thought they made her look unattractive and she simply didn't see well enough without them! She was on night duty at the native hospital when an African woman came in who needed a caesarean. The doctor opened her up and drew the baby out, but it wasn't breathing. He turned to Rose and told her to fetch the Lobelin. The theatre sister said it was in the drug cupboard in the main hospital and told her to be quick. Rose ran through the belt of bushes between the hospitals and peered in the cupboard, but she couldn't read the names. She had to pick each item out and hold it closer to her eyes. She was beginning to panic when one of the sisters came in and asked her what she was looking for, reached in and gave it to her.

Rose rushed back but the Doctor said, "You're too late, the baby's dead." Rose was in tears, but the theatre sister told her not to worry, a Lobelin injection into the heart wouldn't have resuscitated it.

She remembered occasions in the wards when she failed to come up to expectations. In women's surgical one morning, she was told to give a patient, Sheila, who had just been admitted, a bowel washout. Feeling competent she prepared the warm fluid in a jug, took a bucket and the correct rubber funnel a rubber bedsheet and towel to the bedside. She slipped the rubber sheet and towel under her and asked her to turn on her side. Gingerly, she pushed the nozzle into her and began to pour the fluid in. Halfway, she pointed the funnel down into the bucket and nothing came out, so she lifted it and poured the rest in.

Down went the funnel and still nothing came out. She picked up the blankets and peered in. The bed was full of water! Sheila said, "I think you've put it in the wrong place!" Rose realized to her horror, that she had put the tube into Sheila's vagina. She rushed off to fetch towels and clean sheets and Sheila told her not to worry, she wouldn't say anything, which was a relief. Whether there was a problem under the anesthetic, Rose never found out, but she could have kissed Sheila.

It was in men's surgical that she learned a fact of life. One young man had taken a fancy to her and she was unaware of it. He had a gangrenous ulcer on his leg and was going in for an operation in a couple of days. He couldn't move and had to be turned and washed and rubbed on pressure points to prevent bedsores. Usually, it required two or three nurses for this and Rose wasn't one of them. However, when they wanted to move him up the bed a bit, the sister called Rose to help.

She was told to slip her one hand under his buttock and the other under the thigh and wait for them to say "now", then lift him gently.

There were no bedclothes over him and he had no pajama trousers on. As she put her hands under him, up came his penis right in front of her face! Rose nearly dropped him. She hadn't seen anything like that before and didn't know it happened. There was great hilarity in the duty room where the other nurses told the story and explained the reason.

She was shocked to hear that he had had his leg off. He came back from theatre swathed in bandages and Rose was told to call the sister if he came round. She was taking temperatures at the top of the ward when she heard a loud, slurring voice. "Where's Nurse Maason? I want Nurse Maason. I love Nurse Maason. I want to –." The men shouted to Rose "Go outside, Nurse, quickly." They sounded desperate. "Go! GO!" Rose was almost pushed out of the door.

She wished she could have heard what he said but, apparently, it was a bit explicit and the other men were dying of embarrassment.

Rose came on duty one night and the curtains were drawn round a bed in the corner near the door and she looked in to see who was there. A good looking young man was sleeping in the bed propped up on pillows. He didn't wake during the night and at five a.m. Rose was told to give him a bed bath. She woke him and smiled, saying good morning, you slept well. The man didn't answer or smile so she began washing his face and upper body and drying him, wondering why he was so unresponsive. Normally, men chatted to her. When she had turned up the bedclothes and washed his legs, she soaped the cloth and handed it to him asking, "Would you like to wash yourself down there?"

He snatched the cloth and started washing, then suddenly lifted the sheet and looked down in dismay. Rose said, "What's the matter?" thinking he was bleeding or something. He glared at her and complained, "There's too much soap! I can't get it off." Rose was dismayed. She offered to get him fresh water and rinsed the cloth out, handing it back. He snatched it and said it didn't matter. Rose passed him the towel and said she was sorry. In silence, she plumped up his pillows and smoothed the bedclothes. As she left him she turned and smiled. "I wish you would smile, it would make you feel better. You are such a good-looking man and I would love to see you smiling." He just stared at her, so she left, feeling puzzled. She went off duty without looking in to see him again.

The next night, she walked into the ward and immediately looked in the corner to see whether the patient was looking happier. The curtains were drawn back, and the bed was stripped and empty. She went into the duty room and asked the sister where he had gone and what he had wrong with him. The sister said he died during the morning. Rose went to the sluice room and cried. She understood why he was not chatting to her and smiling and she mourned for him. It seemed such a waste. The sister couldn't, or wouldn't, tell her what he had died from and Rose never found out. It haunted her for years.

Another thing that upset her was seeing a tiny dead baby on the sluice room table. Someone had a miscarriage and the five-month foetus had been left there for the doctor to see. Rose wanted to wake it up, it looked so perfect, with tiny little hands and feet, even nails. She wanted to wrap it in a blanket and keep it warm, but she had to leave it alone. At least, someone wept for the little scrap. However, nursing was not for Rose.

EIGHT

THREE WEDDINGS AND AN UNUSUAL HONEYMOON

Rose went to the farm for Christmas again. She scanned the newspaper columns to see what she could do when she went back. The Accountant at the Shell Company needed Accounting Machine Operators and she was interviewed and accepted. The salary was twenty pounds a month and she had been paid fifteen pounds as a nurse.

Dora and Pat had decided to move into a flat in Lonrho Mansions. So they could afford the rent, they needed two others to occupy the second bedroom. Rose and Helen Dillon joined them. Helen's father Charles had begun to court Dora which is how they became acquainted. Helen had contracted T.B. when she was a baby and she was very short, with a tiny hump back. She was much older than Rose, but they became close friends and were happy to share the same room. She had a half-brother named Desmond Bean who visited her. This was the illegitimate child the first Mrs. Dillon had after Charles divorced her. Soon, Desmond asked Rose to go out with him and took her to the cinema and dinner at Meikles Hotel and called to ask her out for the day when he went visiting friends. He wanted to marry her, and she felt sorry for him, knowing about his past.

She found out how Charles felt about him one evening when Des was visiting them, and Charles brought Dora home to the flat. Charles walked into the sitting room and came face to face with him. His face dropped, and he turned and walked straight out again. Helen told Rose that her father was furious. Rose felt that Desmond had been badly treated by Charles and it made her more determined to side with Desmond and continue seeing him. She very nearly agreed to marry him but held back, feeling that it would ruin things for her mother. Dora was seeing more and more of Charles and he had asked her to marry him. He gave her a solitaire, one carat diamond engagement ring. They were to be married in six months.

Sheila Dillon, Charles's other daughter, had married Hostes Nicolle some years back and they had three children. Nick, as he was called, was in a high position in the Native Affairs Department, based in Salisbury and Charles asked him to get Pat's fiancée into Rhodesia by giving him a job, so Mickey arrived in the country and began as a clerk while he studied to become an assistant Native Commissioner. This he soon did and by the time they were married, he was an A.N.C. with a house and office in a district close to the city. He bought a small car and was often at the flat to collect Pat and cement their relationship.

Charles   *Dora*

Dora off to play golf in Gatooma, Rhodesia

Dora and Charles were married in the Magistrate's Office without any ceremony. They arranged to have a family reception in Meikles and Dora, who was called Doreen by Charles moved to the Cam and Motor Mine where she became the first lady, as the manager's wife, living in the enormous Cam House with gardens of twelve acres, several garden boys again, huge lawns, one set out for croquet, a tennis court and every advantage, also many house servants again.

She created the usual beautiful gardens and entertained Sir Digby Burnett, who was put in the guest cottage next to the house. A special cook hit a gong for meals and Dora proved herself a perfect hostess. Sir Digby flew down in his private plane, and on one weekend, before she went to Durban, Rose was there too, and he offered to take her back to Salisbury with him.

By then, he was losing his sight, so he had an untrained African house servant with him in the co-pilot's seat. Sir Digby wore one pair of glasses on his head and another to see ahead and swopped them to see the dials. When landing, the African gave him directions "Lapa side, Baas…panzi – panzi bechaan baas. - PEZOOL! - longele…longele funiga lo." Which was "This side, Boss…down a little down, - UP! - alright…alright like that." and they landed perfectly! Rose, who had been saying a last prayer in the back "Dear God! I'm too young to die!" didn't accept another offer of a lift.

As a wedding present, Charles put five hundred pounds into an account in Dora's name at the bank. This gave her the chance to pay for a wedding reception for Pat at Meikles Hotel, a cake and a beautiful wedding dress. She spent the whole amount and when Charles found out, he was furious. He didn't top it up with more and she was literally penniless. From that day on, she could have whatever she asked for and he would pay the bills, but he held the reins.

Pat as a bridesmad

Pat and Mickey's wedding

Collette Mickey Pat and Rose

Neil age 45

PAt age 18

Yolande age 18

Shortly before their wedding, Mickey and Pat went to the Makabusi river bank for a picnic and Pat relied on him to help her over the rough tufts of grass. He didn't understand how unsteady she was. He took her hand and pulled her forward. Pat lost her balance, fell and broke her leg.

She returned to the flat in a large plaster cast, from knee to toe. What a disaster. The wedding date was the following week and she was determined not to postpone it, so she was married in a wheel chair with Rose as bridesmaid, pushing her into the Salisbury Cathedral which was just over the road from Lonrho Mansions. It was a lovely wedding and a lavish reception for about one hundred guests.

Rose and Helen left the flat at the end of the month. Helen had bought a house in Borrowdale. She had paid a deposit and could afford the monthly payment of the balance on bond. Rose had decided to move to Durban. After working for one year at Shell, she went down to Durban to stay with her great cousin Florence, up on the Berea near her grandfather's place. She had heard of a Professor Fuchs, a singing teacher, who was supposed to prepare singers for a career in opera overseas. She went for an audition and the professor assured her that within four years she could expect to be accepted in London. He had successfully trained one girl just that year and according to him, Rose had a better voice and a four-octave range. The blow fell when he said the fee was four pounds a month.

Rose decided to approach the Shell Company and see whether she could arrange a transfer from Salisbury. The answer was yes, but the salary would not be quite as high. She would be paid seventeen pounds a month for the first year. If she worked in the city, she could probably stay with Cousin

Florence, Uncle Sam and Peggy for about ten pounds a month and have three pounds over for bus fares etc.

Desmond was devastated. He cried, and she explained that this was something she needed to do. She also told him she couldn't bear to place her mother in such a situation with Charles and finally, he agreed. He bought her a beautiful blue suitcase, one that expanded if needed, to almost twice its normal capacity. It was a Godsend, a far more expensive one than she could afford. She spent Christmas and her twentieth birthday with her mother and Charles and a week with Pat and Mickey in Bindura and then she was off by train to Durban with all her possessions in one suitcase and ten pounds in her handbag.

She was to start work in the middle of January and she had no place to stay. Cousin Florence said she had let the room to someone else because Rose hadn't said anything. She would have to stay in a hotel.

She changed trains in Johannesburg and shared a compartment with a group of friends who were returning to Durban. They were appalled to hear that she was arriving that evening in Durban without a place to go. It was the height of summer and every hotel would be fully booked up, they were certain. They insisted on taking her with them to their residential hotel and checking from there. The receptionist contacted a few places and they were fully booked. It was dinner time and they stood her to dinner where they were, then, after more fruitless phone calls, one of the girls said she could share her room and her partner moved in with another man in the group. His name was Noel Strever. Rose couldn't believe her luck. She moved in with Edmay, a little French girl, just for a night or two while she searched for accommodation.

Finally, she found a room to let on the Berea, some distance down the road from Cousin Florence. It was Sunday and she thanked her new benefactors and asked them if she could stand them to a milk shake at the café down the street. Then she was going up by bus to see the room and take it if it was a good one. The shakes cost her more than she realized and when she agreed to take the room, the woman said she had to pay the five pounds in advance.

That meant she had just over three pounds to see her through the month and only half a month's pay coming in then. Rose decided to visit Cousin Florence and see if she invited her to lunch. That was one good meal and she went back afterwards to the Hotel D'urban to collect her things. On the way to the bus stop, she bought a small knife, a half loaf of bread and a pot of anchovy paste. Armed with these, she arrived at five pm and occupied her room. The woman eyed her paper bag and said there was one rule. No food was to be kept in the room because it encouraged cockroaches. She would bring her a cup of tea later and a cup in the morning. Rose didn't say she had fish paste and bread. The tea came at seven and Rose locked the door and had her meal of two thick slices of brown bread and fish paste.

She worked out that she could afford two half loaves a week and a season ticket on the bus, also a couple of necessary items from the chemist and perhaps haunt Cousin Florence every Sunday and have one good meal a week and she would survive. Well, survive she did, but she lost ten pounds in weight! She hid her food in a shoe box given to her by Florence and tucked it away in a dark corner of the wardrobe. The woman must have found it because there were more pointed remarks that if she wanted to keep food in the house, she could use the fridge in the kitchen. She said nothing, and, at the end of the month, she was told that the room wouldn't be available the next month, a relative was coming to stay.

After work, Rose often walked down to the Hotel D'urban to see her friends and a room to share was vacant, so Rose moved there. It would cost her eleven pounds a month and she could walk to work, so there would be no bus fare to pay, but, if she were to start singing lessons, she would have thirty shillings to deduct again because the Professor lived up on the Berea. No way could she afford the lessons. She wrote to her mother asking her whether she could pay it for her and Professor Fuchs gave her a letter to enclose praising Rose's voice as well, but her mother explained the situation she faced having drained her bank account for Pat. That counted out lessons that year and she waited to see what the increment would be after Christmas.

On the train, she had also met a young Rhodesian midshipman named Taffy Evans. He was a tall, good-looking blond with blue eyes and they instantly fell for each other. He asked Rose to write to him and she did. Suddenly, one day he turned up at the hotel. His ship had docked, and he had shore leave. He took her to see the H.M.S. Dorchester and she went aboard with him. He wanted her to become engaged to him and she said she would think about it. She wasn't sure she wanted to tie herself that way and give up her dream of a singing career. The idea of him being away for months at sea also didn't appeal to her. Another man was paying her attention and that was

Noel Strever. He had the advantage of propinquity. His room was down the passage from hers. Also, he had a motorcar, a small Hillman. He took her to meet his sister at Umlaas Road, near Maritzberg. Dorothy was his youngest sister of three. His mother's firstborn was Emily, then came Hilda and then Dorothy. Three years later, she had Edward and then Dennis.

Thirteen years passed, and she was over forty. Her husband was a Station Master and transferred from stations in South Africa to Prieska, on the border between South Africa and South West Africa and the Namib desert. There she acted as a midwife, riding a camel through the desert to outlying sidings where ganger's wives gave birth. One woman was in tears when she went to check her progress. These people were too poor to travel to the towns and shop. They waited for the babies to arrive and if they lived, they sent for a ten-pound layette from a mail order company.

This woman had saved up her ten pounds in a tin hidden in her room, but her husband had found it and spent the whole amount on booze. She was desperate, so Jessie decided that because she was menopausal and so many years had passed since she had Dennis, she would give her the baby clothes she had saved in case she had another child. All the baby clothes were hand stitched by her and there were twelve of everything, also beautifully knitted jackets and shawls and two dozen napkins. Two months later, she was pregnant with Noel!

Noel's sister Dorothy and her husband had a farm called The Gums and at the sprawling farmhouse Rose met her seven children, two girls, two boys, another two girls and a last boy. They spent the day there and had a beautifully cooked meal of roast beef and Yorkshire pudding, with apple pie and large jug of Jersey cream to follow. For tea, the big girls had made a perfect sponge cake, filled with jam and whipped cream. Rose really liked all of them.

Noel took her to meet his favourite brother and his wife. Bunny and Lily, lived down the south coast road in an outlying suburb called Woodlands. Bunny, as they called Edward, was totally different from Noel. He was already in his forties and Lily was fifteen years older, nearly sixty. She had beautiful, naturally curly, silvery gold hair and a plain face and she was old. Rose liked her but wished she would draw breath and let Bunny say something. He was good looking and had crinkly laugh lines round his eyes. Soon she found that he was a joker. He lied and seemed believable and roared with laughter when Lily reprimanded him. Noel told her that he had rented a room in Lily's first husband's house and the husband had found them in bed together and divorced her. He adored her.

Further up the hill, lived Lily's son Douglas Watkins, his wife, Marjorie and two small children. They all worked on the railways. Bunny was a train driver and Noel, who was a World War Two veteran at twenty-three, was three years through his training as a diesel fitter, turner and millwright in the railway workshops. Douglas and Dennis both worked in the main office, in communications. Douglas was leaving Durban and going to Bulawayo in Rhodesia where he would be in signals, and highly paid. They all seemed to feel that Rhodesia was the place to emigrate to because South Africa was becoming so dangerous.

For some reason, Noel avoided going to Dennis and Elaine's house in Durban North. He had lived with them after he returned from North Africa, but he didn't seem to like Elaine and said she was a gossip, always running people down. He had two albums full of family pictures and photos of himself and Bunny in North Africa. Bunny was in the army and Noel was in the air force, both looking very young and handsome in their uniforms. There was a delightful picture of Noel, when about eight months old, lying face down on a cushion, stark naked, frowning belligerently and brandishing an ornamental baby bottle covered in beads.

Soon, Rose and Noel realized they were emotionally and physically attracted to each other. He asked her to marry him. Whether it was love or lust, was debatable! Rose held back and said she would consider it, but she had planned to remain single and become an opera singer.

There were two paths clearly laid before her. The one was a lonely one but unrewarding if, after many years of hard training, she was unsuccessful. At twenty, thirty seemed old to her; she thought she'd no longer be attractive and would be too old to marry and have children. But, if she said yes to Noel, she could say goodbye to her dream of singing. There'd be an endless round of sitting at home tending a brood of yelling children and the drudgery of housework and cooking year after year.

Rose feared that if she didn't say yes quickly, Noel would change his mind and drop out of her life, forever. It had been difficult for her when both her mother and then her sister had married and left the flat. She had felt so deserted and at sea, wondering what to do and where to go. She thought that she was almost on the shelf with her twenty first birthday almost upon her. The following morning, she said yes to Noel and her future was sealed. It was a relief to see the way forward and start planning.

First, she had to contact her mother and tell her and then

to decide when and where the wedding would be. Dora was disappointed, but she feared that Rose might be pregnant, so she resigned herself to the idea. Rose hoped she would come down to Durban and perhaps help her pay for a reception, but nothing was forthcoming, not even a wedding gift of money. Dear Lily stepped into the breach and said she and Bunny would organize a reception at their house as a wedding gift. That meant Rose had only to buy a cake and her wedding dress.

A friend at work said that her mother would make a two-tier wedding cake for five pounds and Rose found a seamstress who would make her dress for a similar amount. Edmay said she would love to be a bridesmaid. Rose had bought a sewing machine and she planned a few new dresses and bought several lengths of material, including some pink silk for a dressing gown and some filmy pale green, flowered material for a nightdress. She should have made her wedding dress herself. She wanted a full-length net skirt and a short-sleeved silk bodice. Net was cheap, and she would have made a net veil as well, but she decided that it would be better if someone professional made it.

She was talked into buying white crepe material and having a short, straight skirt and a top with a fishtailed peplum, scalloped round the edge with plenty of back interest – covered buttons all the way down. She didn't think that a short veil would suit because it would hide the features and she might look a bit top heavy, so she settled for a spray of white rosebuds and orange blossom pinned on each side of her head. She found some high heeled white shoes and decided to wear the pearls she had been given for singing at a friend's wedding. They were to be married at the Cathedral in the centre of Durban in the middle of February and then go by train to Gatooma to spend a week with Charles and her mother then travel to Umtali to stay at a hotel in the Vumba mountains for a week.

The days passed too rapidly and the night before the wedding, Rose still hadn't finished making her silk dressing gown. It was the usual Durban sweltering heat as she sat at her machine, so she turned the fan directly onto her to cool her off. At last she was done, and the glamorous affair was folded into her bulging case. It was three a.m. before she sank into bed and slept. In the morning, she opened her mouth to speak and no sound came out! She had lost her voice. In just six hours she would be expected to say, "I do" and she couldn't utter a sound. The fan had cooled her throat for half the night and that must have done it.

Fortunately, first a whisper, then a croak and finally, as she reached the cathedral, she was speaking normally. Walking in on the arm of Cousin Florence's husband Sam, she saw the small crowd of Noel's friends and relations one side of the aisle and just half a dozen on her side. Auntie Betty and Uncle Fred were by now, bedridden, but Florence was there, sitting with a few of Rose's workmates. Bunny and Lily sat on her side as well as Edmay's fiancée.

Rose took the top tier of the cake to cut at Auntie Betty's house, but Betty wouldn't hear of it. They didn't eat fruit cake, she said, and Rose must keep it to eat on the first anniversary of her wedding. She gave Rose a substantial cheque which was a Godsend. Rose and Noel were feeling the pinch as their small horde was diminishing rapidly. They had a long way to go and much to pay for.

Lily's little sitting room was crammed with people, half of whom Rose didn't know. Cousin Florence had begged to be excused which was a relief. She gave Rose a useful brown zip-up hold-all for a wedding present. It was bound with leather and had two leather-covered handles and was a blessing. Rose had room for several extra items she really needed, and the blue case didn't bulge after all.

Rose hoped to be given a cheque as a wedding present when she arrived at the Cam and Motor mine, but nothing was forthcoming. They didn't see much of Charles because he wasn't well and stayed in his room in bed most of the time. Dora seemed worried about him. Apparently, he had had a slight stroke and his one eye had gone blind. It meant that he had retired, and they were leaving the Cam and going to Salisbury, but Dora didn't tell Rose because she didn't want to put them off their visit. Helen Dillon came down for the weekend in her ancient open tourer. This was to see her father and Rose and to meet Noel. She offered to take them to the Victoria Falls for five days as a wedding present. That was an exciting addition to their honeymoon and Dora packed them a large wicker picnic basket fitted with plates and cutlery and filled with all sorts of foodstuffs, enough to cover meals for most of the days.

A somewhat unusual part of Rose's honeymoon was spent at Victoria Falls with a few memorable events.

Dear Helen, who stood them to a honeymoon holiday at the Falls - and came along!

Open car Helen drove for the holiday to Victoria Falls. An interesting return journey.

Lions? What lions? You mean those loud sounds in the night weren't cows?

Probably, Helen had discussed this with her father, knowing what a strain it would have been for him to have the two of them at the house for long. She went to the falls with them because she didn't like anyone else driving her car. When they reached the falls, they found that the government chalet she had booked was a single large rondavel with three beds in it. All the others were occupied.

It was late, and they had travelled a long distance and were tired out, so they simply pushed the two beds together under one net for the honeymoon couple and Helen's bed was pushed over near the far window under another net and that was that. The following morning, they took the picnic basket and a groundsheet over the bridge to the northern bank to have a picnic lunch at the edge of the gorge, looking over the falls from that angle. They laid down the sheet and Noel carried the basket and set it at one end. Rose sat down and started to put the things on it. She gave the loaf of bread and a knife to Helen to slice and Helen went and stood at the edge of the Gorge for Noel to take a photo of her.

Noel was taking the photos and behind him, wandering around the car, nonchalantly inspecting the tires, was a large male baboon. As soon as Rose took the butter dish out of the basket, he reared up on his hind legs and headed for Helen. Helen had the sense to throw the loaf to Rose and the baboon turned and sat on the ground sheet next to Rose. He had come to lunch! Rose glanced sideways at the baboon, whose face was about a foot from hers. It was not a comforting sight with his bloodshot, beady eyes staring at the bread, the butter dish and the contents of the basket, obviously deciding what he should grab. Noel urged Rose to throw the bread to him and get up and run, but Rose wasn't going to see the baboon dig into all their provisions if she could help it. She held out the loaf to the baboon sideways slowly, with her left hand, without looking at him. Then she slowly picked up the butter dish with her right hand, put it back in the basket and fastened the lid.

Baboon demanding bread with menace. Rose ensured he didn't get the butter!

WILD BABOON at the Victoria Falls with our loaf of bread

Out of the corner of her eye she saw the baboon eyeing her intently, deciding what to do, and there they sat. Finally, the baboon grabbed the loaf of bread and loped off into the bushes. They changed their mind about eating there and returned to the south bank. They decided to picnic where there were other people in future. It was the first time that Rose and Noel had seen the Falls and they had delighted in going through the rain forest to all the various view points along the mile-wide main river. In places, the spray obliterated the view completely and they had to take care not to lose their footing at the slippery edge of the deep gorge and go plummeting down to their deaths. The most remarkable and memorable was the devil's cataract, with its mesmeric mass of water plunging down into the abyss.

Finally, it was time to head back to the Cam. They packed everything in the car and got in, but the car refused to start. Helen tried so long that the engine flooded, and Noel delved into the works to solve the problem. At last, he got it started and they were off, but by now it was quite late in the afternoon, so they didn't stop at Wankie game reserve. They decided to push on to Bulawayo, have a meal somewhere there and drive on to the Cam. They had gone about twenty miles when the engine stopped again. Helen shone a torch while Noel tinkered with the engine, then tried the starter over and over. Finally, they were off again for about five minutes and then it stopped and wouldn't respond at all. They tried push starting, with Helen driving and Noel and Rose pushing, but Helen couldn't get the hang of it, so Noel took over and Rose and Helen pushed.

Getting closer and closer, were the chilling sounds of animals, a grunting, coughing and bawling. Helen and Rose laughed about disturbing the cattle with the noise of the car revving as it started, but suddenly they had a horrible suspicion that they might be lions. To push a car in pitch darkness along a road, wondering whether a lion or leopard was right behind you, Rose found extremely nerve racking. Finally, the car started, Noel revved, the car jerked forward, and Rose nearly fell nose first into the dirt. Noel travelled slowly forward with both Helen and Rose running to catch up and get in and at last they were on their way, with Noel driving and Helen quite happy to let him. They decided to carry on while the car was running well, and they arrived at the Cam at five a.m. Charles, who had been a big game hunter, said that by the description of the sounds, it had indeed been lions!

Their week in the Vumba was spent mainly in bed, as all honeymoons are; They came out of their room just in time not to miss breakfast, went out to see the beautiful scenery until lunch time, then retired to have a rest, managed to surface at tea time, went on tours of the surrounding waterfalls, trout farms and mountain views, had dinner and retired again. They couldn't be bothered with other people's lives as they needed to waste no time on anything but endeavouring to meld themselves together as one. Of course, finally they proved that one and one makes three! Rose was feeling unwell when she got back to Durban and the doctor told her he was sure she was pregnant.

NINE

BABIES, LOVE, AND LIFE'S LITTLE DISAPPOINTMENTS

Rose couldn't believe it. She was sure that her nausea was because the smell of greasy cooking wafted up through their bedroom window at the boarding house at six in the morning made her rush into the toilet and throw up. Even the morning tea tasted vile and she was sure the milk was off! That made her do the same. She was supposed to go to work that Monday, but she asked Noel to phone and tell them that she was sick. They moved into a front room on the veranda to get away from the kitchen smoke and that helped, but Rose spent three months suffering from morning sickness and she lost her job at Shell.

Rose was facing another problem in her early marriage – a rather miserable time because, at the boarding house, she saw Noel pawing the woman next door. She had no idea that he would do it, but the woman was always popping in to chat and plonking herself on his bed next to him. They had no chairs to sit on so that was acceptable, but she always ended up on his bed, not on Rose's. She said that she wasn't ticklish, so he started to tickle her to see. At first, Rose laughed at them but then she noticed that the tickling was a bit more intimate, not just trying to make her laugh. Rose died a little. It destroyed her trust in him and made her want to cry. She turned her back on him and the woman who finally got the message and went. Noel blustered and argued and stormed out. Rose was left alone, accused of imagining it and for a long time, she lay there wondering whether he had left her for good. Finally, he returned and no more was said.

Fortunately, they were moving, and the scene changed. Douglas Watkins told Noel that all the houses up on the hill in Woodlands had been built especially for ex-servicemen and they were leaving for Rhodesia in a month. They had been offered a 100% loan and, as Noel was an ex-serviceman, he could take it over. They went to see it and decided to buy it. The house was lovely. Small, so the repayments were small. The grounds were steep – twenty-two steps up to the front door, with two little terraces and twenty-two steps up to the washing line and servant's accommodation, but that didn't worry them. They were young and strong.

Rose also bought their old baby pram for five pounds. It needed a bit of repair and was a bit scruffy, but they couldn't afford a new one. Rose thought she would spray paint it and improve the looks. She chose a pale grey paint and did a good job, quite oblivious of the danger of using a poisonous substance on any surface a child might chew. The paint was glossy, which was a pity because the result would have looked much better matt.

They couldn't afford a servant either. Rose made meals out of everything possible, poring over the English Woman's Weekly recipes. That little magazine cost a shilling a week and it was her only indulgence. Worth its weight in anything, it had three stories and a serial in it and knitting and sewing patterns. Also, there was an agony aunt, a doctor's column and plenty of easy recipes – everything imaginable had a column. It was small, printed on cheap paper in only one colour but that didn't matter. There, she found knitting patterns for baby jackets and dresses, bootees by the dozen and advice on everything to do with breeding!

Rose loved being alone all day, planning meals and feeling free to do as she wanted, eat what and when she wanted. She controlled the finances. Noel put his salary in the bank and Rose sat and worked out what to do with any amount over, after the house bills were paid. Noel had a couple of pounds to spend and Rose did the book-keeping, with columns for anything else they needed. She spent some of the remainder of the monthly income on wool and material for baby clothes, dresses and even shirts for Noel. She did a lot of sewing on her machine and the magazine always had patterns inside that she used.

All the baby clothes were hand-made by her, which was a great saving. She knitted the baby jackets and leggings from new patterns each week. She used the recipes in a section that helped her plan economical meals. The magazine included three short stories and a serial, so she had something to read each week. They couldn't afford books and there was no library there. Noel took the car to work and she was stranded far away from the nearest shopping centre.

Not once did she think of going to a prenatal clinic and she had no means of getting to one anyway. Fortunately, down the road, lived Noel's brother Bunny and his wife Lily who was years older than he. She was the sister in law who had had Rose's reception at their house as a wedding gift and was the woman closest to her mother's age she knew in Durban. Rose could walk down and visit her and was always welcome. She knew none of the other neighbours and was very lonely. She liked Lily very much although she never stopped talking – not for a minute!

Bunny, Noel's older brother, was full of nonsense. He was much younger than Lily, but he obviously loved her a good deal. All the time she talked, he kept quiet. When she drew breath he'd suddenly tell you a whopping lie that sounded like the truth, and when you believed him, he was satisfied, particularly when Lily was caught believing him. That never stopped either, but they were kind, good friends. Children loved Bunny, he was like the pied piper to them. He drew them round him like a magnet.

Rose was a bit shy of Bunny because Noel told her he had been a lodger in Lily's house when she was married to her first husband and they had an affair, so her husband divorced her, and she married Bunny. One Sunday morning, she was up making tea in the kitchen and the back door was open. She had not bothered to put her gown on as she was getting back in bed to have tea with Noel. Suddenly, there was Bunny, leaning on the door frame and smiling his handsome smile, looking her up and down, grinning and asking for Noel. She knew how transparent her filmy nightdress was and she felt herself blushing all over as she tried to cover everything with both hands rather ineffectually. Curled up, she must have looked like a pink prawn in pale green seaweed. "What are you worrying about?" said Bunny airily "I'm not looking." But he didn't take his eyes off her. Rose made him turn around while she ran to fetch her dressing gown and he thought that was very funny.

Apparently, he had been full of nonsense in the army too. He was the one who sawed almost through the planks holding up soldiers over the latrines, so that they gave in when enough men leaned against them. He got the blame when a two-stroke motorbike shot off backwards underneath the rider "Where's that bloody Bunny Strever! I'll kill him!" Apparently, he hadn't done anything that time! He was the S.M. in charge of a reception dinner for the big brass once. For the normal roast sucking pig, Bunny excelled with a roast baboon in all its hair, arms hanging down over the sides of a stretcher, large apple in mouth and all. The roast pig arrived after he got the desired reaction from the diners. He was the perennial joker!

Noel bought a lovely Rhodesian Ridgeback puppy for Rose, and then a huge black cat with white front and paws walked in one day and made himself at home. She called him Percy.

She had to save up twenty-two pounds for a private nursing home to have the baby in and in due course, one evening, Noel had to take her in and leave her there. The pains had begun but they said it would be hours before the baby arrived. The sisters were efficient but disinterested. They installed her in the theatre, up on a narrow, high bed and left her. She suffered as the pains grew worse and there was no way of turning over or getting off the bed. Hour after hour they went on. She was examined every hour and they said the baby wasn't coming yet and she mustn't push.

Rose felt she was in hell. She instinctively felt she should relax and push gently to allow the baby to come but they told her not to push so she tensed her body against that feeling and held everything in, which doubled the agony. Finally, after twelve hours of it, she was told to push, and her daughter was born. That was painful too, because she tore inside and had to have stitches. It was a grim, lonely experience and no one came to see her or the baby for the whole day. Noel turned up that evening after work.

She spent a week in the home and then he took time of work to take her home and drop her there. He had to go straight back again and there she was, baby and all, alone on the hill. She and the baby had to get to know each other and they spent hours looking at each other in amazement. Rose loved the perfection of those tiny fingers and toes and every tiny hair on its head. She found dark, silky down on the baby's spine and along the top of its ears and hoped her baby wouldn't grow up looking like a monkey. Lily assured her that wouldn't happen. She chose the name Sherry and then thought that sounded like a drink, so she decided to call her Sherrell, which could be shortened to Sherry. Then she added Elizabeth, after Auntie Betty. She thought she would ask her Auntie Betty to be Godmother.

One difficulty for Rose was feeding. For some reason, every time she tried to get her baby to feed, she didn't. She just turned her head away and screamed. Rose, who was bursting at the seams, turned the baby round and tried the other side, pushed the nipple in the baby's mouth and pressed her close and the same thing happened. Round the baby turned and stared out of the window. Rose was in tears. That was when she should have been going to the post-natal clinic, but she didn't know that either. The only thing the baby would drink from was her bottle of orange or water. So, Rose, in desperation got Noel to bring back a tin of Lactogen. She made the formula as they said in the booklet and down it went, to the last drop.

What Rose didn't know was that newborn babies automatically turn towards the light and she had been standing looking out of the window. Sherrell had three months of difficulty with croup and Rose used to put a Cresoline lamp under her cot which helped. Every afternoon, when the top bank was in shade, Rose would take a blanket out on the grass and she and her baby would sit there. Sherrell would be propped up with pillows and Rose would cut the grass with her scissors. There was no garden boy to do it. Percy, the cat, would join them and she would have tea there. Percy had his milk and Sherry her bottle.

On Sundays, they often motored up to Noel's sister Dorothy's farm in Umlaas Road. They had seven children, four girls and three boys. June and Ethne were the bigger girls and they loved holding Sherrell and carrying her around with them. One day, Rose was holding the baby and Noel and the girls were romping on the lawn. He was tickling them and trying to kiss them, and they were screaming "Don't! Uncle Noel." It was all fun until Rose saw that he was again, a bit too intimate with them. They broke away and went off. Rose didn't say anything, but she decided to go away for a while. Pat had asked her to come up and stay for a month or two. She wanted to go to hospital and have operations to strengthen her legs and Rose could look after her little girl Yolande while she was away.

Sherrell was ten months old and Rose made her a warm jacket with a hood and some long trousers out of red flannel to wear in the train. Mickey was stationed at Buhera where he was an Assistant Native Commissioner and their house had a wide long veranda in front where Yolande had a playpen and her toys. She was six months older than Sherrell, so Rose put Sherrell in the pen and Yolande played out on the veranda. One morning, Rose was in the house when she heard a loud screaming, so she rushed out and found that Yolande had bitten Sherrell's finger so hard that it was blue. She grabbed Yolande's arm and bit it, not hard enough to do any damage but enough to put her off doing it again.

Pat was away for two weeks. The surgeon separated part of the strong muscles in her calves and thighs and attached them to weak muscles. She had to do exercises thinking she was drawing her leg up and it would go down and vice versa. It wasn't easy and not fully successful, but it helped. Her knee joints were more stable.

One thing that Rose couldn't bear there was the smell of the dog's food being cooked in the kitchen. The meat smelt of bad fat, and the weather was stinking hot. It made Rose sick. Then, when she suddenly went off tea, she realised she was pregnant again. A month later, when Pat was on her feet and could cope on her own, Rose went back to Durban and started knitting a few blue things, hopefully. She had plenty of white ones. This time, she decided, she'd go to Addington Hospital and have the baby there. It cost only five pounds.

Just before she was due to have the baby, her wisdom tooth gave her trouble. It was not yet through to the surface and Rose felt it bulging up in a painful lump at the back of her lower jaw. She decided to leave it until after the baby was born and ask to see a dentist in Addington where treatment was free. That decision was a bad one as it turned out.

She knew better than to lie for hours on the hospital bed,

she only went in when the pains were coming five minutes apart and walked around until they said the baby was coming. They gave her chloroform eventually to delay the birth until the doctor came and she woke up to be told she had a little boy. Apparently, it was a difficult birth. The baby was coming face first into the world, a face presentation. She had to have twenty-two stitches, seventeen inside. All she saw when they brought the baby to show her was a long, receding head like a rugby ball and four deep wrinkles where the forehead should be. She thought he was deformed but they assured her it would come right soon.

She was shivering from the shock, so they covered her with hot blankets. They took her temperature and then the fun was on. She was whisked into a private ward and they kept asking her if she'd ever had malaria and she kept saying she was sure it was her tooth. She was battling with a large, painful lump in her mouth, where her wisdom tooth was trying to surface. Suddenly, next morning the lump burst. She had to get out of bed and run over to the basin and spit out blood and pus and wash her mouth out with water.

The doctor came and questioned her. She said she was sure it was because of her tooth. She had a burst abscess. He looked in her mouth and ordered injections of penicillin in oil. One every morning for two weeks. The injections stung badly. She asked about the baby, why wasn't he being brought to her, was something wrong? They said no, but he was being kept in the duty room for a few days and then she'd have him with her. She was only allowed to go and look at him and not touch him.

There she saw her baby boy, lying stark naked and blue with cold, howling and wriggling in the duty room. It was winter, and they said he had heat rash. It was nerve racking for Rose, but she had to leave him there. Finally, they brought him to her wrapped up and sleeping and she could cuddle him and look at him. She never fed him, however, he was on the bottle from the day he was born. His forehead gradually moved forward, and his head became normal. He was a robust, beautiful baby with big slanting eyes and a pretty rosebud mouth. Sherrell was a beautiful little doll of a baby and she was just toddling when he was born. Rose named him Christopher James and they called him Kit.

TEN

RETURN TO RHODESIA

They moved to Rhodesia when Kit was nine months old and Sherrell, two. They had a house in Que Que, right next to the bush-veldt and snakes, spiders and other horrors invaded. Noel had found work at the Iron and Steel Company.

One evening she bathed Sherrell, put her pajamas on and took her into the lounge to sit there while she bathed Kit. She came into the lounge with him in a towel to see what she thought was a big yellow dog trying to get out of the door and slipping on the cement floor. When she walked closer, she saw to her horror that it was a huge snake uncoiling and sliding out.

That was a scare and soon there was another. One morning she left Kit sitting on the little veranda on a blanket, came out with his bottle and saw him reaching forward – an enormous, black scorpion was dancing in front of his fingers as he tried to get it. Rose grabbed him and rushed away. After that, they stayed inside with doors closed and she went to the oculist for glasses. Beauty was secondary by then.

They were in Que Que for a year and then Noel was offered a job at the Cam and Motor mine and they moved there. Charles and Dora were no longer there as he had retired and moved to Umtali.

One New Year's Eve, 1951, they went to a dinner dance and saw the new year in. In 1952, nine months later, their daughter Jennifer Anne was born. That was a short pregnancy because the months flew by and suddenly, it was time to book into the maternity home in Gatooma. Noel's mother, Jessie, came up to look after the children when Rose went into the home. Noel had been sent down to Selukwe to oversee some prospecting for diamonds there. He came back before Rose went into the hospital, but he said he had to go back the day after he fetched her and the baby from the home. Rose was thankful that Jessie was there because Sherrell went down with whooping cough and she didn't know how to bring a new baby there unless Jessie could keep the two other children one side of the house and away from her and the baby. Noel drove her home and immediately left for Selukwe again.

One day, Rose came out of her room to see Jessie in the bathroom holding her side. She said she had a bad pain there and, between her shoulder blades, and she felt she should go back to South Africa as soon as possible. Rose sent a message to Noel telling him to return as soon as he could. A week later, he was back and took his mother to the train. She was suffering badly, and it turned out to be cancer of the liver. She died four months later.

Noel told Rose that he had fallen in love with a girl of fifteen in Selukwe and that's why he had gone back. Nothing could come of it because of her age. Rose was furious. She resented his selfishness, hanging around a young girl when she and his mother needed his help. She was hurt and angry, and she lost all respect for him from that time.

She would have left him then, but she had no idea how she could support herself. She couldn't go to work and afford to put three small children into a creche, and no way would she leave them behind. So, she decided to concentrate on the children and ignore him.

Sherrell 6 years, Christopher 4 years Jenny 2 years

Sherrell in the grey pram with Sophie up on the veranda at Woodlands, Durban

Jenny age 8 months at Pickstone goldmine.

Sherrell 4 years, Kit 2 years

Arline   *Colin 11 years*   *Gary 9 years*   *Mike*

Morny   Sherrell   Best man   Yolande
at Mike and Arline's wedding in Umtali 1955

Noel had been asked if he would move to the Pickstone mine as Engineer. This was a small mine about twenty miles away from the Cam, so Rose was occupied in packing up and saying goodbye to all her friends and then settling in to the house at the Pickstone. They were only there for a few months when they decided to leave and move back to Umtali. Noel applied to the railways for a job as a fitter and turner and they accepted him immediately.

There were no houses to rent in Umtali and they had to take anything they could find, first, a most unsuitable communal block near the industrial site and then a house out near Penhalonga. Noel had to take Sherrell, who was nearly five, into Umtali and drop her at the convent where she had started kindergarten and bring her home with him at five. The nuns kept her there all day as a day boarder.

Finally, after some months, they moved into a double-storey house in upper main street, within convenient walking distance of the convent. Also, at the convent was Yolande. She wasn't in the same class. She was in her second year there. Pat and Mickey were living in a large double storey about half a mile away over the hill from Rose. Mickey had been transferred to Umtali and now he was a District Commissioner.

Michael was also in Umtali working at the Jute Factory and Mom and Charles were living in Murambi Gardens. For a while they were all together there.

The first to leave were Pat and Mickey. They moved out to Penhalonga to a border post up the hill near the Portuguese border.

Michael had met an Umtali girl and asked her to marry him. Her name was Arline Jones and she was living with her brother and sister-in-law Don and Barbara and their two children, Cheryl and Terry. They were married in the Anglican Cathedral in Umtali.

Sherrell and Yolande were flower girls, both six years old, looking very charming in frilly pink and blue. Mike looked very handsome and Arline made a beautiful bride. Dora being mother of the groom, dressed in her best finery, wearing a black hat tipped over one eye and her fox fur stole. She was a very beautiful woman to the end of her life. Charles came to the wedding looking smart in his grey suit; tall and upright, he and Dora made a distinguished pair and he was obviously still extremely proud of her. He didn't go to the reception. They were on the move back to Salisbury, to a house in Borrowdale on two acres.

Michael and Arline left Umtali shortly after that. Mike was employed by a farmer/politician at Shamva, near Salisbury, as a farm manager on his second farm. Arline had lost a baby girl, tragically born dead, and they were glad to hear that she was pregnant again.

Rose had her three little ones and Pat had Yolande, incredibly born without a caesarean operation, although Pat's body was so out of shape from the polio. The doctor that attended Pat in Bindura where they lived before moving to Umtali, was confident it would be alright. That same doctor and a friend of his there, both fell in love with each other's wives. Both had five children and it was the common joke about town that they must have lined them up and decided amicably 'You have Mary and I'll have Joe, I'll swop you Pete for little Lily, if you like.' or something like that. So, they divorced, remarried each other's wives and all ten children had one parent and one step parent.

Pat's daughter, Yolande, and Sherrell were closest friends and spent a great deal of time together, mostly at Pat's house in Penhalonga. Rose's only heartache was that Yolande had such beautiful toys. Being an only child, she had a toy car big enough for a six-year-old and a big doll's house with every imaginable piece of furniture inside. She had dolls galore, in all sizes and shapes, huge teddy bears and other furry animals. Sherrell had so little. What's more, Yo was not fond of sharing and if Sherrell tried to use something she refused to let her. She doled out toys as if she were the queen bestowing a knighthood. Rose decided to get Sherrell the best doll she could find for her next birthday.

Rose found a beautiful big doll that could stand and sit, walk if you held her hand and walked her along, her head moved from side to side. She had curly brown hair and moving eyes and she could say mama. She was a roaring success and was called Big Girl by Sherrell. This was something Yolande didn't have. Immediately, Yolande wanted one. Pat bought Yo one with golden curls. Sherrell came back from their house one day with a bald Big Girl! Yolande had ripped it off and thrown it away. Strange, the jealousy of the only child. Big Girl is still sitting in Sherrell's bedroom in Australia, wearing a wig, over fifty years later.

Pat was pregnant again, and the doctor was appalled to hear they had risked a natural birth. Although it was successful, he insisted on a Caesarean operation. The baby lived for only twelve hours and Pat nearly died too. There was some difficulty over the anaesthetic apparently. It was a little girl and she was christened Margaret Mary by a Catholic priest and given the last rites before she died, before Pat emerged from the effects of the anaesthetic. She was buried in the cemetery in the Catholic section.

Pat was not a Catholic and neither was Mickey, but this was a comfort to her. The tiny mite was buried in Umtali. Pat suffered deeply, and she couldn't shake off the effects of the anaesthetic. Mickey had to stay with her and took leave of absence from work. They had a bedroom upstairs without window bars and the fear was that she may throw herself out. Sometimes he had to hold her down and convince her that the little green men she thought were coming in the window were imaginary. It was the time when flying saucers were in the news and that was what she saw, certain they were taking her away. Thank God, the doctors finally managed to give her the right treatment and she recovered her full senses.

Two years after that, she was pregnant again. How worried they all were! The idea of another anaesthetic tragedy was heavy on their minds when she went into the main hospital in Umtali for a caesarean operation again. All went well. Born safely was Neil, a baby boy, big and healthy. Rose was the first to carry him, gently in her car, just a few hours old, over to the maternity hospital. Mickey stayed with Pat to wait for her to wake up and to take her over to join her baby later. She had her pigeon pair, Yolande, and a baby with big, soulful eyes, Neil, who grew up looking and behaving a lot like his father.

Auntie Betty died and left forty-three family members a share of her fortune. Dora inherited four thousand pounds, Rose inherited one thousand five hundred pounds and her silver entrée dish, Pat, two thousand and her silver tea set and Michael, a thousand pounds and her silver cutlery.

That enabled Rose to pay for a new car, purchase a plot of land in Fairbridge Park and put down a ten per cent deposit on a five-thousand-pound house. She went to a building company with a drawing she had done herself and the builder agreed to build it.

Thus, Noel and Rose moved to a good suburb. Jenny was three, so Rose decided to go to work. Jenny went to a crèche and Kit and Sherrell were at junior school. They badly needed extra money now the children were growing bigger and needed new shoes every five minutes, it seemed to her. Much pain is suffered by mothers who are short of enough money to buy their children the toys and clothes other children have.

Noel was earning less. He changed companies, and each time his salary reduced. Rose returning to work solved this problem and caused another. She hated not being at home to protect her children. They were lively children! She came home, once, to find that Christopher had built a fire under the back of their caravan, parked right close to the house. Another day he and Sherrell were walking the tightrope along the ridge of the roof – not Jenny, she wasn't allowed by them to get up there.

They put Jenny in a forty-four-gallon drum and rolled her down the back terraces, bumping and gathering speed. That could have broken her neck. Kit set fire to grass at the showground and nearly burnt the horses! Jenny fell down the stairs next door, landing against a broken front door panel of glass and cut a large slice of flesh half off her finger. People over the road had to take her to the hospital for stitches. Thank God, they were there. Rose wasn't! She shuddered to think what would have happened if she took one step further forward when she fell. She would have cut her throat.

That's when a mother suffers but they needed the money! Rose had a little African nanny there, working in the afternoon, washing and ironing and watching out for the children but she didn't have much authority. Finally, Rose put both older children in the crèche after lunch to do homework or rest like the little ones, have tea and come home when she did. Sherrell, being far too old for creche, took care of little ones for the owners, which made it easier for her having to be there.

After a year or two, it seemed that she could leave them at home. From two to five, was only three hours and they were told to do their homework and then behave themselves for the short time left before she was home. She had sufficient money to afford afternoon tuition as well. She arranged dancing classes for the girls and piano lessons for Kit, then Sherrell, when she stopped dancing. Rose was involved in the amateur theatricals and so was Noel, so the children spent a lot of time with them at the theatre. They loved it. Other children were there, and they were all with their parents. That kept them safe and kept them together as a family.

For Rose, a day was made up of; up, bath, get children to sit and eat breakfast, check their clothes and day's activities, see Kit go on his cycle to school, take two girls to school gates – different schools, get to work before eight, leave at one, pick up girls, go home to lunch, take one to piano lesson, one to dancing or arrange for some other transport, get back to work before two, concentrate, get a moment off to shop for dinner and leave at five, pick up one or two children from school or elsewhere, go home, have tea, sort out dinner and go to the theatre for an hour or two's work on sets, back to cook dinner and see the children are all in and bathed, have dinner together as a family, get ready for a rehearsal, take children, blankets, pillows etc. pile into the car and off to the theatre, rehearse for two or three hours, children galloping around and then settling down to sleep in the aisles, wake them, pile into the car. Back for milk or cocoa, tea for all, teeth, toilet all round and bed! As if this were not enough, life was about to change again.

ELEVEN

AN INTERLUDE WITH DORA

Dora and Charles moved from Salisbury to Cape Town, into various famous hotels there facing the sea, then on again, up the coast to one city after the other. It was in East London that they bought a house in a select suburb next to one of the bank managers. One night, they heard screams somewhere near them and, in the morning, they heard he was in hospital.

This was a city with a port. Apparently, the manager heard screams coming from his native quarters at the bottom of his property at the back. He went to investigate and opened the door, only to get a broken bottle full in the face. It was a drunken sailor from one of the ships, who was trying to rape the coloured servant girl. He nearly lost an eye and needed plastic surgery.

Dora and Charles sold the house, moving to Natal, near Durban. Pietermaritzburg was the name of the town. They lived up Long Hill in a house with a lengthy hillside garden full of rhododendrons and azaleas. People stopped their cars on Long hill to see the amazing sight of a hillside blazing with colour.

Darling Rose, she wrote, I wish you could come down and see! Well, Rose was back at work by that time and had only three weeks holiday a year which had to be used taking three children to the seaside or somewhere like that. She couldn't do it. She always regretted that. Noel was deteriorating in some way and they were on the way towards a divorce. He moved from job to job, each time earning less a month, until Rose was earning more than he.

During those years, Dora and Charles yet again sold up and moved to Natal, Pietermaritzburg. Then again to the South Coast, Scottborough, near Durban. They spent some time in a south coast hotel and became friendly with the Indian waiters there. It appeared that Charles believed in tipping the waiters well and they hadn't had any treatment like this from South Africans. The Indians repaid him in a strange way later.

In 1960, suddenly, Charles dropped dead. Over the telephone Dora sounded desperate for help but didn't ask. Apparently, she had heard a thump on the bathroom floor and went in. There was Charles unconscious on the floor and she quickly phoned the doctor. He confirmed Charles was dead.

Michael and Rose immediately said they would be with her as soon as they could. Noel and the children drove to Salisbury to drop her at the airport. Michael and Rose flew down to fetch Dora and attend the funeral. They stayed to help her pack up everything for the removals van, collect the ashes and drive her up in her car to Rhodesia.

Dora seemed strangely charged, as if she might suddenly explode. There was a tenseness in her although she was quiet and busy with everything necessary for leaving. She didn't want to be left alone.

They helped her and bolstered her as much as they could. She grieved, but in her controlled way. It was building up inside her, unfortunately. She had much to arrange and do before they could set off for home again. She and Charles had a combined will, leaving everything to each other. She made a new will leaving everything to her three children.

None of the Dillon family came to the funeral but the Indian waiters from the one hotel Dora and Charles had lived in, were pall bearers; they had asked to be, which touched Dora's heart deeply.

As with all losses, there are moments of hysterical laughter and they had them. Rose leapt out of the car in Durban to see the undertaker and fetch the ashes for them to take to Rhodesia for the Dillons. Rose waited in the reception room at the undertakers, sitting there, with a table in front of her, listening to soulful music until they brought in a little wooden coffin about a foot long! Then she cried. Charles had been a big man, over six feet tall and she had never seen anything like this before. All she could think of was him, squashed down into that! She'd only been to cemetery burials before.

Reverently and carefully she carried it to the car and it was placed on the floor at the back. She kept quiet about her image of Charles being concertinaed into a small man in there, telling Mike when they were alone. It was horrid, but it relieved their tension laughing about it. The box was wrapped in a cloth and put in the one wardrobe temporarily to be put in the car when they left.

The next day the transport company collected the furniture. Suddenly, they recalled the box in one wardrobe! They whisked it out just in time. The wardrobes were off to the second-hand shop to be sold, so just imagine the result if someone bought that one and opened the surprise wooden box in it!

They set off next day, Mike and Rose taking turns driving. Dora paid for their hotel rooms and they reached the border town of Messina in two days. It should have been one, but on the long, straight stretch before crossing the mountain pass, they changed drivers. Neither Mike nor Rose looked at the petrol gauge, so they ran out of petrol!

What red faces they had, trying to flag unwilling travelers down but, at last, a big, fat travelling salesman in a big, fat car stopped and carted them to Bandolierkop, the next little dorp or village. They were delighted because the hotel by the same quaint name was one Mike and Rose had often stayed in. It was charming!

Round the rambling ranch type hotel, there were rondavels, huge, round, thatched rooms with the back third, divided in half, with a walk-in wardrobe in one side and an en suite in the other segment. These, they booked into and met the salesman for a drink before dinner. He had driven Mike all the way back to the car with fuel, so he deserved their hospitality.

Several drinks later, after hearing the sad reason for their travels, he suddenly launched into a joke he was reminded of – about Mac, whose friend Jock asked him to pour a bottle of whiskey over his coffin when he died. At the graveside, Mac was busy swallowing the whole bottleful. As he downed the last drop, he urinated on the coffin in the grave. Hamish asked him why and his answer was "Och! I'm sure he won't worry if it passes through me kidneys first!"

Mike and Rose looked at each other. They couldn't believe he'd come out with that, but they had to laugh politely. Dora just sat looking rather pensive. They went in to dinner before he could rake up another thoughtless joke.

The miniature coffin was tenderly placed on the floor at the back of the car again and they set off for the border but the delays there made them too late to cross, so they returned to Messina, just ten miles back. There they booked into the hotel for the night. Dora paid for the rooms and dinner for all.

Once again, they carried the box upstairs to their room and put it in the built-in wardrobe, went to dinner, slept comfortably and rose early as they were in a hurry to get over the border, jumped in the car before realising that the ashes were still in the one bedroom!

Panic, in case the bedroom cleaner had found it and stolen it, followed by relief and mortified disbelief that they could forget, made them very careful to get the remains to Helen's house without further delay. There, they parted company with it and left Dora in Helen's care. She was moving to a flat near Helen, right in the little shopping centre where everything was at hand. The flat was on the ground floor, in a lovely little block of four in the best suburb in Salisbury and her furniture was already waiting at the depot. All seemed well.

Noel and the children motored up to fetch Rose and see Dora, who gave the four-year-old Jenny a beautiful big teddy bear and they returned to Umtali.

Noel was building the theatre sets Rose designed and she was painting them. Sherrell and Jenny were dancing on stage for their school performances and Christopher was getting piano lessons from Rose's singing teacher, an old Afrikaans woman who called herself Madame G. She was a very good teacher, having been taught by some opera singer in Berlin. Rose practiced with her before singing in the Eisteddfods and that helped her get the highest marks. Kit was about nine and she made him kiss her goodbye after the lessons. He didn't put up with that for long! He said she had a hairy face and that was that!

He wanted to learn the trumpet and later brought one home when he moved to High School, but the racket was mind bending for everyone and, apart from that, he got fever blisters on his lips. Rose was afraid of cancer and she turned down the instrument. She should have let him try the flute. He was very musical but, somehow, she thought he'd have refused to try such a little instrument as a flute.

The Mountain Theatre Club took the musical 'Oklahoma!' to Beira that year. In Portuguese East Africa, on the coast, it was exciting to hire a whole coach for the large cast that could sleep in it and use it to sleep in at the station. Rose was singing in the chorus, understudying the lead and organising the trip, also helping the producer, Doug Hill, who happened to be the owner of the stationers, where she did the accounting. His wife, Maureen, had a new baby to care for, so she stayed at home. Noel helped too, dismantling the set and getting it into the goods van of the Beira train, after stage managing for the seventeen performances in the Courtauld Theatre in Umtali. Rose always thought Doug should go on stage as a leading man. He was a tall, handsome man and she saw him playing the lead in Noel Coward's play, 'Private Lives' and several others, but he just laughed and said he preferred producing.

Rose had the job of billeting the cast in compartments and they took all three children in one big compartment with six bunks. It was great fun. Beira heat overcame their excellent Ado Annie in the stuffy dressing room. Rose was dressing next to her when she heard a noise like a pumpkin dropping and splitting on the floor – it was Audrey's head! She had fainted but recovered without much more than a lump on her head.

The men, who had been downing beers at a phenomenal rate, found a fire extinguisher on the wall, set it off and directed a stream of foam on top of her, and the rest of the ladies! They kicked the revelers out of the dressing room, who then turned the extinguisher onto the garden of a house next door to the theatre, covering all the vegetables with foam and causing a war, almost, between the Portuguese and Rhodesians.

There was trouble between "Rhodies" and "Pork n Beans" from old, because Rhodesian hotheads went over the border to see the bullfights and, roaring drunk, jumped in the bullring to grab the poor little scraggy bulls by the horns and get them down on the ground, thus depriving the Toreador of his kill.

In their drunken haze they fought in Beira, got themselves incarcerated in jails and paid fines to get back for work in Rhodesia on Monday. They called that fun. The Portuguese lost face and were infuriated.

Time to go on stage and the performances, afternoon and evening, played to full houses and were a howling success. They had one person staying with the children – about ten of them – and they had a lunch provided by the hosts. Jenny was presented with a skate wing to eat. She was in tears when Rose got there after the rehearsal. There was nothing to eat on the skate wing! Rose gave her a small portion of her own dinner and bought her something tasty at the beach.

After the after-show party, they all embarked on the train which set off for Rhodesia. One thoroughly irritating old female lead had a coupe compartment to herself and refused point blank to share. That left someone in the corridor, sleeping on the floor in a sleeping bag.

She barricaded herself in and that was that. Perhaps she snored like a trooper or noisily passed wind all the time! They laughed it off rather than going for her. Anyhow, the children had a great day at the beach and the fun of the train trip. Then, they settled down to work again.

Sir Stephen and Lady Courtauld lived over the Christmas Pass in a beautiful place up the hillside, half way to Penhalonga. They named it La Rochelle. Finally, after their deaths it was bequeathed to the state. Courtauld rayon fabric had made their fortune and they retired from England to Umtali. It was the theatre company's luck to have them pay half for the building of the Courtauld Theatre for the Umtali Players. Lady Courtauld had been a chorus girl before he married her, and they were told she had a snake tattooed round her leg – all the way up!

Seating nearly five hundred, the theatre was equipped with everything of the best, including a revolving stage and a high proscenium arch. It was a joy to design and build sets there, also the lighting equipment was excellent. The Players only had a bond on half the cost and playing to full houses for a run of nearly three weeks soon cleared that. They had full houses most of the time.

Beautifully set in the mountains of the Vumba, with an ideal climate, although Umtali was a small town, it had drawn retirees from overseas who were talented and wealthy. Truly, it was a little gem of a place. They put on 'The King and I' and Rose understudied the lead, Anna. Her final show was in 1964 and that was Sound of Music. She took the part of Maria four times with Alan Baker as Captain von Trapp as well as designing and painting the massive set. It was a time of terrific stress and Rose had appreciated that outlet for her pent-up misery and despair. Alan made a handsome and talented captain, and his attractive wife Ann understudied Liesl. Rose also took the part of Sister Margaretta for the other fourteen performances, and Jenny played one of the children, Louisa. In fact, it was the only show in which Rose's whole family had been involved, with Noel and Sherrell working backstage, plus Christopher, who also took the part of a German soldier. It was the last show she had anything to do with in Umtali.

Often, Rose saw Pat, Mickey and Neil but they had moved from Umtali to Enkeldoorn. Yolande went to the same Convent in Gwelo, at which Rose spent four years. They had built a new Convent out of town and called it the Regina Mundi. Civil unrest had started in Rhodesia, and in case they were attacked, the nuns carried shotguns when they took the children out in crocodile formation for walks. Mike and Arline, Colin and Gary were still on Hayman's farm and they spent a few days with them when they could. Mike was hankering after a farm of his own but hadn't the money for a deposit.

Suddenly, Helen rang to say that Dora had a massive heart attack and lay almost at death's door in Salisbury Hospital. They rushed up there and found her in a public ward, flat down in the bed, looking so small and vulnerable. Apparently, her blood pressure had risen to dangerous levels when Charles died, and she had been suffering from stress staying on her own in her flat. She had a dog, but thieves had broken into the flat next door and she was constantly afraid. Both Pat and Rose rushed up to Salisbury to be with her.

Pat and Rose stayed on in the flat and they were amused

to hear Dora's story of coming out of the coma she had been in at first. She opened her eyes to see a long black object above her. It was some equipment they could bring down for some purpose or other, but she thought it was the lid of her coffin and they were about to bury her alive!

However, they had her moved to St. Anne's when she told them about the little trainee nurse who woke her and told her to get up and have her breakfast at the table. She had the sense to know this mustn't be done. She was lying flat in the bed and was told by the doctor not to even try to sit up!

She had made up her mind to leave the flat and told them to share everything between the three of them, very cleverly arranging the order as well. The large box of linen and the lounge suite were for Rose, and then Pat was to have first choice, Rose second and they chose something for Mike third, trying to be scrupulously fair. The new piano was to be returned to the music shop. She kept the car and decided to go to the farm and live with Mike and Arline and the two boys Colin and Gary. She gave Rose the neat little lounge suite knowing she didn't have one.

They were sad for her but realised this was for the best. She had been more afraid and stressed than they knew, living on her own in that flat. Pat and Rose both wanted her with them any time she liked. She was precious to them and they had nearly lost her. Rose and Noel's house was compact, but Christopher had a good little bedroom to himself and the girls shared the third double one next to them.

Just at the back, a couple of steps from the kitchen door was the caravan Noel had built. This, the children loved to sleep in, so Rose decided that Kit could give up his room and move in there if Dora came to stay. He was happy, more so than Rose, but there was no way of adding an extra bedroom to the house.

Rose and Noel took a few days leave and spent a little time at the farm with Mike and Arline who now had two young boys, Colin and Gary. Colin was a hyperactive child who had distinguished himself by breaking his own nose with his knee. Gary was a cheeky young devil, very like his father in looks and behaviour and extremely artistic. Rose shared a room with Dora who told her she was going to stay with Pat and Mickey soon. She told Rose how she felt, years before, when she had no money and Mike was a small boy at Prince Edward's School. He could run like a deer and, played rugby well. He had to play bare footed because she didn't have the money to buy him running shoes. Remembering this, she decided to use six thousand pounds to pay half down on a farm for him. He could manage a Land Bank loan for the six-thousand-pound balance. She did this and then moved to Enkeldoorn to live with Pat. They had been like sisters long ago and wanted to be together.

Mike, Arline and the boys were happily moving to their own farm at last; something they never thought possible. The farm was in a derelict condition and the house had been attacked by termites and not repaired, but at the asking price it was still a bargain. Michael couldn't wait to get there and start building it up into the beautiful showpiece it became. He was an excellent farmer and soon built a store there. Gradually, he built up the house and put in a swimming pool. He stopped growing tobacco and grew maize, sunflowers and paprika, putting in a good deal of irrigation which increased the value of the farm considerably. Noel, Rose and family spent many holidays there and it became the hub where all the family gathered.

Dora settled in with Pat and Mickey and all was well for some months until a frantic call came to say Dora had collapsed and "died". The doctor injected adrenaline straight into her heart and got it beating again. She and Pat had been having a disagreement and that had suddenly happened. Rose went up immediately and took her mother back to Umtali. Hastily, Rose cleared Christopher's room for Dora, and Kit moved into the caravan.

Poor old Pat was going through a rough patch of her own at the time. She was suffering a sort of nervous breakdown and no-one realised it. Her letters had become full of references to God that they disregarded. They should have shown them to a doctor. Later, they did so, and Pat went for treatment in a private hospital in Bulawayo.

When she was better, she told them about one woman who was in the ward with her, describing what had happened to her. Her abusive husband used to stub out cigarettes on her breasts. After she was cured of her anxiety and submissiveness, she went home, and he did it again. She waited until he was asleep and brought a heavy frying pan down in his head. After twenty stitches or so, apparently, he was "cured" too. He never did it again!

Pat was once more her lively and humorous self. She had great stories to tell about her spells in hospital which were so frequent. She seemed to have everything wrong with her and Rose had nothing – it seemed so unfair. Once, when she was recovering from an operation, a little woman came in who had never been in hospital before. Pat, the knowledgeable, informed her that first the anaesthetist would assess her and then the doctor would see her before she went into theatre.

Sure enough, a white coated figure peered in and looked around the ward. She smiled expectantly at him and he came over and said to her "Well. What seems to be the matter with you?"

"It's me loomps, doctor," she answered. The doctor smiled uncertainly.

"Well, open wide!"

Pat said it was the woman's eyes which opened wide then and she looked rather confused, but obediently turned over in the bed, bared her bottom and lifted her leg. Her operation was for piles! It turned out that the "doctor" was an equally confused, and very embarrassed young dentist who had come to the wrong ward looking for his patient with wisdom tooth problems.

Dora wanted to come and stay with Rose, so they fetched her immediately. All was prepared at home for her and Kit was installed in the caravan, suited him fine. She asked Rose to choose a new bedroom suite for her as they had little good furniture except for the lounge suite she had given them. Rose chose a pretty dressing table, stool and chest of drawers painted a soft dove grey, which her mother loved when she saw it.

Rose and Noel were still short of money. Dora's shares had climbed rapidly, and she was quite wealthy by then and loved good things around her. She put up her pretty chintz curtains in the little bedroom and it looked transformed. She contributed her share of cost of living and brought her car with her. The children called her Morny so that's who Dora became.

Rose was having trouble focusing on everything. She had another man in her life. She was trying to keep it from everyone because both he and she were married, and this seemed something to hide until they finally were free. Her marriage with Noel was over in all but name. He and she no longer cared for each other, but it was difficult for Rose to think of separating the children from their father and breaking up their home. Her mind was on the other man constantly and she was happy only on the rare occasions when they were together.

The arrangement was that they would wait until the children were grown and no longer needed a home. Rose knew that his wife was considering leaving their marriage too. And in her own case Noel had let her down within a month of their marriage and many times since. His blatantly informing her that he fell in love with a girl of fifteen had been a pointer. She no longer wanted him in her life. Seldom did she and other man get together anywhere. Their lives were so set in their own households and even at work and at the theatre. Mainly, he wrote love letters which she had to read secretly and there were no secret places. She had to wait until everyone was asleep and then sit in the lounge reading and answering the notes and screeds. The man had tiny writing and filled foolscap pages. Rose was overwhelmed and almost hypnotized.

She told her mother and explained why she was sometimes distant and not concentrating. Dora understood. She, herself, had loved another man while she was married to Rose's father and it had caused a frightening night and nearly ended in tragedy. They had parted for a while and then Dora came to her senses and realised that her romance had faded, and she returned to Bert. Rose felt better about it, knowing that her mother supported her.

It was wonderful having her with them and she was a favourite with the children so her years there were good ones. They shared the love of theatre and Rose had bought an old piano in good order. Dora's playing filled their lives with special intense pleasure. Rose was overjoyed to find that the children developed a love of classical music. Dora was unbelievably talented and trained, and she was an excellent accompanist. She accompanied Rose at the Eisteddfod in Salisbury that year.

Rose was singing Caro Nome, which has repetitive runs and trills in the middle. The second time ended differently and that enabled the song to move forward to the next part. Rose didn't change to the second and then realised she was repeating the first bit. She turned and looked at her mother and both corrected. The adjudicator didn't seem to notice, and Rose received honours. They were both busting to laugh but they managed to contain themselves until they got off stage.

They laughed together, almost uncontrollably sometimes. It was a family failing that got them into trouble frequently. Dora went with Rose to her singing lessons. Once, old Madame G leapt up from the piano as Rose was singing high scales, stuck her rather dirty thumb in Rose's mouth, up at the palate and said "Here! You've got to get your ARSE UP HERE!" She had that sort of accent – she meant ah's of course. Dora and Rose looked at each other, unfortunately, and she could hardly sing! They were busting to laugh again.

Madame G had a huge, male Alsatian too, that lay at her feet. Madame said, "To get your top C properly, get down on the mat on all fours and try the scale and you'll see." Rose obeyed, with Dora looking on with the look she knew so well. The dog got up as she began the scale, and she suddenly realised his intentions!

There was Rose, running up a scale to top C and beyond,

and busy kicking out backwards with one leg to fend off Fido's amorous advances, all the while knowing Dora was in fits sitting there watching. No wonder Rose got top marks in the Eisteddfod that year. She was an excellent teacher, old Madame Gera. Perhaps she had trained her dog to keep her students grimly concentrating on getting the high C, come what may!

One morning, when Dora was still in bed, she called Rose. "Rose, what do you think this is? She looked and there was a little beetle thing walking casually over her mother's sheet. She stared hard at it but didn't know. Rose had never seen one like it before. She picked it off the sheet and put it in a glass.

Finally, Dora said in a small voice "Do you think it's a bug?" Well, Rose had never seen one of those either, so she rang pest control immediately. Up came a man and confirmed that it was! Hells bells, they thought, and a frantic search began. None in Dora's bed or room, the man confirmed, so where had that lonely wanderer come from?

They immediately began to itch and scratch! The specialist walked around nonchalantly with his eyes up to heaven, He looked as if he were sleepwalking but there was a reason. Assuring them there were none in each room so far, the last one was the girls' room at the back. Up in the corners of the ceiling he found the nests. He told them that they waited until lights out and then walked down the wall and into the beds for a feed. Disgusting!

He found them in the native quarters where he said they had originated, so both places were fumigated. Rose made up her own and Noel's beds, and Dora made up hers, but the children's beds were made by the servant as they were a bit lazy about doing it themselves and of course it was always such a rush in the morning for all of them. So, that was how the little monstrosities came in.

There were many shows to see and friends to visit. Dora and Rose often went to visit the Goldbergs. They lived twenty miles from Umtali on their ranch. Leigh Ranch was a revelation. There, in their colossal ranch house, lived Rachel, Sarah, Mick, Haim and Maurice. Benny lived in Salisbury. He no longer farmed as he was a Minister in Parliament. Jack had his own farm. They had a 100-year old parrot that could speak Yiddish, English and Chishona, the local native language, and a Steinway concert grand piano in their huge lounge. Up on the walls of their veranda were the mud nests of dozens of swallows. They simply painted over them every year, leaving a round hole for the swallows to go in. Later, when they were away somewhere, the terrorists burnt the ranch down, including the Steinway, but they left the parrot outside. The parrot was taken to Jack's farm in the Penhalonga hills but some months later, the terrorists burnt that house down too and poor Polly perished in the flames.

Benny had only one ear. The other was sliced off in a car accident on the main road to Chipinga. They couldn't find it although they combed the grass verge and raked the surrounding sandy area. It is strange for an ear to disappear without trace, some small animal must have snatched it!

Jack, the youngest brother, had married a Christian girl, so he was not really one of them. He farmed elsewhere, up near Penhalonga. He was the only one who married and had children, two sons, but they didn't count as they were on the wrong side of acceptable in Israel. That meant the line was dying out. The sons were fine young men. One was killed the war, leaving only Simon to inherit any possible fortune.

They had come to Rhodesia when Bert was in management on Rezende mine. They had nothing, having fled from Europe. Bert let Mick build a shanty next to the mine compound to sell goods on tick to the native workers. Each week, on pay day, he could collect payment right there. Thus, the Masons started the Goldbergs off in life towards making millions.

They prospered and often descended in a flock of chattering, noisy bodies, for afternoon tea and music, which drifted into sundowner time. It was taken for granted that they imbibed at sundowner time and then stayed for a big dinner. Rachel sang, and Dora played for her. Hymie acted in plays Dora produced. As with all Jews, they loved music and theatre and gravitated to Dora and Bert.

Bert had a goose with a long, bent nose called Hymie and when the family came to visit one day, Rose suddenly saw the likeness and said, "We've got a goose called Hy...."

"Rose, GO and play outside!" Quickly her mother broke in, "Let the grown-ups talk and come back at tea time." Rose thought her mother had been unusually rude not to let them know such an interesting coincidence and went off with an aggrieved flounce. Trouble was averted that time but when Dora innocently and inaccurately remarked that Jews were Asian, there was a general offended exodus and they didn't communicate for about three months until the misconception was cleared up and normal relationships resumed.

Passing a mile of enormous fields of maize or tobacco, all irrigated, Dora and Rose approached the house. Somewhere, far out of sight, there were perfect houses for their large African community of workers who wanted for nothing and were highly paid. Where are they now, those farm workers, now that 95% of Africans in Zimbabwe are out of work? Do they regret the past? They were all kicked off the farm when so-called 'War Vets' rampaged in and evicted them, burning the house down as well.

Although it was a difficult period, there were still children to consider, so they went on holiday to Scottburgh. This was where Dora and Charles had lived until his death. Rose drove her car for her as they took both cars and the caravan, and they travelled in tandem all the way from Umtali to South Coast, Natal. They also took Yolande with them. Dora had her new Wolseley 16/60 serviced and the engine steam cleaned for the journey. The big Wolseley 6/90 could pull the caravan and it was kept in perfect order by Noel. Steam cleaning was a luxury it didn't have.

Sherrell and Jenny at Scottburgh
nar Durban

Kit at Scottburgh

They were travelling in front and well ahead of Noel, on the last leg of the low veldt journey to Beit Bridge and the border crossing over the Limpopo River to South Africa. Suddenly, the car began jibbing and then stopped altogether. There they were, stuck with Kit and Jenny in the blazing heat with no traffic passing and no sign of Noel, Sherrell and Yolande. All food and water supplies were in the caravan and they had to wait. It was pleasant there, listening to the wild doves making their typical coo kurru coo in the bush and all the little sounds and rustling in the quiet surroundings. One or two cars passed but didn't stop.

Finally, a man stopped to help them. He opened the bonnet and fiddled about with everything – no joy. Then he took the distributor apart and drew out some little part with a long metal needle-like protrusion, held it up to the light and declared that it looked crooked to him. Rose was praying that Noel would hurry up, and she kept telling the stranger that he should leave it for Noel. He was looking for a hammer to straighten the bent piece when at last the others appeared.

Noel couldn't fix the problem, so he took the caravan on to Beit Bridge and left it outside the hotel, came back the fifteen miles and towed Arabella, Dora's car, to the Customs building. They cleared their papers through Customs and explained the situation, then Arabella was pushed into position with Rose steering. Noel edged the big Wolseley up bumper to bumper behind Rose, and with the caravan hitched behind, carefully and expertly shunted the smaller car across the bridge into South Africa. All the customs and immigration staff cheered and waved them on and they made it!

Noel drove straight to the first garage in Messina and Arabella was towed in and checked. They had to book Dora into the hotel for the night and, after she stood all of them to dinner and a bottle of wine they went off to the caravan park and slept there.

All morning, the mechanics puzzled over Arabella's problem and, finally, it was discovered that the steam clean had cracked the distributor top – just an invisible hairline but it was enough to short everything. So much for steam cleaning.

It was soon repaired, and they were off again through Wylie's Poort, winding through a narrow gorge next to a river and up to the Mountain Inn, perched at the edge of a drop with a spectacular view across the land below and right in the clouds. It was too late to go any further. They had expected to be five hundred miles closer to Scottborough by then, but the view was worth the delay. Sundowners on the veranda overlooking the world's view as the sun set, was breath taking and in the lounge and dining room huge log fires crackled. They all bathed in Dora's private chalet with the caravan parked in front and they rose early to see the dawn.

Finally, they reached Scottborough which had a wonderful beach with smooth rocks at the side, ideal for children's safety and Dora staying in the hotel to the delight of the Indian waiters who recognised her, thoroughly enjoyed herself as did all.

Back in Umtali, they would often go up into the mountains on the weekends or sometimes to Hot Springs in the winter, when the mountains were freezing. It smelt a bit of Sulphur at the springs, but they could all swim there and the Hotel was quaintly old-fashioned had a thatched roof.

At lunch time, in the heat, there was a 'punka wallah' sitting outside the window with a rope tied round his toe, cheerfully pulling it. The rope led up to the ceiling where a large palm frond fan waved back and forth over the diners and cooled the air. They did it in India for the Colonials there. In India, the punka wallah was an Indian but in Hot Springs, it was an old native man happily eating his sadza and nyama, which was their staple diet of stiff maize porridge and meat, with his big toe going back and forth, automatically. Another case of these mad white people! Fancy paying for this simple activity – and free food thrown in!

Once, on that road, they stopped for a giraffe right at the road edge. The engine was a bit hot and sounds of boiling could be heard. This fascinated the giraffe, so he spread his legs out wide, bent his long, long neck until his head was near the grill and listened intently, cocking his head from side to side.

Dora had been in Africa all her life and had just said there was one animal she had never seen in the bush – a giraffe – and there was one, a couple of feet away from her. Giraffes have the most beautiful big eyes and long curly eyelashes. He then put his head right near her and peered through the windscreen.

So, they filled Dora's days with them with all they could, and, in turn, they enjoyed every minute of her company. Sherrell was growing up and Dora used to take her on her own to a special restaurant and treat her to mushrooms on toast on a Saturday morning. For Jenny, she sat at the machine and made her some pretty dresses. Christopher came into extra pocket money on many occasions. Everywhere Rose and her mother went and everything they did together they enjoyed. Dora was so beautiful, and her clothes were chosen so well that she looked fifteen years younger than her sixty years. Even a week before she died, when her weight had diminished to seven stone and her face was distorted by Bell's palsy and she wore a large dressing on one cheek, she went to the hairdresser and had a titian tint and set. She didn't give up for a moment. Never once did she complain. Only once did she say to Rose "I think I've had it!" Rose assured her that Doctor Kay had told her it wasn't cancer. Rose was the one in denial. she wept inwardly for her mother, wanting her to recover with all her heart.

Dora woke one morning and couldn't stand up. She was bent double having slipped a disk. Off to the hospital they took her, and she was stretched out with a thick wooden block on her soles, bound on with thick layers of plaster. The wood had rope round it attached to heavy weights which dangled halfway to the floor over the rail at the bottom of the bed. That was to stretch her spine and re-position the disk.

She slept on her back and had a troubled dream. She was in the jungle, tied to a pole with rope round her feet and chest. The savages were dancing round a huge fire, on which was a large cooking pot bubbling. She had to get loose to get away! She was going to be stewed!

She tore the thick plaster off her feet in her sleep, dreaming she was struggling to get the ropes off and escape. This she felt she had done and her dream continued with her running through the bush and getting away. She woke finding that her disc was back in place and Rose took her home.

Suddenly, one morning she called Rose to her bedroom. The whole one side of her face had drooped and was numb. It was Bell's palsy, they said. The beauty was marred completely. Then, a few weeks later, she felt a small lump on her cheek which was excised, and tissue sent away for examination. It wasn't cancerous, they said. Dora made light of the face problem until another came up on her other cheek. The first had been excised more than a year before.

It was a terrible year. Doctor Kay said Rose's mother was the bravest woman he had ever treated. She lived each day without referring to illness and they continued sharing their travels and holidays with her. She just had this non-healing place on her cheek, covered with a neat dressing and special plaster. It was only opened and dressed once a week and it was growing bigger.

Rose drove her everywhere around Murambi Gardens, the best suburb in Umtali, because she wanted to buy a house there. She hankered for a house of her own saying that it was something that she'd never had. She wanted them all to live in it together. Rose could see problems with Noel because she knew that they were probably separating soon.

The children were very good to her towards the end, caring for her in whatever way they could. Sherrell found her a special cup with a drinking spout at Red Cross now that the Bell's palsy had made drinking difficult.

Strangely, Dora had no pain in her face or head. Rose asked her, once, and she said it was just an odd feeling. Occasionally, but very rarely, she would jerk her head and draw in her breath. Then, Rose feared it was painful, but she denied it. They were glad of that, truly glad.

One morning, as Rose was about to leave the house with the girls for school and work, she called out "Rose! Rose!" Rose rushed into her room where she was horrified to find blood gushing from her mother's cheek. She made a thick pad of cotton wool and pressed it on.

Dora was shaking with fear, so Rose held her close and

calmed her. The bleeding stopped, and she was in a quandary, wanting to stay but knowing she must go quickly as the children were late. Rose had taken time off from work too, on other days, and dreaded losing her position in the company. Dora told her to go so she phoned the doctor about it first and rushed off. It never happened again, thank goodness.

Then, at last, a bed was ready for her in Bulawayo. Rose took a week of her leave and they motored down, all the way to Bulawayo Hospital. At last, Dora was to have radiotherapy there, seven hundred miles from home. They passed every town she had lived in on the way down and spent a night at the farm with Michael half way, to break the journey. They stopped in Gatooma for tea, and had a break in Gwelo, places she knew so well, and then they settled her in her private ward in Bulawayo Hospital where they laughed with her over her ordering a cold beer. That was what she felt like, after the heat of the journey. She was so frail and tiny. Rose had to leave her, feeling very heartsore that she couldn't stay. The sister provided the beer. Rose sat there with her for as long as she could, held her hand and promised to come and fetch her in three weeks when the treatment was complete and said, "Be good!" She smiled a little and answered, "I'll try!" Then Rose kissed her goodbye reluctantly, having to motor back home to work and the children.

Dora had to travel in an ambulance every day, in the searing heat, to the native hospital for radiotherapy where the finest oncology unit in the southern hemisphere had been installed. However, she was too weak to stand the therapy and slipped into a coma a week later. Rose, Mike and Pat were called back urgently. Rose held Dora's hand and spoke to her gently telling her they were all there with her. She slipped away quietly in the early hours of the morning, having never regained consciousness. Doctor Skinner, the American specialist in charge of the unit, told the desperately grieving Rose not to wish that her mother had stayed alive any longer as the cancer had invaded her brain. She didn't suffer any pain, thank God, and she was in command of all her faculties to the end.

Dora's wish to be cremated and her ashes scattered was put in her will. Rose recalled her in earlier, healthier days saying "I don't want to be buried where my family have to come and mourn over me. Just remember me as I was." Another thing she said came to mind then "Don't ever put an 'In Memoriam' in the paper for me. I'm afraid I might get 'The trumpet sounded! St Peter said come. The pearly gates opened and in walked our mum!'." That was Dora, valiant and humorous to the end.

Rose found that the house her mother bought in Murambi Gardens was left to her in her will. That changed their lives. Somehow, she changed all their lives completely for the better.

They moved into the large house in Murambi Gardens and sold the house in Fairbridge Park to their friends, Jimmy and Avril.

Her mother had died before she could occupy the house with them. So, her room, en suite in the best part of the house, enclosed between all the other rooms for protection and looking out onto a rose garden, was never occupied by the one person they most wanted in it. Sherrell had the bedroom Morny would have had for a while, then she moved to Bulawayo to start as a trainee nurse and Jenny moved into Morny's room.

Rose saw much more of the other man in her life, the beloved Roy, once she was living there. Noel was hardly ever home. He'd go out after dinner and not come back until the early hours. Sometimes it was Police Reserve duty in Sakubva African Township protecting the ordinary workers from Joshua Nkomo's thugs. They had begun what was called 'necklacing' indiscriminate individuals they accused of not supporting N'komo. They would jam a tyre down over the head and shoulders of the victim, fill it with petrol and set it alight. Where Rose worked, they had a frail old tea boy called Tickey, and they feared for his life when he went home. They let him off early and instructed him to make a detour, way round the industrial sites, and not walk down the usual routes to get home. The Police Reserve wore a hard hat and carried a truncheon, that's all the protection they had but they saved many from a frightful end.

On other nights he went to his "youth club". He had fitted out an industrial shed as a dance hall for teenagers, theoretically to keep them out of trouble. Unfortunately, his idea of dark, ill lit corners and big cushions for couples to loll on, lighting only a central dance area, made Rose uneasy. She had nothing to do with it, but the closing time was ten p.m. and when he didn't come home for hours after that, Rose asked why. He said there were those who had no transport and he took them home. Rose's friend Molly had a daughter, aged thirteen who went for a while but finally she stopped going. She said it made her feel uncomfortable. Molly said Noel was concentrating on one girl of fourteen and always took her home. He was there at all hours of the day and night and, apparently, was having an affair with her mother.

Noel and Rose ended their time together for good. He passed a derogatory remark about everything wrong with their relationship being the fault of her 'bloody mother.' This was a

215

week after Dora had died and it caught Rose on the raw. He said it again of course. Strangely, he had been good to Dora all the time she stayed in their house.

Rose had warned him if he ever said that again after her gift to them of the house in which he was standing, he must get out of it. Of course, he couldn't control himself and he said it again. They separated for a year. Then, just as she was considering having him back for the benefit of his children, she became aware of more about him that sent her into the lawyers' office for an immediate divorce. It had been a time of deep turbulence, but there were to be very rough waters indeed, downstream!

TWELVE

TO SALISBURY WITH FORTITUDE!

Rose started to organize her life on her own with the two younger children, Sherrell having gone to try out nursing in Bulawayo. She employed a new house servant and started to work out her new routines.

One day, while alone in the house with the new servant, she found he wasn't working properly. Among many other issues, her precious music tapes, many of which featured Dora playing the piano and Rose singing, had been thrown in the dustbin, so she told him to go and pack his things. She was dismissing him. To her horror, he straddled across the passageway from the bedrooms to the dining room and entrance, with no room for her to pass. He demanded his money. She was afraid, but she tried to avert trouble. She said "I must go to the bank and get your money. I haven't any in the house." Then she just looked at him as though she hadn't noticed how he was blocking her that way.

Fortunately for her, he decided to move aside. She quickly sent him to wait in his rooms at the back, locked the house and drove to the bank. There were several incidents of women killed in their houses by servants. With the terrorist war beginning, it didn't pay to employ just anyone. Rose had been careless. That is when she took on Margaret, her dear little maid.

She bought an Enterprise yacht and joined the yacht club. She couldn't handle the Enterprise, but at least her sixteen-year-old son had the pleasure of learning to sail, up in Inyanga on Lake Alexander. Christopher only wanted his girl-friends on board, so she bought a Yachting World pram dinghy for Jenny. Very much like an Optimist, it was safe for her and she had lots of pleasure in it. For herself, she bought a manageable class boat, a Mirror. She drove them up there nearly every Sunday in Dora's car, taking a picnic lunch. She sold the lovely big house and bought a small one when Kit left school and went to work as an assistant to the Government Medical Officer in Fort Victoria. Then, only Jenny and Rose were still at home and three bedrooms were enough. Fort Victoria was where her Uncle Pluff, Dora's brother Bertie, had been the G.M.O. years before. It seemed as close as her son, with only a Senior Cambridge certificate, could get towards becoming a doctor. Rose had asked Kit when he was eight, what he wanted to be when he grew up? He thought for a long time and answered "Mom, how much do doctors make?" Sherrell was in Bulawayo, finishing her second year of nursing, however she'd had enough of it and when her cousin Yolande left to get married, she came home again.

Loss again was a major feature in Rose's life. First the terrible loss of her mother, then the predictable loss of her marriage and finally with great shock, the loss of Roy. Rose walked into his office one day and caught him snatching his hand away from under another woman's skirt, looking so guilty that she knew it was the end of him for her. He tried to make light of it but for Rose, he was walking dead. She spent a wretched few months trying to punish him and make him suffer as she was suffering, but it was behaviour that she regretted later when she got over the shock and misery.

She saw the doctor when she became so depressed she contemplated suicide. She swallowed a handful of aspirin tablets one day and her heart began to pound as if it would burst out of her chest. Her head pounded, and her ears rang so loudly that she felt afraid she would explode. This wasn't expected: she thought she would go to sleep and slip away from life and suddenly the wish evaporated. Suddenly, she was frantically clawing at life. She was panicking about her children and what a dreadful thing she was doing to them, and she prayed to God to give her a chance to recover. She rushed into the kitchen and drank glass after glass of salt water hoping to vomit out some of the aspirin. That didn't work, and she gave up and relaxed, just praying and hoping. Gradually, she came out of it and made a vow that never again would she do anything so stupid and selfish.

There was just one way she had to go to solve this. She should have left her job and left Umtali. Stubbornly, she was determined to remain and force Roy to be the one who suffered the loss of his. She carried her pistol around in her bag and let her friend, Vangie, know she was contemplating putting a bullet in his crown jewels! She knew Vangie would pass it on. The fact was that she really wouldn't have done it because she couldn't bear to hurt him, she still loved him. He warned her that she would get the sack if she didn't stop behaving the way she was, and she said, "Go on, do it!" She couldn't understand why everyone seemed to accept his behaviour in the office.

This was a predatory man conning women into trusting him and nailing scalps to his belt. Surely the manager knew this? Surely, they would know how she had been conned. She was determined to remain in her office until she got rid of him.

She was disliking herself so much that she began crying suddenly at work. She went to see her doctor and he sent her to see a psychiatrist in Salisbury. She had two quarter-hour appointments and faced a big, old man with black, horn-rimmed glasses, behind which were the kindest, wisest, big green eyes. She immediately wanted to tell him all and that is what he asked her to do. A wave of relief flooded through her and she told all, howling all the way, for the full quarter of an hour. He listened, simply passing tissue after tissue to her out of a box he had on his desk. Finally, he passed the box over, making a note in his pad – probably ordering another box full!

Rose felt she was understood. Finally, she asked him what she should do? He hesitated, then said she must make her mind up herself. That was disappointing, Rose expected more, so she persisted. Did he think she should divorce? What should happen to the man who had let her down? How should she behave and what would he do in her place? He stared at her for a minute, blinking as he decided how to answer this outburst. Then he made up his mind. He was careful to say that this was not what he usually did, and she must decide whether to do what he would do if he were she.

He would divorce, most definitely. The letters from Roy should be destroyed and if she brought them in, he would help her burn them. She should move away from both work place and town. Rose argued, how could she burn those precious letters, they were all she had left. He said that was his advice and she must go and think it over, then come back to him if she didn't take it, goodbye. He gave her a prescription for some tablets and that was that.

Rose spent the weekend with Pat and Mickey who had moved to a beautiful house in Avondale. This one was their own, not the Native Department's. It was a very pleasant weekend and they said they hoped she would move to Salisbury as they were permanently there now that Mickey was high up in the Head Office of the Native Department. Rose studied the house sales adverts in their Sunday paper and two small adverts caught her fancy. Ballantyne Park, three acres plus old cottage needing renovation for $10,000. It seemed too good to be true, particularly as Ballantyne Park was in Borrowdale, the best suburb of Salisbury. She didn't realise that she was already moving towards doing what the psychiatrist had advised. She noted the address and decided to go out there before going back home. There she found an absolute gem. A tumbledown cottage set below three towering pale lilac bougainvillea trees, it seemed, although bougainvillea was normally a bush! In front, down a grassy slope were large willow trees, dipping their branches in a small lake. $10,000? Rose couldn't credit it! She went back immediately and phoned the agent again. He said he wasn't sure whether it was still on the market, but he'd find out and ring her.

She mulled over what the psychiatrist has told her and at first, she couldn't bear to take his advice, except for the divorce. That, she did immediately. She didn't have to wrench herself away from her job. She was asked to resign! The letter was signed by the manager, not Roy. It satisfied Rose because she knew it hurt him a bit. He had made several overtures towards smoothing the shattered relationship between them and she had rebuffed him every time. She longed to make it up but realised that he would never change. She would never be able to trust him.

The letters were different. Finally, she had to decide whether her reluctance was in some way harmful. She reflected on the fact that that a highly trained specialist's advice should be taken. She brought out her boxful and started tearing them up and weeping simultaneously. Then she fetched the wheelbarrow and piled the fragments in, lighted a match and watched them go up in flames. There was no epiphany of relief. It was more like a cremation. It was certainly the death of a dream. But it was done and that was that. She wrote a note of thanks to the psychiatrist and waited for news from the estate agent.

The news, when it finally came, was that the farm cottage in Ballantyne Park was on sale again. Rose told the agent to draw up the agreement immediately and secure the purchase that day. She'd be up there to sign in the morning, first thing. Sight unseen and voetstoots, she meant it and she'd pay cash on the dot!

Rose as Maria with Alan Baker as Captain Von Trapp

Rose in front of Chapel scene

The Swiss Alps scene

Sets designed and painted by Rose for The Sound of Music

There had been plenty of time to think. Rose was like a hermit in the small house in Umtali, just ferrying Jenny to school and back and not going anywhere that Roy would be, so that meant dropping out of the theatre as well. Her final show in Umtali had been The Sound of Music, not very long after her mother had died. It was so sad for Rose that Dora never saw her play Maria with the handsome and talented Alan Baker playing Captain von Trapp. Dora would have also delighted in the beautiful sets Rose had painted for the show. In fact, it was the only show Rose did in which her entire family was involved, on stage or off, and it helped as a temporary distraction for her difficulties

Rose was alone. The only man who came to find her during this period was Tony, who used to supply the music department in the store with records, and she had met him at Roy's house. He had come to her house one evening when she held a dinner party. He spilt red wine down the front of his shirt and Rose went into the bathroom to try and wash it off. Suddenly, he leant forward and kissed her, and she was shaken because she liked this tall, handsome man. Now that she was alone and unhappy, he came to see her and take her out and she grew very fond of him. She knew that she would see him in Salisbury if she moved there. He was married but was contemplating divorce, so her future was possibly with him.

It became clear to her, then, that her life had changed every seven years, and another change was due. She was forty-two when she moved to Salisbury. That was the first half of her life – would she last to eighty-four, she wondered?

Rose sold the little house and the yachts, keeping the pram dinghy for Jenny. She was sad about the Enterprise, because her son loved it, but she couldn't cart it everywhere by herself. She found friends who would board Jenny until she finished her schooling at the Umtali Girls High. She went to say goodbye to the Ropers, who had bought the house she had designed in Fairbridge Park she and Noel and the family had lived in for ten years. They were looking after Jenny for her and she asked Jimmy Roper if he knew who could bring Sherrell's car to Salisbury. She was introduced to Tom, the widower of Daphne who had just died of cancer. Daphne had played the organ in the orchestra for Sound of Music and Rose knew her but had never met him. He said he was going up to Salisbury to stay with his daughter and would drive the car up for her so that was a relief.

She had found the property in Salisbury and her luck was changing. She now owned an extraordinary find in the most beautiful part of Borrowdale, in Ballantyne Park. There, perhaps, she could build a home and have her children there again. Three acres with a little lake, and a quaint cottage cost her only five thousand pounds! Her last memory of Umtali and Penhalonga where they had all lived and where she was born, was packing her trailer with the last of her pot plants and garden implements with the help of her little African maid, Margaret, who couldn't come with her. She had found Margaret a highly paid job with the prison service.

She was a dear little woman who had been let down by a policeman who had abandoned her when she got pregnant. Rose said she would make him support the child, but Margaret wouldn't let her, "He will take little George away from me, madam, if I take money from him. It's African law!" Rose hugged her as she got in the car and her parting words were "Goodbye,

Madam, go well!" Then, as Rose started to drive away, she ran to the car and said this: "It's always worse for the one who is left behind".

Then, Rose said farewell to the shades of the past and set off to face her future.

THIRTEEN

BIG MEN, SMALL MEN AND A
LITTLE SWINE OR TWO

Well? What next?

Here she was. Rose had no key for the front door and it was already seven o'clock at night. This was her new home and it was in a different city in a different province. She rose stiffly out of the car and stretched. Too tired to unhitch the trailer, she took one suitcase out, decanted little Aggie, her Scottie, and the cat box containing Cindy, Jenny's cat. She locked the Wolseley, she had named Arabella, giving the car a little pat on her bonnet for pulling the heavily laden trailer a hundred and fifty miles without faltering.

Summertime, and it was still light enough to see the little lake in front of her and the fantastic pale lilac Formosa bougainvillea towering over the top lawn and almost dwarfing the little cottage beneath it. The full moon was just rising on her right between massive gum trees on the perimeter of the three-acre property. Her heart felt the first delight it had, in years.

Where was her son Christopher? She had left him in the place and expected him to welcome her. Kit, as Rose called her son, had left Fort Victoria for good and had been transferred to the Head Office of the Health Department.

She had bought her daughter Sherrell an old Borgward car which would be driven up on Sunday by the new acquaintance Tom, and which would ease the transport problem. In the meantime, Kit had no car, so why wasn't he here? She tried the windows and found that the bathroom one was a little ajar. With a stick, she managed to lift the latch and climb in without any difficulty, making a firm resolve that bars would be added without delay. That had been far too easy.

She tried the light switch. Fine. The electricity was on. The furniture van would arrive in the morning, but she had a bed in the end bedroom and Kit's bed in the first one, also a table and chairs in the huge kitchen at the other end that she had brought up previously in the trailer, enough for them to cope with until the morning. With her flask of coffee and the sandwiches, all she needed to do was let out the little cat and fetch the animal food and milk from the car. She had brought cat litter and a sandbox, so she shut Cindy in her end bedroom. Aggie was fine and after a visit to the lawn again, the little dog settled down under the table and Rose put the dog's bedding down in the corner for later. Strangely, she felt quite safe there, no sense of fear at all.

The telephone, she found to her surprise, was still working so she phoned her sister Pat who lived on the other side of the city near the University. She said she had to stay where she was, so Pat and Mickey motored over with some spare bedding for her, some groceries and a bottle of wine. They had a quick drink and left her to get to bed early. After a hot soaking in the quaint bathroom, she slipped into bed and slept flat out until a car brought Kit home at midnight, shining its lights into her bedroom window. It turned out that he had thought she was coming the next day, following the furniture van. Sherrell would be arriving soon and she would be able to give him a lift to work every day. Jenny, too, would be home on holidays from school. Rose had other beds arriving. She just had to decide where to put them all!

Daylight came in the most unexpected way. Her eyelid was opened with a claw! There, peering in her eye, was a skinny little black cat. "Min?" she mewed, "Min?" It seemed to mean "Are you there?" When Rose said "hello, who are you?" she ran in the bathroom and hid under the bath. She belonged to the old lady who had sold the property to Rose. She crawled in where it was bricked in with a small gap near the pipes where she could squeeze through. She stayed there mainly, going outside at night and just coming in for a meal or early in the morning to give all of them a wake-up claw. Nobody came to collect her, and they called her Min. She was very old and just disappeared one day.

Rose bought Christopher the promised car. Sherrell's would only be brought up at the weekend by Tom who was coming up from Umtali to visit his daughter. He was much older than Rose and seemed to be almost fatherly, kind and trustworthy. Her friend Avril praised him and told her how he had cared for Daphne. Rose felt glad she had met him. He was not the usual type of man she was drawn to. He was a Londoner; a Cockney from the Thames wharf, now out of that element; and living for years in Rhodesia had made him stand out as different and interesting. Rose wanted to get to know him better. She recalled seeing him once, driving past in his large car in Umtali; this large, black-haired man with a big, curved nose and a bigger, jutting chin. Rose had a sensation of some future link between them. Then she had moved away but he was, by some strange quirk of fate, bringing the car to her door that weekend.

Suddenly, there was a knock on the back door. "Morning Missus. It's Joseph." There stood a huge African with a smile showing a set of the whitest, finest teeth. He was towering over Rose and must have been at least six-foot-two and built like a boxer. He stepped back and went down on his haunches suddenly. This threw her for a moment until she remembered that Africans find it impolite to be higher that the chief, they literally crawl, and he was a simple village African from the tribal trust lands.

"Morning, Joseph. Yes, I remember you. Yes, you can start work now, for the same money." Joseph made a surprising leap in the air, landed with a spin, stamped the ground and headed off to the garden shed. Rose thought that he must be a Matabele, and she was right. The Matabele were bigger than the Shona and were an offshoot of the Zulu in Natal. Rose well recalled the Zulu uprising against the Indians in Durban when she lived up the hill on the South Coast near Durban, where her first two babies had been born.

The Indians had started the uprising when an African bus driver ran over a little Indian child that ran in front of the bus. In retribution, Indian cane cutters, coming home on a lorry, lopped the heads off a couple of blacks as they passed them on the Berea hill. The climb out of Durban on the Berea, was called Jacob's Ladder and all the Indian shops lined it, so the Zulus came down in a mass, stamping the ground in their war dance and smashing windows, looting, killing and setting fire to buildings.

The ground shook with the stamping and it was quite terrifying for those living near there. Noel drove to work and back into the city and out, after dark. Once, on the main bridge, he was stopped, and a knife held at his throat, as an Indian peered in with a torch and then let him go because he was white.

Rose saw the fires in the shops along the road below their house. Apparently, the Zulus were shutting Indian families in and setting them alight. The Army was called in and had orders to shoot to kill any Zulu who crossed the bridge below them.

Rose had an African maid called Sophie who complained bitterly because she had left her chickens with an Indian woman down there, Rose told her not to try to cross the bridge to retrieve them, but she went down. There she saw a mob of Zulus storming the bridge, with the Army lined up the other side firing at them. She came back to Rose looking as white as any black woman could possibly be! She had seen several of her friends killed right before her eyes! The Zulus were famous warriors, but they couldn't beat the bullets. Those were Joseph's forebears.

Rose didn't quite know why Joseph disappeared until she dressed and went outside. He'd unhitched the trailer and moved it up to the little wall behind the house. The wall was just the right height for the trailer to be supported and there it stayed. She was soon to value Joseph more than any servant she had employed before. Obviously, he was a Matabele. She asked him, and he was delighted to tell her because she was so clever he was glad to be working for her. Could he please beg her for a small advance because he needed to go to the shebeen, the beerhall on Saturday, if, of course, the 'Inkosigaas,' the lady "chief" gave him Saturday afternoon off? Also, if she had any, could he please have one aspirin? He did not need more. He knew the way to get happy down at the shebeen. He only bought one beer – one bottle. That's all! Then you pop the aspirin in and shake it. That's enough to keep you happy all day! Rose obliged. He was irresistible.

Rose told him he could have Saturday afternoon and all Sunday. This he refused to do, so she insisted he only work Sunday morning until she told him to go. This was the only African she knew who wanted his own way and hated to be away from his garden.

He decided to teach her his way to get rid of moles. He dug away the top of the last mound and inserted his dirty old sand shoe, first smelling it and assuring her it was strong "Its sterek, Missus and it will work." Later, he called her. There was a little, furious, furry creature trying to jump out of the watering can, blinking its tiny eyes at the light. She tried to pick it up, but it did its best to bite her.

He was just about to cut it in half with a spade when she stopped him and told him to take it far afield and let it go. He thought it was a crazy thing to do. Little edibles were prized by him. They went into the pot! The little animal disappeared and was later discovered when he tried to use the can. The mole had hidden up the spout. Rose was so impressed with it she made Joseph put it back in its hole. That nearly sent him into a fit of despair. These white people! Were they totally mad? Just 'penga'! Mad!

The view out of the kitchen window was blocked by the biggest fig tree Rose had ever seen. It was the shape of a monster cabbage and covered with thousands of small, green figs. She could hardly wait to try them. Then suddenly after a month or two it began to wilt and die. She didn't know what to do. Then, a large branch fell off and when she examined the base, to her horror she saw huge, wriggling white cut-worms crawling out. She shouted for Joseph and the moment he saw them, he ran for a spade and set to, digging flat out until the whole tree toppled over. The whole base was alive with the wriggling things. Rose was terribly disappointed but not Joseph! He collected the bucket and shovelled all the disgusting things in – for his dinner. Apparently, they were very tasty when toasted – well, after all, white people eat prawns!

He told her that the 'old missus' made jam, lots of jam out of the figs. He said the man from the council came and sprayed the tree for her for nothing and she gave him lots of jam, more than she should have, in his opinion. Rose regretted not knowing about this or she'd have contacted him. Joseph planted small branches of it and she at least made some green fig jam with the biggest fruit.

That led Rose into meeting the man who allowed her to make the most extensive building alterations to the cottage without more than a rough plan handed to him. She enjoyed carte blanche with great pleasure. He was the building inspector and just let her do what she wanted, seldom checking and never criticizing. The fig tree, he couldn't save. Rose made him cakes and bought the odd bottle to thank him, absolutely astounded at his casual attitude. He came and checked once or twice and then left her to it giving her advice if she asked, as to where to buy building material etc. Rose measured and drew plans for the alteration.

The furniture arrived, and Joseph made it simple, hauling huge articles into any place she chose without even straining himself. Fortunately, she didn't have too much furniture that couldn't be stored in the shed. Hers and the children's beds, the odd wardrobe, a big sofa and dining suite filled the whole interior with little room to walk round. The kitchen was easy. The old lady had left a huge kitchen table in the middle and a couple of kitchen chairs and everything fitted in there with masses of room all round. It was a real farm kitchen. Rose wished she had an Aga cooker or an old wood stove.

The entrance was at the side of the front verandah. It was half walled along the front, with pillars. Big windows had been fitted all along the veranda room between the pillars, looking out at the front lawn and the bougainvillea. Through these you could see the little lake with willow trees all along the edge. The place had great charm. It was like the Garden of Eden. The floors of the cottage were red, shiny polished concrete, as were so many old Rhodesian houses. Rose had several mats and small carpets and she fitted the large, comfortable sofa in the veranda room.

Up a step and through a French door, there was a long rather narrow lounge/dining room in which fitted the oblong dining-room table, a few chairs and the sideboard. A step led down into the big kitchen on the west side. The ceilings were low and made of rough asbestos board, sagging in one or two places so you could see the flattish corrugated asbestos-cement roof through it. Replacement was necessary, but Rose relished the thought. She had bought the whole place for almost nothing. She spent her evenings drawing up plans for alterations.

A door led through from the dining room on the left to the

bedroom section, and Rose was glad this could be locked at night for safety. This was 1968 and the war against the terrorists had been intensified. There were incidents in the outlying suburbs and a fear of terrorist incursions so one had to be cautious. First and immediately burglar bars had to be installed. Christmas was coming and suddenly she would have all three grown children with her.

Sherrell had decided to give up her nursing training having become thoroughly disgusted with the attitudes in the profession, and her son, Kit, realising that becoming a doctor to 'make the money doctors make' in the small town of Fort Victoria, was a pipe dream, asked for a transfer to Salisbury. Jenny was due home for the long school holiday as well.

Rose had to plan how to fit them into the cottage. It was miniscule! There was no passage. The dining room door opened to the first bedroom, a very small one. That led straight into the second, also small, and that led into the bathroom, and then, into the last bedroom, a bigger room that had been added on. All the ceilings were low and falling apart except that one, so she had set her bedroom furniture it. She put the girls' beds in the next one, so that she and they had the bathroom almost en suite. A large wardrobe, put sideways, divided the third little room in half. That gave Kit a narrow semi-private bedroom with a wardrobe, away from the females surrounding him. She and the girls walked through behind the wardrobe, using the space as a passage to the dining room and the rest of the house.

Of course, all three brought their precious acquisitions with them and stashed them away in the cottage. Rose had other possessions of theirs already there, brought from the big home in Umtali. Then it rained! It just poured down for days and the roof began to leak! It didn't just drip – it poured on the beds and all over their precious radios, radiograms and speakers. She rushed off to buy extra buckets as they all howled out in rage over wet books and clothes.

They were cooped up, miserably squashed in a small space, so quarrels were bound to happen. Once, her dear son passed a particularly snide remark about her which made her cry. Sherrell, who didn't usually say much, suddenly leapt up, pounced on the unfortunate Kit, screaming like a banshee and pinning him down. Rose saw tufts of dark hair flying in every direction as she pounded him! Rose had to stop Sherrell defending her before her darling boy emerged totally bald! She was very proud of him as he didn't hit back, he just covered as much of himself as he could with his arms and hands. She had a flashback to Umtali, when he was sixteen and he and she were alone in the house.

He had passed an equally unpleasant remark about her and she lost her temper, made a fist and hit him on the jaw, an uppercut, as he was nearly a foot taller than she. By the time her fist met his jaw, it had lost much of its momentum. All he did was raise one eyebrow which made them both laugh. He just felt bound to stir things up.

Rose remembered how he could stir his father into a rage. Once, at the dinner table, when a large ox tongue was about to be eaten with relish and his father had put the first piece in his mouth, Kit said airily, "Just think! A week ago, this tongue was up a cow's nose!"

His father slammed his knife and fork down:

"Jesus CHRIST!"

Back went his chair, turning over on the floor as he stormed out.

"Christopher!" said Rose, accusingly.

"What?" said the innocent, "What did I say? I only said – Last week -" Rose quickly broke in "Don't you dare say it again!"

Kit took off looking aggrieved. None of them could face the tongue after that. Rose didn't buy it again for years.

A break in the weather enabled her to see the roof. It was made of asbestos cement sheets and some were damaged. Quickly, she sent Joseph up with bitumen and strips of canvas to plaster up all the cracks he could find. That made a successful temporary mackintosh for the whole house until she could raise enough funds for improvements. The shares her mother had left her were taking off in value and dividends were doubling. She also had the rent money from the house in Marlborough.

They were all fast asleep one night when Sherrell suddenly screeched and Sherrell's screeches were enough to wake the dead! Rose shot out of bed shouting "I've got my gun!" She grabbed her pistol from under her pillow and started running on the spot. She was in such a blue funk, she couldn't move an inch forward "There's somebody in my room!" yelled Sherrell.

Kit said "Go back to sleep, you're dreaming. There's nothing there!" He had no intention of getting up.

Then Rose realised she was in the full moonlight in her shortie pyjamas which were brief.

"I'm coming, I've got my gun!" she yelled, still running on the spot.

This was no time for modesty or holding back! She finally got traction and rushed in, cocking the pistol on the way, searched the bathroom and both the children's bedrooms and there was no one. They switched on the lights, put their gowns on before going through to the front rooms. Christopher slept on regardless. It was four a.m. and he didn't even bother to join them. He turned over and pretended not to hear.

Then they noticed a window open in the veranda lounge. One pane of glass was broken so they knew how the intruder had opened it and entered. What's more, together with the strong polecat odour of sweat, there was a strong smell of brandy and a broken bottle on the floor under the window. Rose aimed the pistol out towards the water and fire one shot into the darkness. There was that creepy feeling that someone was lurking outside. Unlikely given Sherrell's spectacular top C and Rose's shot, but the feeling persisted.

She checked the drinks cabinet. Another bottle was missing, and she found a small amount of cash had gone from her handbag. She had very little in it, so that was not much loss. Rose kept trying to rouse Kit but after asking what had gone, he refused to budge. She just wished her big son would be a man and support them – lazy beast!

It was impossible to go back to sleep, so they locked the middle door again and rested until time to rise and dress for work. That was when Christopher found his trousers had gone with a five-pound note in the pocket. Then there was a wild flurry of interest. "Why haven't you phoned the police? Phone them now! The thief will be miles away by now!" They had, of course, already done so and the police arrived at that moment. There was little for them to do except take details and dust for fingerprints and then they were off again. Kit said the five pounds wasn't his money, it was a collection for someone at work's parting gift. He was supposed to buy the present that day and he only earned a few pounds a month. Sherrell gave him five pounds after a lecture about daring to pick on their mother for not phoning the police sooner!

Sherrell was working for African Distillers and Kit was still in the Health Department main offices. Rose had bought them an old car each, the best she could afford. Kit's old Rover was divine to look at. It guzzled oil, but it looked up-market and it got him about. Sherrell's Borgward was fine but Kit's Rover was driven at top speed by him until the engine seized. He was about to go into the Army to do his national service for two years, so the demise of his Rover didn't worry him. It was sold for scrap for almost as much as it cost Rose and he banked the money.

Kit and Sherrell finally left to live in the city. Sherrell and her school friend Alanna shared a flat and Kit moved into the Tally Ho, a large hotel run by old Mrs. Gold, who stuffed young people in, two to a single room and three in a double and charged them a bit less. Thus, she simultaneously made extra money and helped the teenagers. The meals were filling, plenty of meat and vegetables and there was a big swimming pool there. He soon charmed her into letting him have a large room to himself which he decorated with enormous speakers to play his music at ear splitting volume.

Rose sold some shares at a premium and purchased others that seemed about to rise, increasing her portfolio considerably. Also, when she had sold the huge house in Umtali that she inherited from her mother, the purchase of which had depended on her accepting as deposit a big bungalow they owned in Marlborough, Salisbury, rented to a doctor for a year and she still had that monthly income.

She planned extensions and changes to her new place. About 25 feet away on the left and almost parallel, was a colossal brick structure divided into four big rooms with an iron roof and a solid cement floor. Attached at the far end of that was a separate building with a lower sloping iron roof. This had a large extension, open to the east front room, down one step, with a concrete floor and a long window facing the lake. The back section appeared to have been a workroom or dairy and it had an earth floor and three phase electricity with several plug sockets. She decided to tackle that first. Without any difficulty, it could be converted into a new bedroom section of three large rooms in front, a wide passage down the centre and two modern bathrooms and a separate toilet at the back. An iron door would open at the end of the passage into the workshop section which would become a large double garage or a fourth large bedroom en suite with walk in wardrobes.

She had temporarily stored all her extra furniture there, but there was still room to use half of that section as a kitchen for a while. Rose was puzzled to see a pipe sticking out of the wall with a couple of thick wires sticking out. She was delighted to be told that that was for an electric stove. Obviously, the previous owner had been converting the place into a house to replace the old cottage. All Rose's boxes and bits and pieces from Umtali were piled on one side.

Rose envisaged joining the two buildings somehow with a veranda room full of plants and, perhaps, a small pond. She paced it out and jotted the measurements down, making rough drawings of what she planned and when she was satisfied that she had an idea what the house would look like, she tried to make architects drawings like she had of the house in Umtali. The town planning office would require these, she knew.

It was rather lonely there, on a three-acre corner block, set away from all the other houses, with huge gum trees down both sides of the triangular plot, and the lake in front. All her neighbours lived in massive houses on big plots. Most of the houses were double storied and owned by the wealthy and prominent section of the community - doctors, lawyers and various millionaires and politicians. She felt bound to construct something impressive.

She almost achieved her aim of "something impressive" although not quite in the way she imagined when one day, she decided to cut down an enormous Australian blue gum with nothing but the aid of Joseph the gardener. Joseph set to with a will, chopping madly at the broad base of the tree. It took him all morning to remove a large V more than halfway through. By then, some neighbours had gathered over the side road, one in his Jaguar in the driveway of his house, to watch the intrepid proceedings of this new neighbour. To her dismay, gusts of wind started to blow. The huge tree began to sway, this way, that way, this way again, and Rose saw to her dismay that "that way" included a trajectory right across the neighbours, the Jaguar, his fancy house and all! She wanted to race over and yell at them to get out of the way, but mustering both courage and dignity, directed Joseph to cut a V into the trunk on the other side a little higher than the first. The tree began to groan, and after what seemed to be an eternity, slowly toppled over straight down her long lawn, to the applause of the onlookers. Rose smiled weakly, congratulated Joseph and retreated shakily into the house for a cup of tea, or three!

Her neighbour on the right, over the bridge and up the hill, was Sir Somebody or Other who owned race horses, had stables on his large acreage and an enormous palace of a house. There was one other house up there, in front of which was a large pool which once suddenly detached itself from the earth after heavy rain, rising right up in the air like Noah's ark and looking as if it would be floating down to the lake. Finally, it subsided again but it had to be taken out and replaced. Over the road on her left was an English diplomat living in a double-storey mansion. He was deported for spying for the British during Rhodesia's independence years.

Before she decided to buy, she had driven up from Umtali to view the property with a friend. Audrey had laughed when Rose looked around to make sure the neighbours seemed suitable, and the houses were upmarket.

"I like that!" she said, "This is what you're buying and you scrutinise those!" Rose supposed she was being ridiculous, but she had dreams for the future and told Audrey she had no imagination! This was a place loaded with potential. She changed the name of the property from Sedgemere to Seven Springs after the place near the source of the Thames named 'Seven Springs' in England. The man-made lake was beautiful, with its willow trees reflecting in the water, the geese swimming in it and a couple of huge, friendly and greedy white swans. Streams ran into it all round, except on her little hill where her friend in the municipal office told her the foundations were solid as a rock. On the other side of the road, behind her and up the hill, there was a little shopping centre - a row comprising grocery, butchery, bakery, liquor store, oculist and garage. The main housing section was up behind the shops and there was a parking area in front, leading to another smaller dam and tiny game park. The little lake was being fenced on the front boundary by the Council. She had envisaged having to do it herself and it saved her the expense. It was about half a mile long.

There was a doctor living over the road above her and some retired MDs, so she wasn't devoid of neighbours. However, they were all strangers at present. She joined the Reps Theatre group, but the theatre was eight miles away and she wasn't too happy about coming home late at night. Rose had always been afraid of the dark, always feeling something would jump on her from behind, so she was glad to have the little F.N. pistol that her husband had bought for her and had taught her to use in Durban.

There had been burglars almost nightly in their suburb in Durban and it was dangerous to live there. Sometimes, the intruders were stark naked and covered with grease, making it easy to wriggle out of capture. Once out of the windows, they melted into the black night being relatively black themselves. They carried sharp knives and stabbed, killing one man who had been living behind Rose and Noel's property. Another thieving trick was to fish clothes and handbags out through windows, also car keys. It was dangerous to grab the sticks they fished with. A couple of men had been badly slashed by razor blades attached to them.

Rose and Noel's little car was fitted with an alarm and they were often up in the night, staring out at the car in case it was stolen. Finally, they packed up and left Durban after three years in the house, after the car's rear window was broken and the radio stolen. Sherrell was two and Kit was a baby then.

Seventeen years and one divorce later, Rose was alone, and the night held the same lurking, invisible dark menace!

Rose had planned what she intended to do, so now she needed a builder. She told Joseph and, like magic, next morning a master builder appeared at her back door. There stood a dapper little black gentleman wearing a brown trilby over one eye, a walking stick and shiny boots. "Morning madam, my name is Phillip, the builder." This was no Matabele, that she knew. He was shorter than Rose, about 5 foot nothing, with a pale brown complexion. She thought this was an unlikely candidate for quick brickwork and mixing concrete. He understood exactly what she told him however, so she thought she'd just try him on the first alteration. He walked off nonchalantly saying he'd be back at seven a.m., having first checked the piles of sand, stone and bags of cement she'd bought. He said order bricks, one thousand commons, and went. She needed bricks, so she ordered them anyhow.

On the dot of seven a.m. there was Phillip, dressed as before but with the addition of large sunglasses. Trailing behind him was a small gang of labourers, about ten of them. She told Joseph to work round that side to watch out for them and see what they wanted, show them his toilet etc. and he agreed happily, feeling a bit superior. She also told him to watch out that they didn't steal anything. He knew Phillip, of course. Rose gathered that, but they didn't chat to each other. Out came her wheelbarrow and shovels and soon Phillip had chosen a hard surface for cement mixing. The gang got busy – hose pipe, water taps, where were they? Now what to do? This was moving faster than she expected. Out came her big hammers and the mallet, everything Phillip found he needed by riffling through her things without a by-your-leave! The bricks arrived and were piled at the back. She chose the first project and described it to Phillip. He was away with his orders to the gang and then he sauntered off!

Soon, she realised she had to be the 'boss boy', standing there in the midday sun, supervising 'dagga boys' mixing the sand and cement, making sure they didn't yap so much to each other that the cement leeched out of the mixture with too much water being poured in. Three or four labourers mixed a huge pile of cement and the others set about the walls that had to be broken into for doors and windows etc. With only Rose's rough plan, Phillip had instructed them, and Rose found they were doing everything quickly and correctly without her supervision. Within a day or two, the iron door leading into the long, wide passage from the future garage was in place. This was a requirement in Rhodesia in case of fire. And so, they progressed, Phillip, his gang and Rose, acting foreman. The walls were high, so she put in the ceilings nearly three metres up. She added picture rails for all her paintings. Finally, the result was passed by her friend in council. He approved wholeheartedly, and she was free to move everything into that side using the one big double room as lounge-dining room and the other as her bedroom – a lovely, big room with a view of the lake.

The door at that end of the passage near her bedroom, led into a small brick lean-to and Rose put the telephone extension there. It had a low tin roof that needed replacing later. She added a long, narrow glass window, placed high up near the ceiling, so nobody could look through. Rose's bedroom was opposite the bathroom that end, and she knew that there would be times when she went from bed to bathroom without a stitch on. The new window was only 18 inches in depth. This room she called the vestibule. Behind this, a high wall extended from the bedroom section to the cottage and behind that, was a covered veranda facing the road. This, would be the back wall of the veranda room facing the lake.

When she needed plasterers, those arrived. Then carpenters or face-brick specialists were there immediately. Phillip was quite amazing. Rose realised he went off because he was building other houses elsewhere. His charges were exceptionally low, but she had to supervise in his absence. That was just taken for granted.

She got busy drawing up a plan for the cottage alteration. First, the roof of the cottage had to come off. All Phillip's labourers were delighted to cart away anything she threw out, even broken pieces of asbestos cement roofing. Anything and everything was vacuumed away. It brought home to her the reality of their relative poverty and she sorted out anything she didn't want in the way of clothing and threw it in. They were delighted and worked diligently on her building. Nothing was stolen, absolutely nothing. The floors in the bedroom section had been put in by a flooring company. She chose a lovely, light wood block floor right through and she planned that for the living rooms too. Phillip had produced carpenters for the woodwork. Those, too were lined up for the future; first came the breaking down of the existing interior walls to create the large new lounge, TV room and kitchen then the building up of the walls for a new tiled roof with higher ceilings.

Rose had met Tom and had married him. Tom, the huge, burly, old Cockney ex-boxer wasn't the type she intended to marry, if ever she did, but he'd set his mind on her, so she married him. He seemed such a quiet, kind, helpful man when he brought Sherrell's car up to Salisbury for her. She so badly needed someone to listen to her and be a companion. It was a mistake, but she was so emotionally battered by her previous disasters of the last seven years that she yearned for a big-daddy relationship. There were signs, however, before the marriage that the 'big-daddy' façade could slip. Rose should have been warned. She said something he didn't like once, and suddenly he shouted and his hands were round her throat, shocking her deeply. It wasn't an argument, it was just a sentence, as she talked to him. She couldn't understand why he turned on her. She asked his doctor, who said it wasn't the Tom he knew. Probably, it was because she hadn't said yes to his proposal. This decided her, and she married him.

Once, the blow up was about a cat's saucer of milk outside. Neither cook nor gardener picked it up and Rose said one of them should have done so. Weeks later, at full moon again, she was accused of meaning him! "Admit it, you're a bloody liar!" he'd pushed her over backwards, so she lost her balance. He frightened her with unmerciful bullying. This increased after she stupidly married him, and she should have heeded the initial warning signs.

Always, contrition and crocodile tears followed, then a hasty departure, back to his place in Umtali. It didn't stop, it just increased in severity. He'd rant and rave and scare the daylights out of her. The danger was that he was a powerful ex-boxer and he would suddenly lash out and push her backwards so that she lost her balance and went careering backwards and down. Once she landed on the sofa which had a solid back and arm-rests. Her head snapped forward with such force she thought it would snap off. Apart from that, she found it degrading and damaging to her nervous system. She came out in little lumps on her arms and fingers that had to be cut out by a skin specialist. They seemed to be from stress.

Tom had a huge Akai tape recorder he'd turn on full bore, so loud that the windows rattled, and the cat's hair stood on end as it took off through the window. He'd click his fingers and say, "I'm in a vindictive mood now!" Rose would curl up inside with fear what may come next, the violence of which intensified with time, then he'd be off again to Umtali in his big automatic Westminster. Everything he touched he kept in perfect condition – except her, Rose realised! Once, when they went to his daughter's house for a party lunch, Tom went to see the female visitors out of the gate as Rose carried a pile of borrowed plates out to the car. The steps were slippery with rain and she fell, saving the plates but catching the base of her spine on the corner of the step and damaging the bone at the base of her spine. It was agonising. Tom looked round and didn't even bother to come and help her up. It was then that she realised that he did not love her.

Rose was in dreadful pain next day and could hardly walk. Tom went to the city without a word and, at lunchtime, feeling a bit better, Rose went out to plant something in her rockery. She was down on her haunches there when he returned. He came over to her and she smiled and said hello. Without speaking to her he put a hand on her chest and pushed her over so hard that her legs went up in the air and her dress went over her face, baring her legs and showing her underwear, and she nearly went over in a somersault. The pain in her spine was so bad she could hardly get up. It was totally degrading. He turned on his heel and went.

She rolled over and managed to stand, feeling stabbing pain as she limped inside, greatly relieved that nobody had seen her from the road, and as it was Sunday, the garden workers and builders weren't around. Rose couldn't understand why she couldn't raise the strength to end the relationship immediately. The fact was that she was afraid. His threats were cowing her. She seemed to have no one to turn to and no way out. Tom had disappeared in his car again and Rose didn't hear from him for a few days. She began to deteriorate in health. More skin lesions came up and the specialist removed them one by one. They were tested but benign, thankfully. She was developing a bigger internal health problem that happened later.

Of course, he was back eventually, without apologies, and everything was resumed as if the incident hadn't occurred. Rose realised that if she bore this degrading behaviour without complaint, life would continue just as if nothing had happened. There were many aspects of this union that were worthwhile. She admired his extreme sense of order and clean living and he had an earthy sense of humour. Rose really enjoyed his company when they went to his daughter and son in law, Gillian and Wally. They taught her many card games like 'Chase the bitch' and they made up a foursome at bridge. He was good with her children too and Rose felt that they were safe with him.

They travelled to Beira several times in his superbly comfortable Westminster and stayed at the Estoril Hotel on the beach front. He had business interests there and they were invited to dinner by the owners and managers of companies he dealt with. Having the rail spur in Umtali, he handled the importing of wood from the M'tao Forest which was cut by a Company owned by a Portuguese man from Oporto, in Portugal, a billionaire who couldn't speak English. He invited them to a dinner party at Johnnie's, the celebrated restaurant in Beira, and communicated with them through a Portuguese Army Officer he used as interpreter, so the evening was a success. Rose had lobster thermidor for the first time and they drank a Portuguese vino verde, a green wine called 'mouro basto'. Adding a little humour to the party, Rose asked innocently: "What's mouro basto? Does that mean Dead Bastard?"

The reaction from the officer astonished all of them. He laughed so much, holding his stomach, that he fell off his chair and rolled on the floor. The whole party's attention was riveted on him and he had to interpret for their host who was equally delighted. Rose hadn't expected it to be the highlight of the evening! A year later the timber exporter built a road around a town near the border after a row with the Municipality over being taxed for taking his huge timber trucks on the road through. Then he disappeared altogether back to Portugal after a scandal over the pregnancy of his niece, so it was rumoured.

Tom was the Vice Chairman of the Umtali Players and a member of the Beira Club. On the strength of it, they had reciprocity so that was a pleasure. The clubhouse was on the upper floor of one of the oldest buildings in Beira, right on the bay. Downstairs, there was a huge Chinese restaurant and their kitchen had an open well to the club at the top. One could lean over the railing and watch them cooking. Occasionally, there'd be a first-class fight with Chinese shrieks and swearwords and knives literally flying at each other. It was good entertainment on a steamy evening and Beira was nothing if not hot and steamy!

'Beira tummy' was a killer. It was in Beira that Rose first found the wonderful remedy, Chamberlains Colic and Diarrhoea mixture - full of chloral! She had tried prawns in the Chinese restaurant, not knowing that one must take out the black vein along the back or leave it at your peril. It is their exhaust pipe to the rear – full of killer bacteria! She was doubled up and the chemist gave her a teaspoon of Chamberlains in half a glass of water. The whole of her interior was immediately suffused in a hot glow and every killer bug died instantly. The prawns served at the restaurant were wonderful, but they came from the bay where all the town sewerage poured in. From then on, Rose refrained from eating prawns there. To look down in the water of the bay, at the passing 'floaters' plus her experience of Beira tummy, had put her off for life.

The Club balcony extended over the bay and at low tide thousands of flamingos settled in the shallow water, put their long necks down and riffled in the mud for prawns. At sundown, it was magical up there, drinking your sundowner and watching the pink cloud of birds settle, their reflection mirrored in the still bay. Sometimes there were clouds in the sky and as the sun went down, the sky turned a lurid orange and red and the water turned a rippling gold and red. That, plus the flamingos flying out in a cloud was unbelievable. Suddenly, it would turn to a mauve red and black silhouette and then die as the stars began to twinkle and the electric lights reflected there instead.

Inside, there was space for dancing and groups of chairs round small tables with a large bar at the corner. There, all the important people in Beira who were not Portuguese, all members of the Club, met and imbibed vast quantities of expensive liquor on their expense accounts, no doubt. The main business transactions were made 'in vino', and wily old Tom was happy to use his company funds for the benefit. He could drink any of them under the table. They seemed to lavish plenty of attention on Rose as they all got more and more under the weather and he realised what an asset she was.

At the time, a British warship was patrolling along the coast in full view, making sure sanctions against Rhodesia were not breached and no fuel reached the embargoed country by sea. The British Embassy staff propped up the bar in the Club and even Rose was questioned rather amateurishly by a fat, sweaty, pink faced Vice Consul who thought he was obtaining information from her about sanctions busting. He was blinking owlishly, drunk and rather ridiculous. Rose gave him misleading stories about the source of their fuel and true ones about how well they were surviving in Rhodesia despite sanctions. She didn't mention the first pantyhose a factory had created – some had one short leg and one long! They soon got it right. A new company, was producing good chocolates and the whole country had begun manufacturing items that couldn't be imported.

Tom didn't bother to dance but she had one partner who delighted in taking to the dance floor with her. That was Ben, the Managing Director of the Holland Africa Line and Honorary Consul of Holland. He was great fun and the more he drank the more he danced and very well too. Rose was grabbed unceremoniously for the Pasa Double and she did her best. There was Ben, whirling her about and holding out his invisible red cloak for the 'bull' to run past. She drew the line at that!

However, it was fun, indeed. Tom ignored her. He was making business contacts.

They saw a lot of Ben because Tom had shipping and storing contracts with the Holland Africa Line. Ben invited them to a luncheon before they left Beira. They met at Johnnie's and Ben brought a Dutch captain of one of their cargo ships with him. He was a very pleasant young man with a wife and children living in Perth, Australia. Talking to him, Rose heard there were passengers, only twelve, taken aboard his liner apart from the cargo shipped. They all travelled first class and sat at the captain's table, away from the crew. She thought it sounded great for some future holiday overseas and very reasonable in price and tagged it in her mind for future reference.

However, she couldn't imagine going with Tom because of his tempers, so it was a forlorn hope. She recalled when for a honeymoon gift, Tom had bought tickets to go on the Pendennis Castle from Durban to Cape town on the ship's last voyage. All went well until they boarded. Her young daughter, Jenny, wanted to see her off as she was on holiday with her father there. He brought her down to the docks but kept well out of sight. Rose leaned over the rail waving to Jenny as the Pendennis sailed away with all the ships and tugs sounding the last farewell and everyone throwing streamers, ship to shore. It was exceptionally touching and special for Rose, but she didn't know what was brewing and seething in the head of the man next to her. He was in a jealous rage.

She was charmed by this generous gesture. To her, at that moment it was a wonderful honeymoon. When land was out of sight, they went down to their cabin. There, Rose decided that she would shin up to the top bunk. She was fifteen years younger, slim and agile and she considered he was old at nearly sixty! He didn't say much but Rose suspected nothing. She changed into one of her best evening dresses to go to dinner, proud and happy to be with him and thought he felt the same. He was very silent, and he didn't look at her. After dinner, Rose thought they would go on to the dance floor and Tom would dance with her, but he was so abrupt with her, she asked him if he was feeling alright. He said no, so she thought it best to go back to the cabin with him. She was feeling a bit queasy too. The ship was stabilized, but it seemed that she was seasick.

Once in the confined space of the tiny cabin, he suddenly turned on her and shouted about Jenny coming with her ex-husband to the docks. She became terrified as he stood over her threatening her and shouting. He had his hands on her throat again and Rose thought her last day had come. Then he suddenly flung himself on the bunk, turning his back. Rose was devastated. It took her an hour, sitting in the ablution block on the edge of the bath, before she crept back to the cabin and changed silently into day clothes. Then she climbed up into the top bunk where she felt safer. Finally, she dozed and woke to find she was still seasick. That, and the general misery of the situation spoilt the whole trip for her.

Tom was back to normal in Cape Town and she enjoyed the rest of the trip, but she was on tenterhooks all the time. So, there were good times and there were many of them, interspersed with the bad times. But the bad times grew more violent. Rose decided that it was the brandy he consumed when he went to the pubs in the morning. He would be away for hours and never seemed drunk when he returned, but she knew that he drank a lot. To walk in and immediately attack her and then slump on his bed and sleep, was one indication. Or else get in his car and leave for days and then walk in as if nothing had happened and work flat out 'helping' her. Oh! How he helped her, whether she wanted help or not, and she was too afraid of him to argue. His help included woodwork. He was very talented at it and it was his hobby.

In return, she bought him a $1,000 collection of power tools, the very best of everything, because she didn't want to feel she owed him. That was a substantial gift from her because the price of a good house in the suburbs was only around $4,000 in those years. For Christmas, Rose received a huge cookery book inscribed inside "from the Big Bully". That was funny, really, in its way. She still uses it, forty years after their divorce and the inscription is still a reminder.

Tom gave her eighty dollars a month towards the bills. That paid for the drinks and some groceries because they carried bottles and baskets of groceries to his daughter's home when they spent the evening with them. Rose was very fond of Gillian. She was clever, amusing, very organised and she kept her house like a new pin. Rose immediately felt welcomed there by both Gillian and her husband, Wally. Wally was fun and great at a party, assuming the character of anyone, even pious nuns, when he told rude jokes. His facial expressions were hilarious, and he would have made a great comedian. The money also paid for Tom's cook, Tickey, who moved up to Salisbury with him. Sometimes, he said, as he handed the money to her with tears in his eyes "I've had no income coming in this month." and she just handed it back. It was the way he put it that fascinated Rose, – so poetic! "No income coming in!" She knew he had quite a lot. She thought he was just testing her. However, in case she was wrong, she didn't want the money. He saved her a lot, doing the carpentry.

One day, in front of the cook, Tickey, he grabbed her frock at the neck and tore a strip out, right down to the waist. Horribly embarrassed, she pulled up the piece of material and quickly tried to cover her bra from the cook, saying "the boss is feeling a bit sick." To her surprise, he said airily "Oh, Madam, that's nothing! The old madam used to run screaming down the road!" She could hardly believe it! It was probably then that she realised that he didn't need a reason to go into a rage, it just happened. She knew Tom had looked after Daphne so kindly and carefully when she had cancer and died. She had died in the same great, heavy wooden bed Tom brought up to Salisbury for their bedroom, which was a bit daunting, but Rose understood his sentimental attachment. It was super king size, so at least there was room to spare between them. She didn't really like double beds and she was beginning to wish she didn't have to share this one.

Tom had been trying to find something to do in Salisbury and Rose, to assist him, had bought a five-acre property in the beautiful Mazoe Valley, near the dam and the citrus estates with all their rows of orange trees. Situated in the tiny village near the hotel, it had a three-bedroomed house on it and a butchery, far from the house down the hill. There were five butchery licenses, one for a butchery next to the hotel as well.

She didn't have the ready money for it, but she saw the value at $10,000! To her, it was a gift. She sold some shares and bought it. The butcheries were for Tom to make use of, hiring a butcher to manage them. Tom didn't keep a proper eye on his business and the butcher began salting away profits. It hadn't anything to do with Rose, but she had handled credit management in a large organisation and she checked the figures and tried to help Tom not to go under. Somehow, she said, he had to get rid of that butcher and try another.

Rose had major health concerns by this time. She was bleeding very heavily and urgently needed a hysterectomy. The specialist said there was a growth, possibly malignant. However, she developed a bad dose of flu and couldn't go into hospital until her cough cleared. Ordered to stay in bed and try to control her cough, because coughing made her almost bleed to death, she was ordered by the doctor not to move out of bed at all.

Without warning, Tom went out to the butchery and suddenly he returned with the butcher. He brought this stranger into the bedroom and accused her of saying that he was a thief. Then he turned on his heel and left. Rose and the butcher were both embarrassed and finally she got the butcher to leave. Tom carried on shouting at her and she said that they must part company as soon as her operation was over. He picked up the side of the bed, with her in it, trying to roll her out on the floor. Then he dropped it from nearly vertical and she rolled out. He didn't care a damn about her.

Her operation was a total success. A large, benign, fibroid growth had been causing the trouble, which was a huge relief to her. Going for a short walk up the road behind her house, she met the doctor who lived in the house behind hers. He stopped her and ribbed her "I believe you've just changed your nursery into a playpen!" he said. It took a minute for Rose to realise what he meant.

The cottage section had now been converted to a large lounge with a fireplace and a large dining room in the front and a pantry, kitchen, scullery and laundry at the back. Rose decided on a light wood ceiling in the lounge and Tom made an excellent job of it.

The company completed the floors once the ceiling was done and the large picture windows were glazed. The east wall of the lounge now had a large fireplace and the chimney jutted out into the space between the two buildings. Rose found that half the area between the two buildings was big enough for an extensive veranda room with the ceiling raked up at the front, with fully glassed sections between narrow pillars so that the winter sun would warm it. A French door in the centre formed the front entrance to the house and the floor was tiled with slate in colours matching the bougainvillea slightly in a muted violet-grey. She envisaged putting masses of indoor plants and a small fishpond in one side.

Extra wide patios with pillars were added in front of the two main sections of the house and they were tiled in slate as well. That tiling was done by an African who approached her himself. He didn't work for Phillip. He produced a 'situpa' a form of work portfolio, with his photo on it stating he was 'Raphael the Well Digger'.

Rose already had a well in front that Phillip's boys had bricked up in a circle with two pillars for a little hipped roof and a rope with a bucket to wind up water. He assured her he could tile the verandas with slate, so she tried him out, knowing he needed some work. He was very good. Later, she was to see him again under somewhat different circumstances.

She and Tom were not communicating much. He was busy pounding on his typewriter in the dining room, in which he had put an enormous desk without discussing it with her. What he was writing, she didn't inquire. She saw little of him. She suggested to him that they should part company, but he simply shouted that if she tried to divorce him, he'd 'take her for every penny she had!' and that he'd been to court and won cases before and he knew how to do it. Also, he said that if she tried to tell them what he had done to her, he'd just plead provocation.

Was she just hanging on because she expected him to stop? She saw an element of it in the way she drifted back into the same situation over and over instead of forgetting any faint thought that things would change. She had walked into the marriage as casually as she did the first one, without heeding her own inner voice of reason.

Strangely, as it turns out so often in life, she was picked up by an unseen hand and dumped out of it quite unceremoniously. An incident began one Saturday when her sister-in-law was spending a few days with them. She was recuperating from a back operation and wanted to see her son act in a play at Churchill School, so Rose said she would drive her there and watch her nephew Colin acting on stage as a British officer in World War One. He was excellent. Tom said he wouldn't come with them. When they got home at eleven, Tom was still up making tea for them, which was a surprise. Arline started telling him about the play, but he wasn't listening. He brought in the tray and a plate of sandwiches. He gave Arline tea and brought Rose a cup stirring it vigorously. The cup was half full of sugar. She didn't take sugar. The plate of sandwiches was dumped next to her and he shouted at her to drink the tea and eat the sandwiches or he'd 'stuff them down her f...ing gullet!'

Then he turned to Arline and talked to her pleasantly as if they were in totally different rooms. He paced up and down shouting at Rose until Arline began to cry. She needed to get to bed but she had never seen Tom like this and it frightened her. He asked her if she wanted more tea and she said yes as she didn't want to leave Rose alone with him. She told him she must get her tablets to have with the tea and he walked out to the kitchen for hot water. Quickly, Rose whispered "Put some of your diazepam in his tea if you can!" It was a strong sedative.

She did so, putting lots in, which worried Rose rather, and stirring it as he came in with the teapot. Rose kept pretending to drink her tea and eat the disgusting sandwiches, then stuffing them under the sofa cushions when he turned his back. They were made of inch thick bread with a quarter-inch thick layer of butter filled with large slices of cheap, fatty corned beef, bought for the dog, and could not have fitted in her mouth. They were to make her fat, he said, seeing she was dieting. At last, at three a. m., the diazepam took effect he started to flag and to get weepy about the past. He turned and shuffled off to bed. Arline went too. Rose thought it was over because he was snoring heavily. She curled up on the sofa, but she felt Tom was alright again. In the morning, Arline, Rose and Tom had breakfast normally and she left for the farm. He saw her out to her car.

The 'phone rang, and he went to answer it and called Rose. It was an African policeman complaining about her painter who took an old pram from her Pise house he was painting. The policeman said the tenant gave it to him when she left. Rose was telling the policeman she would speak to the painter, when Tom passed her and locked the door, taking out the key. As he passed her again, he ran his thumb down her cheek, hard, saying,

"I'm going to slit your face with a razor!"

He walked away and suddenly she panicked. He just might do it! She spoke urgently to the African policeman "Send someone, quickly, my husband's threatening to cut my face with a razor!" She didn't hold out much hope that the young policeman understood her and would do anything about it. She went back to the sitting room and sat far back in her chair, so she couldn't be pushed over. Tom brought in a huge mug of tea and the sugar bowl. He began screaming abuse again, ladling spoon after spoon of sugar into the cup and stirring. More huge sandwiches were brought in and the same performance began. She tried to get up and was pushed violently back. No razor blade, she was thankful to see. She prayed for the police to come.

In a remarkably short time, a car drove up the driveway and Tom turned around. Rose saw her chance, leapt up and took off, out through the kitchen, mug in one hand and sandwich in the other. Round to the front she ran and parked there was a police Jeep with a young policeman getting out of it, followed by a police woman.

What a relief! She hid behind him as Tom came out with his trousers unbuttoned and unbelted. He looked dreadful. The policeman said quietly:

"What seems to be the trouble, sir?"

Tom tried to look collected:

"Officer, you don't understand the circumstances."

"I'm not interested in the circumstances, sir. This lady seems to be in a state of fear. Shall we go inside and talk about it?"

He led Tom into the house and the police woman quietly told Rose to come into the house with her and pack a case of necessities as quickly as she could, and they would take her with them to any place she wanted. Rose packed a few things and they dropped her at the Tally Ho Hotel where her daughter, Sherrell, shared a double room with an English girl named Joan. Joan was happy to move into another room, so Rose could share with her daughter.

They sat at a long table in the dining room with several of Sherrell's friends, one of whom was a policeman named Chris. One morning, there was a telephone call for Rose and it turned out to be the wife of the padre who had built an A frame church in Avondale. She invited Rose to tea that afternoon, which puzzled Rose until she told her that Tom had been to see her husband in tears, and he had begged him to try and persuade Rose to go back to him. They had built an A frame house next door to the church. They listened to Rose carefully and then told her that they felt she should not go back. In their opinion Tom was possessed by the devil!

This shook Rose. It was the last thing she had expected to hear, and she found it so peculiar that she had to ask what they meant? This sounded to her like something out of the middle ages. It reminded her of the play written by Arthur Miller, called The Crucible, in which Elisabeth and John Proctor are accused of being possessed by the devil and hanged. They said from what she told them about him and how she had lumps removed from her arms and had an operation on her tongue and then a hysterectomy and a large cyst removed it was obvious to them that his sudden rages were caused by demons in him controlling his actions. Some of the demons were trying to get to her and manifesting as cysts and lumps.

They said they had received tapes from New Zealand and were going to play them for a gathering at their house that night at eight and they hoped she could come and listen to them. Rose arrived back at Tally Ho just in time for dinner and she couldn't wait to tell them what had happened. When she said there was a meeting that evening, the policeman Chris said that was his church and he was going there at seven, could he give her a lift? She wouldn't have gone there alone but with him she decided to satisfy her curiosity. Sherrell didn't want to go so she and Chris set off alone.

The sitting room had been cleared and they were busy setting benches in rows with an aisle in the middle leading to where there was a step up to a separate section behind an ornamental wrought iron grill. It was a hot night and Rose chose a bench near the open French door, leading to the veranda. When Chris had finished helping Don with the benches he joined her. He explained that Don would begin with prayers before he played the tapes. When the room was full of his parishioners he stood up on the step and said "Let us pray, brothers and sisters. Bow your heads and close your eyes and I will lead you."

Rose looked about to see if there were any prayer books but there weren't. Chris had his head down and his eyes shut, so she did likewise. The Reverend Don began, "Almighty God, help us to renounce the devil and all his works. Keep us on the straight and narrow path and let us guard our thoughts and not let the demons in lest we fall from grace." This was such extraordinary praying that Rose had difficulty absorbing it. Suddenly someone near her called out "AMEN!" and someone else shouted, "SAVE US, LORD." Rose suddenly wanted to giggle. She was glad her mother wasn't with her or she would have been unable to control it. Chris was praying with his eyes shut so Rose closed her eyes and covered them with her hands just to be on the safe side.

Finally, the prayer was over, and Don went to start the tape. It was about the number 666 being the code number of the devil. You would find it on everything you bought, all the code numbers showed six broader stripes and eventually, there would be a microchip on everyone's forehead or wrist and all round the world you would be controlled by the devil. This had to be resisted with prayer. You had to control your thoughts so that you didn't let the demons in. Millions of demons were out there just waiting for you think of murder or fornication and they would get into your brain and weaken your resolve. Rose found it more than peculiar at this stage and she wanted to get away and go home but she had to wait for Chris. The tape finished, and Don addressed them again. He said they needed to pray again and those who felt that they needed to be cleansed must come up to the front and he would lay hands on them and pray for them. "Brothers and sisters, bow your heads and pray with me, close your eyes and concentrate.

"Come forward, anyone who needs to be cleansed, come forward." There was a shuffling sound, and someone was walking up the aisle. Rose opened her eyes and looked through her fingers, trying to see who was going up when Don called

"Don't give in to the demon of curiosity, brothers and sisters, bow your heads and continue praying. Down went Rose's head smartly and she had to listen hard rather than be a little devil and look! Someone was mumbling and gabbling but she couldn't understand a word. Don, said "What's that you say, brother?" More mumbling and gabbling, "What's that? The demon of murder?? COME OUT, you foul thing! In the name of God, I command you, COME OUT!!" The gabbling and mumbling continued. "What's that you say? Demon of fornication?? COME OUT! Demon of masturbation? He shouted, COME OUT! In the name of God come out, YOU FOUL THING!!

Rose opened her eyes slightly, she was getting a bit tired of just listening to the Reverend Don who was beginning to sound a little desperate. Then she saw a movement next to her, and she saw a tiny mouse had come in the door and was sitting up on its haunches listening. The next time Don shrieked out "COME OUT, YOU FOUL THINGS!" the mouse turned and scurried away as fast as it could, jumping over the edge of the veranda and disappearing. Rose thought of the Gadarene swine and all the demons being transferred to it.

Was this the Gadarene mouse?

It can't have been much of a demon!

On that somewhat irreverent thought, Rose stifled a giggle and returned her concentration to the carry-on in front. However, nothing had changed up there with Don and the demons. There was a sudden scuffling as Chris got up and whispered, "Stay here." He went to the front and Rose wondered what on earth was happening. She looked up and saw Chris and some others carrying someone down the aisle and along the veranda and into a room at the end, where she could still hear a faint "Come out, you foul thing." The lights were switched on and a rather grim Mrs. Don said, "Come over here and have some tea." Rose was relieved. She had tea and then another cup and a couple of biscuits before the door opened at the end of the veranda and out came Chris and the rest of them, including a short, fair haired young man, looking a bit dazed and silent. Chris said sorry, but he had had to go and help. Shall they go? They said goodbye and as soon as they were in the car Chris told her what had happened. The small man was a university student and when Don had started calling out the demons, he put his hands round his own throat and tried to throttle himself. Don said it was the demons doing it. It took four strong men to pull his hands away. On reflection, Rose decided that she certainly had a fair idea of what the little man did in his spare time!

When she asked what all the mumbling and gabbling was, Chris said he was speaking in tongues. Rose wouldn't have missed a moment of that evening, but she never went back. She had a lot of respect for what they were doing, but she decided that it wasn't for her.

FOURTEEN

THREE DOWN, MORE TO COME

Tom was given a warning and her lawyer saw that he received an order to vacate the premises. Instead of immediately, Rose gave him a month to pack up his possessions. He tried flowers and apologies, but she had the sense to resist any idea of trying again. He left on the last day, sending a message that the key was in the door. She went there and found that the door was open. Wondering what she'd find, she was relieved to find all seemed in order. Only when she looked at the walls did she notice a kind of emptiness. Then she realised all her paintings had gone.

Rose is an artist and had several large paintings, one very precious, as she had painted it for her mother who had just died, after which it had been returned to her. It pictured her white Spode vase full of her favourite flowers, anemones. At one side was a small, framed picture of her mother when she was seventeen. Nothing could have upset Rose more. It was irreplaceable. Her mother had treasured it. They were not the sort of things an African thief would choose to steal but just before Tom had threatened her, they had visited a friend of his who was leaving the country. He was taking paintings as he said they were valuable assets to sell in another place – He told Tom "You just cut them out of the frames and they will fit into a suitcase, a light and easy way to get money out. Paintings are valuable things to collect." That friend skipped out of the country and was wanted by the police!

Rose's lawyer contacted Tom and he denied having them and Wally said he didn't think Tom had taken them. That was that. His car was parked outside in the road for hours. He was warned and ordered to stay away. She proceeded with the divorce which was finally granted. She claimed no alimony, but the lawyer added a small clause of one dollar per annum, in case she needed to claim at any future date. That had been all she claimed from her first husband as well.

So, in 1973 she was alone again and having to build a new life for herself on her own once more. The builders returned, and she resumed finishing the central veranda room. She had her three children in town and could see them often. She began painting again and joined the operatic society, but she didn't go out at night much, being a little afraid of returning at night all on her own.

Rose designed and painted many sets for the theatre shows as well because she could use the theatre during the day. She was awarded a silver cup in Umtali and a silver medal in Reps which was satisfying. In great demand for sets, she found it amusing to wait for the approach by the various producers – all the praise and 'Rose darlings' that preceded the requests. She had plenty to keep her occupied which was a good thing.

Of course, she had romantic moments. In the theatre, the choices are unlimited, but she just wasn't the type for casual affairs. She was looking for someone who wanted a lifelong partnership. Married men were off limits as far as she was concerned. One good looking singer really appealed to her because he was divorced and very attractive. Unfortunately, he was paired off with her on stage in the chorus of 'The Merry Widow' and she had to listen to him telling her about his ex-wife, who lived in his house with his three daughters and his one girlfriend! He mentioned having a flat in town with another woman in it, also he 'had relations' with the theatre secretary who adored him. His house was called 'The Harem' and he wanted to leave it and come and live with Rose! As far as Rose was concerned, three's a crowd, let alone six and she had no intention of becoming the seventh! He was a charmer; a wealthy, good looking one too, but his love affair with himself was the last straw. He thought he was the best tenor in Rhodesia and the perfect lover, wanted by all!

He once turned up at her house at nine at night. Surprised, she let him in, which was idiotic of her. He was rolling drunk and thought he was welcome in her bed, such was his image of his popularity. She said no, thank you, and he pinned her down on the sofa and tried to force her. He was so inebriated that it was totally limp, and it began to strike her as ridiculously funny, so she just laughed at him and that, apparently, was totally deflating. Finally, she persuaded him to desist and pushed him out of the door again. What stayed in her mind was his persistence over a period of two years. It seemed he needed to prove that he was irresistible.

One of her friends, a comedienne in Reps, referred to him as 'the passionate prick'. Rose seemed unable to find a companion of the opposite sex who wasn't either married, peculiar, impotent or dangerous. Then there were the ardent suitors who bored her to tears. Perhaps that was her trouble - she needed someone extraordinary and unusual. In his way, Tom had been an extraordinary and unusual man, but he was prone to domestic violence. Years later, his daughter told Rose that his father used to beat him when he was a child. His father drank heavily and boxed him so hard on the ear that he burst an eardrum and was deaf that side. That probably explained it.

She decided to go on an extended holiday overseas to get away from it all. Her three children had gone their own ways. Sherrell and Yolande, Rose's niece, shared a flat in the city, Kit had moved to South Africa with two girls, one of whom, he finally married. Jenny was in Johannesburg studying midwifery. She didn't need a home to come to at present, so Rose felt free!

Tom had collected his facts and figures, a lot of it typed when he sat in her dining room, commandeering it as his office before he was evicted. He instructed his Greek lawyer to proceed with "taking her for every penny she had." That had been his threat when she suggested they part company. Her lawyer was Tim Tanser, the son of Tony Tanser who had been her headmaster in junior school, and who had acted in plays her mother produced when he became headmaster of Gatooma School. Tim had handled her previous divorce and her conveyancing. Tom claimed $35,000.

In 1974, that was enough to buy three or four good houses. The lawyers were fascinated because he was her husband at the time, he claimed an amount per hour, eight hours a day, for working on the house and standing about ordering her gang of workers to level the ground in front of the house. The fact that she had already employed the workers and paid them wasn't considered. They were 'garden boys' and were already doing just that without his standing there.

In addition, Rose had bought another large property in the city with an old house and twenty rooms built on, plus bathrooms and toilets. Rose had decided to cement the area between the buildings and she had Phillip's gang there. Tom elected to stand over them and supervise, not that they appreciated it. This, he also reckoned up as his work and charged accordingly.

The house in Marlborough lost its tenant and she found it needed a lot to be done prior to sale. The pool was dirty and needed scrubbing and refilling. The whole place needed a coat of paint and one bedroom had housed a motorbike. The floor was stained and scratched. Rose paid people to do it, but Tom had insisted on being there and supervising. She had let him because she didn't dare argue with him at this stage. She was too afraid of him. Also, she didn't dare tell him he was wasting his time there. They could do it without supervision. She had no idea he was totting up his hours there as well or she might have risked it. He had prepared well for this eventuality.

So, her lawyer prepared her defense. She had to consider going to face a judge and had to spend many hours preparing sheets of costs and counter arguments. Of course, she had paid the builder, Phillip cash weekly for years. Fortunately, she had made him sign dated slips for the money. It required her finding invoices for everything she had bought – sand, cement, stone, wood, wiring and much more; paint and everything. She racked her brain, as nothing else could be done but prepare her papers. The $35,000 came down to $20,000 if she settled out of court. Still, her lawyers held out. It was reduced to $15,000. In early 1975, the claim had dwindled to $11,000. Tim

Tanser had found the best Advocate in Salisbury, but he had to recuse. It turned out that he was friendly with Tom's son in law and daughter. They found another Advocate and Tim still considered Rose would win. Finally, there was such a delay that she was told she could go on holiday. Nothing would be settled in court for the next few months.

She had wanted to go overseas to England and then she remembered the ship's captain she met in Beira. She tried writing to Ben Ubbink in Beira about the captain of the Holland Africa liner and found Ben had retired and gone to Holland. Her letter was forwarded to him and suddenly he replied. He told her how he had felt about her in Beira. He was as attracted to her as she to him, but they were both married and that was that. He was still married but had been separated for many years. He wanted her to come over to Holland if she intended to go overseas, and promised to take her everywhere, mentioning Cannes on the French Riviera.

She found travel brochures for Cosmos Tours and was amazed to find they cost half the amount of any other company's Tours. It was exciting to see that she could spend three months overseas and travel by coach into and through thirty different countries for less than three hundred pounds. That was $600 in Rhodesian currency. It seemed incredible – breakfast and dinner included and private shower.

She booked a sixteen-day tour through France, Switzerland, Italy and back up the other way through Austria, Germany and Holland, staying in all the main capitals, two days in Capri, Venice, Rome, Paris. Then eight days in Greece and a third tour through southern Spain and over to Morocco. She added a fourth one for good measure to Russia. It was through

Scandinavia to St. Petersburg, down to Moscow and to Berlin and back through Holland, Belgium and London. She finally cancelled the tour of Russia after the other three because she was worn out! She spent that last month in England and London.

In the month before she boarded the plane for Heathrow airport, she began to prepare in earnest. Ben had been asking her to come to Vlissingen when she first landed. He said he'd come to London and escort her over the channel straight from London docks to Flushing. He asked her to spend a week with him and he'd take her to Cannes by car. When she asked him to book her into a hotel near him, he assured her that she wouldn't lose her virtue staying with him because he was impotent! He said she sounded Victorian over staying where all his visitors did. She found him so delightful, amusing and sophisticated, she was terrified she wouldn't be able to live up to his image of her.

Cannes! That was on the Riviera, the playground of the rich and famous! How could she dress and even fit in wearing her miserable rather cheap clothes? These were the millionaire's babes with figures to die for and all of them probably young and gorgeous. It was all yachts and beaches and night clubs and glitz, judging by the glossy magazines. So! What should she do? Back out? GO for it?

Of course, she couldn't resist it! Ben was too astute not to know that he'd held out the right carrots. The second one may have been a limp one, but that suited her nicely and the first one might have been daunting, but she decided to do her best to copy the styles in magazines showing the stars on yachts and on the beach etc. and not disappoint him. She also began to skip most food daily, nibbling an apple or chewing a lettuce leaf and pretending she was full. She exercised madly and stitched fancy bits of braid onto scanty tops. She went to every sale and found two fantastic dresses – one with a slit right up the side and another a new line, a butterfly winged, see-through affair in a vivid orange. A third, a full length, simple black sheath with narrow straps, just pleated across the breast and bare shouldered, made up her glamorous wardrobe. That one looked fantastic and she was suitably emaciated for the first time in her life. Suddenly, things were looking up. She packed and weighed and panicked and stitched and Sherrell came out to help her, bringing Yolande, Rose's niece along too. They took over some stitching there and then and Rose finished the packing.

Sherrell had just come back from a Cosmos young people's tour of Spain, France, Italy and Austria. She lectured her mother. "Mom, I know you! Don't talk to the first black you see in London! London's full of them and it is dangerous!" Rose felt so impressed by her daughter's concern, that she dutifully promised. She had found a colossal black suitcase with wheels to accommodate most of the clothes she thought she couldn't do without. She had a little hand case for the cabin and a capacious handbag, plus a middle-sized case containing a lovely cream coat and a brown fitting raincoat with a flared skirt, long brown leather boots, short black boots and several pairs of high heeled shoes and sandals. a fur stole and a special leopard skin cap and scarf. With all this, she had treated herself to the latest sunglasses and a great white panama hat that folded up in the suitcase. She had evening bags, long, narrow leather clutch bags in tan and black. She had everything but the kitchen sink!

The girls took her to the airport and she was off. Rose was travelling on T.A.P., the Portuguese airline they mocked as 'Take Another Plane' and she found out why later. As she crossed the channel into British airspace, she looked down at the 'green, green hills of home' and she was in tears! All her colonial life, they had referred to England as home, and there it was. They landed at Heathrow and she went to wait for her luggage to come off the roundabout. She waited and waited then went to the other one and waited, then she went back to the first again. Rose was there for an hour or more. In the end, she wandered back to the main section of this colossal place that was totally strange to her. She had no idea of what to do.

She was so lost and distraught by then that she just stood in a corner, turned her back and started to howl. Everything had gone into the hold. She only had her handbag and coat with her. Finally, when she was considering slitting her throat with her nail file, she felt a tap on her shoulder and a kind official asked her what was wrong. She led Rose to the information desk where others took over. Yes, they said, the luggage had gone astray. Hmmm, "Take Another Plane" indeed!

They said she could buy a small case and necessary articles of clothing for the night at the duty free and arranged her transport to the hotel, the Great Russel, the hotel she had booked into in Russell Square, where Ben was to meet her in two days. Rose arrived at the Great Russell Hotel at five in the evening. The hotel was a gracious old one with an impressive entrance to a red carpeted reception room with high pressed steel ceilings. She was shown into a large double room with glamorous chairs and a colossal double bed with a high wooden headboard. She loved it! She had a quick bath in her private bathroom and went out to see Russell Square, chosen by her because Mom's friend in the war years, John Pemberton had a publishing company there. It was a link with home and he wanted her to meet him when she got to London.

She didn't know London then. This was Holborn, away from Piccadilly and Oxford Street. However, when Ben arrived, he would be somewhere in that area on business, so she thought it would be convenient for him too, not realising that anywhere is convenient because of the Underground tube stations.

Russell square has a little central park, one of the small enclosures of trees which give London much of its charm. Rose strolled down the street in the bright sunlight, seeing only huge buildings fronted by high iron railings and entrances to basements. Just as she thought of turning back, she saw a strange sight, a group of black men talking on the street corner. By their faces, she judged they were from Central Africa.

This made her feel so at home that she went up to them "Excuse me, but can you tell me where you come from?". One huge African turned to her, "I come from Zimbabwe!" Rose was amazed! This was the first person she spoke to in London and he came from Rhodesia – which it still was. She said without thinking "Well! That puts us on opposite sides of the political fence, doesn't it? I come from Rhodesia!" They all murmured together for a minute and the others drifted away. This one carried on talking to her. Where did she live and what was she doing in London? She told him and asked him the same. He said he was on business there and lived in England.

Suddenly it hit her. She had done exactly what Sherrell said she would do. She began to move back towards her hotel, feeling a need to get where she could see the doorman standing on the steps. He questioned her about conditions at home and the politics. She argued with him that Rhodesian's knew the terrorists were brain washed in Russia and China by the Communists and he argued against her, trying to convince her that they were not. Stirred up, he grabbed the railings and stood on the foot-high concrete wall the rails were set in. He linked his arm through the railing and hung there, swinging like a monkey, earnestly talking. Rose wished she had a movie camera. It was fascinating to watch but she really needed to get into the hotel. She was getting tired of his persistent effort to make her see his side and it was after midnight. She said she must go in and he moved to come in with her, so she ran up the steps, asking the doorman to stop him, which he did.

She wasn't sorry they had talked but she kicked herself for doing what Sherrell had said she would. It was so strange to think that this African came from the same city she came from in the middle of Africa, the first man she spoke to in London, out of several million!

Up in her room, she turned down the bedding and was about to sink into it when she saw a suspiciously curly black hair! The sheets were creased as well so she realised they were not clean. She was furious. This was an expensive hotel.

She phoned the reception number and complained loudly to the man who answered. He came up and she found it was a doddery old night porter. The rest of the staff were off. He brought clean sheets and she helped him make the bed. At last, she could get to sleep, and determined to leave the hotel the next morning.

Next day, she moved just one block down, to a very modern ten storey hotel called the Continental. She booked into that immediately and left the Russell with an indignant flourish. This hotel had adequate rooms, clean and satisfactory, with a restaurant on the top floor. There was a message from Heathrow Airport. They had located her luggage, and they would deliver it to the hotel later. It had been left in Lisbon by mistake by T.A.P. which lived up to its reputation.

She walked around Holborn for a while and called in to see John, but he was up in Manchester as he was also an editor with the Manchester Guardian. She hoped to see him when she was again in London. After wandering around for a while, she went back to the hotel and found her luggage was already in her room. She had a rest, bathed and put on a short, black dress. Up in the resident's bar she thought she'd have a sherry and something to eat up there as well, overlooking the city lights.

Seated at the bar was a man on holiday from America and they chatted for a long time. He asked her if he could sit at her table for a light meal. They continued talking about America and Rhodesia, comparing their lives until she said she felt very tired, so he offered to 'walk her back to her room'. That was a quaint Americanism that amused her and down they went to the fifth floor and her room. He leaned forward suddenly and kissed her lightly on the forehead. She reversed and shut the door quickly, thinking "Oh yes, my boy? This may be holiday high jinks, but you can forget it!" She was in bed and dead to the world in a few moments.

Suddenly there was a wild clanging noise, enough to make her shoot out of bed and put on the light. It was three a.m. and the perpetual clanging was deafening. She put on her dressing gown and slippers and heard a knock at her door. There was her friend the American! It was a bomb scare and he'd come to fetch her, to 'walk' her safely down! The fire alarm was still clanging. They were all told to assemble, hundreds of them, in the courtyard downstairs as quickly as possible. She grabbed her handbag plus passport etc. and off she went, very glad the American had been kind enough to worry about her. They stood there for three hours while the police searched everywhere for a bomb before deciding it was a hoax. Back they went to her room and she said a quick ' thanks and goodbye.' He looked rather hopeful as he said he was off early in the morning, but Rose didn't care. She was only interested in sleep and soon forgot his name.

She slept until ten next morning when a call came from Ben. He'd be in to fetch her in the afternoon. Be ready, he'd have a taxi and they'd be off by train to catch the ferry for the channel crossing. He didn't bring his car to London, it was at the docks in Vlissingen. Rose had the luggage carried down to reception and went out to see if John Pemberton was there but as he wasn't, she wandered around the square and park enjoying London itself.

At four, there was Ben as promised. It was strange in a way to be gathered up in his arms for the first time. Rose felt quite shy. They sat for a while in the hotel lounge and just enjoyed being together in person and not in print. Then she was bundled into the taxi, all cases stowed in the boot and on the back seat without her lifting a finger and they were off to the station. There, they had to carry the small items only, as Ben booked the big cases into a cloakroom while they went to the hotel for a drink and light meal. Ben drank only soda but ordered her a sherry. There, they caught up with their lives since the Beira days.

Rose told Ben about Tom and his unacceptable behaviour and Ben told her what had happened to him. He was on A.A. and wouldn't even eat Christmas cake with brandy in it. In Beira, with all the high living she had witnessed in the club, he had ended up drinking more than a bottle of whisky a day. Finally, he was at death's door with blood pressure so sky high the doctors said they wondered that he was still alive. Unfortunately, he told her it had made him mentally imbalanced, so he had to retire. Also, it had made him impotent. He had tablets to keep him stable and they seemed to work.

Suddenly, it was time to catch the train and Ben manfully pulled her huge trunk along on its wheels and carried the other case, which was heavy, leaving her to bring the smaller items. They caught the train and in no time, they had to change trains, heave all the luggage out and rush to another platform, getting everything pulled on just as the train started to move. Ben heaved all the heavy cases out at the dockside and, again, it was a scramble to reach the ferry. There was almost no time and she was running next to Ben, trying to keep up. She felt like Sancho Panza, running along with Don Quixote on his horse! Ben looked grim with his jaw jutting out and he was muttering to himself and moving ahead. She just caught one sentence, muttered under his breath.

"I'm not going to be a hewer of wood and drawer of water for any fucking, bloody Rhodesian girl!"

Apparently, the massive trunk was a mistake!

At first, she was shaken, but then she realised he was thinking of the fact that they had black men doing all the carrying of cases in Africa. She guessed he was a bit appalled at the amount of heavy luggage she had dumped on him. Anyhow, they managed to catch the ferry and relax. There were porters on the other side to carry the luggage to his car to get everything to the Boulevard de Ruyter where they took a lift to one of the most exotic and beautiful apartments on the first floor, with a veranda almost leaning over the sea, where they could watch the sun rise and set over the water. Obviously, Ben was a wealthy man.

The walls, tables and floors were covered with silk Persian carpets. Everything in the place was expensive. Ben poured Rose a drink, but he had something non-alcoholic himself. He made a supper dish for them and when it was time for bed, he stepped up into a second lounge and pulled out the base of the second leather sofa which converted into a double bed for her. He brought her cases in and pressed a switch at the side wall, which closed two full length, heavy curtains across the opening, making a superb bedroom.

She had been wondering where she would be sleeping – not with him, she hoped. She realised that she was shyer than she had thought. She was afraid that she might snore, or she might sound off in some other direction in her sleep! They still hadn't got fully acquainted. To her relief, he seemed to take it as read that he'd sleep alone.

Gradually, over the next day or two, they became more relaxed. Rose was really attracted to Ben and he seemed the same. He took her all over the place, to see the windmills and dykes and little villages. They walked along the streets in the evening, where all the houses had their curtains open and all of them seemed lacy ones, tied back in pretty drapes. People inside sat around tables eating their meals or in the lounges, in full view from the road. Ben said they never closed the curtains as people might think they were up to something odd inside. They all looked like dolls houses.

They visited his married sister in Delft and Rose was sent off with her husband to see the old town and university where he worked. Ben had business to discuss with his sister. Apparently, he was telling her what a problem he had and asking her advice. There was one place Rose soon found she wouldn't see and that was Cannes! After they left, he told her his doctor didn't want him to drive all that way, so she said that she didn't mind at all. She told him that she had been really worried about going there and that was the reason she had the huge case full of clothes. He asked her to take some of them out and put them on to show him, so she treated him to a mini fashion parade. He loved it and she loved showing them to him. He was feeling very guilty about having to break his word about the Riviera.

Gradually, she began to enjoy everything. She felt as if she had been married to Ben for years; a strange, comfortable, happiness. After lunch, she curled up on Ben's bed with him and they had two hours of total, loving, companionship. Seldom do men realise the value of this but Ben did. Had he not been impotent, it would have been different, she knew only too well.

Ben told her about the war. He had been captured, with thirty-nine others, by the Germans when they invaded Holland. He was still a teenager fighting in the resistance army. They were all taken to a school and locked in two dormitories with small, barred windows, twenty to a room. The Germans were waiting for a train to take them to Germany to a concentration camp. There were basins in the rooms and they found that they could communicate with the others by tapping the pipes, using Morse code. They were heavily guarded and had to fold their outer clothes at night and pile them on a chair outside the doors, where the Germans counted them to ensure none of them could escape.

Ben and another young one in the other room were both very thin and found they could get their heads through the bars. The others helped them plan. On Saturday night, they made nineteen piles of clothes into twenty with clever folding and, when they heard the guards shouting and laughing, obviously getting drunk, the two young ones squeezed through the bars and hid in the lavatories. Ben said he was terrified. The guards kept banging on the doors, shouting at them not to be so long in there. They were sure they'd be discovered but, luckily, they both had learnt German at school and could answer the guards who were rolling drunk. There were plenty of other lavatories, fortunately.

In the early hours of the morning, when all was quiet, they crept out and set off on foot. They separated, and Ben made his way down to the coast. Finally, he found a rowing boat and managed to row himself over the channel to England. He handed himself in to authorities and was immediately interned as a possible spy. Three months later, they had verified his story and he was told the fate of the others. The other young man was captured and when the guards found out the way they escaped, he and several of the older men were lined up and shot. The rest went to concentration camps in Germany.

Ben was trained to spy for the British and then dropped by parachute back in Holland. He was decorated after the war by Britain and Holland. Prince Bernhardt became a firm friend.

The Dutch had prepared a T.V. series of the whole episode but, unfortunately, Rose never managed to see it. She didn't know she had met such a famous man who found her worthwhile. She felt very proud of him and was thankful that he knew she had not been aware of his past. She had visions of being on his arm in one of her special evening dresses, looking as glamorous as she could as she met Prince Bernhardt and, perhaps, the Queen! And thus, do optimists knit their future hopes and dreams in the mind.

Suddenly, on the fourth day, she was rudely disillusioned. Ben suddenly changed. He began shouting and raving, not in English. Rose skidded out of sight into the bathroom, wondering what on earth was the matter? He suddenly appeared in the doorway and loomed over her threateningly. His eyes didn't focus on her. They just stared through her. His face changed strangely. He wasn't a good-looking man in any case. He had quite a bulbous nose and fat lips and a slightly receding jaw. Rose normally found his face pleasant and good humoured. In any case, she avoided over handsome men. They always seemed to be walking around themselves in admiration.

However, at this moment, poor Ben looked as if he could murder her and she was afraid. It was an extraordinary Jekyll and Hyde transformation. Shouted invective poured out against her in English and it wasn't pleasant. She began to tremble, thinking of Tom, wondering whether she'd live to tell the tale and whether she could manage to get out and away. He didn't touch her, thank God.

Suddenly he turned and vanished. She peered round the door and along the passage and quickly made her way to the room where her things were. She began gathering up and packing, still feeling he might appear with a knife or gun.

Her mind reeled with plans for possible escape. But where to go? She knew nobody! Must try to placate him. At least, get her old friend Billy Cartwright on the telephone and then somebody would know where she was. At that moment, nobody did! Why had she been so stupid?

Finally, Ben appeared out of his bedroom. He seemed normal and asked her if she wanted tea? She certainly did! This reminded her of Tom too and she guessed things were alright for now, but she was still on edge and the atmosphere was tense. Ben brought the tea and a cake. He apologised rather sadly and said that he should have taken his tablets that morning and stupidly, he had forgotten. He went on to tell her that this was part of the result of his illness. He wasn't healthy. He said that he'd arrange for her to go back to London right away if she wanted, and he would pay for all the expenses. They had tea and she asked if he would let her telephone Billy and Dorrie in Folkestone and tell them when she would be there, giving details as soon as she had them. This he did, handing the phone to her as soon as the call was answered.

"Hello, Billy, is that you? I wanted to tell you I would be in Folkestone in a day or two. Where am I now? Can you write this down?"

Billy sounded surprised, but he said she was to go ahead. She carefully told him who she was with and where. Then she added "Thanks Billy. Expect me back as soon as possible. If you don't hear from me, ring this number and ask Ben. Please tell Sherrell in Salisbury. Her number is —. Thanks so much.

See you soon, bye." Rose felt relieved and thanked Ben, feeling very miserable about everything.

Ben said little and they had more tea. He asked her to come out and sit on the veranda and went on talking about his deep regret. He said she must do exactly what she wished but rest assured she was perfectly safe with him. His rage and words were not directed at her or anyone really. He realised she was shocked but, if she would only stay a few more days, he'd like a chance to take her to Amsterdam and to meet his other sister near there. He so wanted to heal the breakdown in their relationship. He always religiously took his medication and couldn't account for the lapse.

Having had Tom Sheppard in her life, she agreed. Perhaps it was stupid of her, but she knew she would be leaving at the end of the week in any case. They still longed to be together and her day in Amsterdam was memorable. Ben cheered up and took her there in his lovely Audi. They lunched at a restaurant of his choice and Ben ordered palling, which was eel. It was a specialty at the restaurant and they both had it. The chunks of eel were thick and gelatinous and steeped in oil. They were stewed, with potato chunks and onion and were delicious, but very rich.

Rose vowed she'd never have that again. It was far too loaded with calories. After that, Ben led her over a bridge and walked with her up a road to show her all the prostitutes in windows in the red-light area. She had heard about it and wanted to see them once in her lifetime. They were mostly coloured girls and almost bare, also most alluring. They went into one sex shop and Ben was amused to see how shocked she was. She skittered out as fast as she could and saw things she didn't know existed or what they were for. Further up the street was a billboard pointing the way in to see a 'Fucky-fucky' show. Rose took a photo of that to show everyone back in fuddy-duddy Rhodesia! She was heartily glad they had censorship back home!

Then they dropped in on his sister on the way back. They weren't speaking English but there was much laughter and Rose asked Ben what it was all about. He said his sister had asked "Have you managed to get it up yet, Ben!" that made her laugh, but it showed her how they thought and spoke to each other. Rose didn't think his sister was aware of the extent of his troubles. She put it out of her mind for the last day with him.

On the previous Thursday morning, she had woken suddenly, surprised to hear bells chiming everywhere. It was only four a.m. but the dawn was already showing faint light. She leaned out of the window towards town but could only hear the bells more clearly.

"Turn again Whittington, Lord Mayor of London," chimed on one side and then from elsewhere came "London Bridge is broken down, Dance over my Lady Lee. London Bridge is broken down, with a hey lay dee." Then a wild tumble of all sorts of other bells. It was fascinating. Ben suddenly joined her. "It's market day," he told her. "Get dressed and we'll go down and see them, if you would like to." It was five a. m.

He made early coffee, then down they went, taking the car to the market place and then strolling hand in hand, through the mist, along cobbled streets where everything imaginable was displayed. There were girls dressed in their striped dresses with white apron, wearing clogs and pretty lace caps with points sticking out sideways. It was their national dress. There were tall, gangling fishermen picking up raw herrings and lifting their heads to swallow them whole, like seals. This was Holland as it should be seen.

Ben bought fresh fish and some caviar for later and they picked their way through the crowds until they felt hungry and went home for bacon and eggs. Ben even had South African marmalade for their toast.

This was May and there was a considerable chill in the air in the morning. They watched the sun come struggling through the mist and turning the grey sea lilac and gold and all was beautiful.

Later, they walked to the town centre a fair distance away, Ben trundling a small shopping trolley. He went into the supermarket to buy a lettuce and Rose waited on the pavement. She was fascinated by an organ grinder at the roadside, turning a handle on a quaint, old fashioned barrel organ producing tunes. The organ was on wheels, so he could push it from place to place, and was painted dark red with old fashioned bunches of flowers and gold scrolls painted on it. He even had a little monkey dressed up in a uniform. The monkey took off its little round pill-box hat and passed it round for a collection. Rose wished she could take them home with her. The old man seemed weary and hard up so Rose waited for the monkey to turn her way, delved in her purse and found a florin. The old man looked hopeful indeed!

That went into the hat just as Ben came back with his purchase. He nearly dropped dead when she said she had given a florin. She was just asking him if it was enough? Enough! For the rest of her stay, everyone he knew had to hear his tale – how he'd walked down to the centre and bargained for a lettuce in the shop. That had cost him the equivalent of tuppence and there was Rose outside, calmly handing a florin to an organ grinder, of all people! It really amused him, and he made a great display of being so indignant with that laughing glint in his eye that she enjoyed so much

On her last evening, they dined at a lovely restaurant and he invited his great friends to join them. They were South Africans who had settled in Holland near him. They had a wonderful evening, and all came back to Ben's apartment for a nightcap. Out revolved a section of one wood-paneled wall and there was a complete cabinet with all sorts of bottles of whiskey, other spirits and liqueurs, everything. Ben made Turkish coffee and handed out small edibles and chocolates. He drank soda, and he played mine host with all the suavity Rose remembered. She only wished…. But then she put that in the back of her mind. This was farewell.

In the morning, Ben drove her down through Belgium. They lunched in Brussels in the square and then they travelled on through France to Calais, for her to board the ferry that would take her right to Dover, near Folkestone. He held her tight and made her promise to come back if she could. He said she must write but never tell him about any other man in her life. Rose was just sad. She really loved Ben, that she knew, but this was another closed door!

Arriving in Dover late in the evening, there were no porters anywhere, so she had to get all her luggage over to the other side of the rails by crossing the overhead iron foot bridge. She faced twenty steps up to the metal bridge, dragging all her cases on her own. She thought she would have a heart attack! She left the big trunk at the bottom and went up with everything else. Then left everything smaller in a pile at the top and ran down to drag the trunk up, step by step. She kept thinking of Ben, loaded with her luggage, muttering about not being a hewer of wood or drawer of water for any bloody effing Rhodesian girl. Finally, she made it out and had to take a taxi all the way along the coast to Folkestone where she had booked a hotel room. She arrived there late at night, but they were holding the room for her. It had been a paid for, she found, by her dear Ben.

The following morning, she walked up the cliff walk and along the Leas, overlooking the channel and France in the hazy distance. The gulls were swooping and mewling around her as she passed the little pavilion where the band played every afternoon and caught sight of the Grand and Metropole, two huge, red bricked, old fashioned hotels that had been converted to apartments.

Billy and Dorrie had bought one of the apartments and retired there from their farm in Rhodesia. Billy was amused to hear the reason Rose phoned him. He said the moment he heard her voice he knew something dire had happened. Couldn't she keep out of trouble? Must she always rush in where angels feared to tread? It seemed to be the story of her life and she should write a book!

They were just what she needed there to help her relax and raise her flagging spirits. Old they both were, but Billy she had known since she was a baby. He was like a second father to her. Their farm was her second home and she had lived there for school holidays and any time they could when Dolly was alive, they all stayed there.

Then he married his oldest friend's widow, after Dolly died.

Strangely, she was called Dorrie. Rose didn't know her well. They had no extra bedroom but had booked her into the Carlton, the best and most expensive hotel in Upper Folkestone, just a short way down the Leas from them. At least, she could leave her huge black case and the other big one with them and borrow a small one from Billie for the rest of her travels. Those big cases were another source of amazement for Billie. What in God's name did she have in them? They were amused to hear about the Riviera and Cannes.

Rose contacted Ben and wrote as well, thanking him for everything then she cancelled extra days in the pricey Carlton, parting with a large wad of her holiday money. The two days cost her half of the price of the Cosmos tour of Italy and over twenty other countries. She arranged with Cosmos to meet them in Dover and cross the channel again for the coach trip Number one.

FIFTEEN

LONG REACH OF THE ORACLE

When she disembarked in Calais again, Rose followed the other travelers to the left to go through customs. When she reached the front, she read the sign on the wall 'Cosmos Tours' arrow to the left and to the right, 'Other Tours'. She realised why it cost half as much as other tours. They had 36 Cosmos coaches outside waiting to collect people for different tours all over Europe, fifty-eight people in each coach.

Soon, they grouped in fours and sixes of like-minded souls and Rose, who had only just managed to book the last seat on that tour, timing in with her other tours, was sharing a room with two young girls about the ages of her two daughters. She apologised to them but they were fine with it. A lanky young man joined them on the coach. He was keen to go to galleries and all the art he could for his final year at college.

To join the four, came a Malaysian doctor and his wife, both very young. They had left a small baby with a grandmother in Malaysia and the wife just yearned to get back to her infant. She would have left the tour gladly, but her husband was enjoying it and he was great fun to be with in any place they went, making sure they had bottles of wine and snacks and he was full of the sort of jokes doctors tell – very funny and rude.

Rose tried to let them go sight-seeing without her, feeling so much older than they were, but they wouldn't hear of it, saying it wouldn't be such fun without her, which was flattering. They spent nights in all the big capitals; Paris, Zurich, Rome, Florence, Naples, Capri, San Marino, Venice. Climbing over the Alps, they suddenly caught sight of the wonderful Glass Mountains. The driver stopped so they could take photos and Rose felt a feathery, cold touch on her face. She realised it was snow. Then she saw it – tiny flakes drifting down, the first snow she had ever seen. They spent the night up there in a beautiful hotel where the snow was falling outside, yet it was warm in the lounge and dining rooms. They had full length picture windows with a view of the glass mountains all rose and gold in the light of the setting sun. The snow was banked up on the bottom of the windows, about a foot deep.

In Munich, their hotel was right near a nightclub open to the pavement, so they went in and were treated to a floor show that was totally unexpected. Little tables and seats surrounded a small dance floor. A disk jockey was playing the music and they ordered drinks. Lights were lowered, and they saw, at a table a little way from them, two transvestites with long red talons and blonde wigs.

On closer inspection, they saw the disc jockey was wearing makeup. Two men got up and danced together and Rose and the others were glued to their seats watching what everyone did. Apparently, they were the only 'straight' ones there. When the two blondes began screaming and trying to scratch each other's eyes out, they decided to slide along the wall to the door and out. That was Munich, possibly staged for their benefit.

Paris again, and they had an evening in a bistro and a special farewell dinner that Cosmos provided. Rose had Bisque d'Homard for the first time in her life and it remained, perhaps, her favourite food. Thick lobster soup, delightfully rich and creamy, 'beautiful, beautiful bisque!' Then she tried frog legs, strange little legs like miniature chicken legs with a faint flavour of fish!

Back in London, she caught a double decker bus and went to Cambridge to see where her father was born and went to school before he emigrated to Rhodesia. She had found a string of Red Lion Hotels scattered over England and they offered reasonable rates. The room was noisy as it faced the main road and huge trucks rattled past all night, but the food was good.

She found the house, No. 1 Fair Street, where her father was born in 1883, and his school, called The Perse. It was quite a famous old grammar school, built of red brick. The new school was built further out of town and his school only housed the books and papers, she was told. She strolled about University and the river Cam where he had once punted, then caught another bus and went to Huntingdon, Grantchester so reminiscent of Rupert Brooke, and Ely. It was nostalgia all the way for Rose. In two days, she had to be in Luton to fly by Olympic Airways for her second Cosmos tour - to Greece.

Rose had two days free in Athens, just wandering around. Then they were taken down the Corinth Canal and over in the coach to see ancient ruins and the Amphitheatre at Epidaurus, where they were told by the guide to climb up to the top tier of seating. He stood in the open arena at the bottom and tore a piece of paper in half. It could be heard quite clearly at the top. The very age of everything affected Rose and wrenched her heart strangely. She dragged her mind back to the present as they boarded their coach and she chose the single seat behind the courier, Maria, a quaint little thing who wore white framed sunglasses and a large, floppy white hat, managing to look picturesque and artlessly attractive.

Next to Maria was the driver and he was introduced to all as Yianis. He was grey haired and ruggedly handsome, with his bronzed skin and blue eyes. He greeted them briefly and got on with the business of checking all the cases, quickly stowing them in the lower compartment of the coach as if they were feather light. Then he sat at the wheel and waited for everyone to be checked in by Maria. Rose's greatest friend in Umtali was Greek. Vangie was Rose's secretary and they had shared nine years of their working life together. They became close friends out of the office as well. Rose spent a lot of time at Vangie's house and had picked up quite a few basic Greek words and phrases.

When she came out with a word or two, Maria was intrigued. She immediately singled Rose out of the other tourists and asked her to share the special table where they sat - Maria, Yianis, the beautiful guide, Danae and a couple of other drivers. Unfortunately, Rose found that her dozen or so Greek words were useless. She couldn't gather what they said. However, she was treated to little plates of the food they ordered for themselves, special fasolakia, green bean salad with oil and vinegar, a little dish of octopus or calamari and the delicious cod roe mashed with oil and bread Vangie often made, called

Taramasalata. That, eaten with crusty loaves and garlic and olive oil, instead of butter, was delicious. All the other tourists were dished up with English food.

Yianis spoke no English and seemed a strong, silent, taciturn man. The girls were fond of him and the other drivers seemed to look up to him in some way. With them, he came out of his shell and laughed a lot. It turned out that he had a part share in a small ship together with a Greek friend who was the captain. That surprised Rose and she wondered why he was a coach driver. Maria said that Yianis loved driving and he preferred to continue working for Cosmos, rather than constantly sailing to the same three islands that were included in the Cosmos tours.

The next day, they crossed over on the ferry, to motor up to Delphi, taking the coach on board with them. Then it was a steep climb up the mountain to beautiful, magical Delphi – perhaps the most beautiful place on earth. Known as the navel of the world, where the Delphic oracle had sat in ancient times, pensively rubbing a large stone 'omphalos', a phallic symbol, in mists of the past, making her predictions for the benefit of all who sailed from distant lands to consult her. Rose tried a tentative rub of the rather vulgar, waist high stone edifice but she didn't get any prediction – not at that point anyway.

However, perhaps Rose had called up the shade of the Oracle and the Oracle took a 'shady' hand '! Did a few angels become a little nervous of treading?!

They all trailed up the mountainside to another Amphitheatre, and she walked up the steps to the top on her own, to see the fabulous view between the mountains to the sea. The land fell away steeply to the charming little village down a chasm almost in the blue depths of space before rising to the crags opposite.

Unlike the mountains of South Africa, the massive, jagged Drakensberg; the Dragon's mountain, the Greek mountains were dry, grey blue and sparsely strewn with white rock, aridly towering up to the sky. Rose had the sensation that she could fly and soar like an eagle, down, down to the sea in the depths below.

When they all returned, the tourists found themselves in a different hotel from Maria and the other Cosmos coach staff. The rooms were good, and Rose had a shower en suite which was great. Dinner was not included, and they chose their evening meal wherever they wished, wandering about the village and checking the Tavernas on their own.

In some of the main cities, dinner was not provided. Delphi was a quaint little village on a steep mountain side – with steps up between the little houses and narrow lanes with tiny Tavernas offering all sorts of tempting meals. Rose wandered about in the lingering dusk and came across Maria and Danai who immediately gathered her in and begged her to join them. With a couple of other coach drivers, guides and couriers, they were going down the road to a special restaurant they liked for a meal.

Off they set, a group of about eight walking down to the restaurant, but it was dark, and Rose couldn't see the rough road. Maria said something to Yianis and she felt a strong arm go around her waist. That was a surprise but more than welcome.

Half way there, suddenly a donkey brayed loudly near them, when one of the men said something loudly and Maria answered him. Yianis then said something in Greek. All of them shouted with laughter except Rose of course, who couldn't understand. Maria explained that her boyfriend had said something suggestive and she had told him not to say such things. Immediately, the donkey brayed again and Yianis told the donkey not to disobey Maria much to the group's delight. That was their simple humour, totally without vulgarity and very engaging to Rose.

She only wished she could have understood and joined in at the time. They reached a lovely little restaurant plus night club, without any of the tourists in it. Large picture windows overlooked a sheer drop to the valley below and the little village with masses of twinkling lights. It seemed that this was a private Greek hideout where tourists were excluded, so Rose felt highly privileged. Looking up, there were a million stars and the moon on the sea, light enough to etch out the mountains opposite Delphi and show a diamond path on the water. This was their place. There, she was in the real Greek atmosphere and dancing wordlessly to real Greek music with Yianis who turned out to be an excellent dancer. They didn't need trivial conversation to enjoy their evening. Rose loved them all!

There is something about the Greeks that catches at one's heart and soul. They know the true meaning of Philadelphia, the all-embracing love of everyone. They are so earthy and humorous, seemingly without malice, although she realised that they were well capable of stoning to death anyone who committed a thou-shalt-not! They took their Greek Orthodox priests seriously.

Yianis seemed to have decided that she was his responsibility and she couldn't pay for anything no matter how hard she tried. Wine flowed, all chosen by the men, retsina must be tried by

Rose, also a powerful little glass of ouzo – for her to see how it went milky when water was added. Little dishes of this and that strange Greek concoction came to the table to be picked at by all, and then a huge platter of seafood, Greek salad and hard, crusty bread. The lights grew dimmer and dimmer and the dancing more intimate. Rose let her hair down and enjoyed every moment. It needed no words between herself and Yianis to interpret the feeling developing between them. He was an excellent dancer.

No doubt, she was slightly under the weather when they finally set off up the hill with the men singing and joshing each other. Yianis, by this time, automatically half carried her along with his firm, strong arm making her feel safe on the stony road. It was so dark by then that someone lit a match to see the time. It was two in the morning! They had to drop Rose at her hotel along the way. The moon had dipped behind the mountain and a faint glimmer of dawn was rising in the east. A slightly sobering thought for her was that before eight, they had to be up, bathed and have had breakfast, ready to board the coach.

At her hotel, the door was firmly locked! They pressed the bell and banged on the glass, over and over, but nothing! She was suddenly feeling rather guilty. What could she do? She told Maria and the others to go on. She would carry on ringing. She would be alright. They needed their sleep. They would be fit to work the next day. They wouldn't hear of it. "No, no, no, definitely not, you come with us, come, we are not going to leave you, we want you to come with us!"

So, the Delphic Oracle played her hand and along Rose went for Turkish coffee and a Greek conference about her situation. Yianis disappeared. Finally, the others drifted away, and Maria had a dish of fasolakia – green beans in tomato sauce at three a.m.! Rose had nothing. Yianis returned and spoke to Maria who told her "Go with Yianis, he has a room for you." Rose kissed her 'good morning, thank you' and Yianis took her hand.

He showed her into a large suite with an inviting looking double bed and a mezzanine floor with a large, glassed-in shower room. With a few words he knew, he ushered her into the shower, handing her a little towel. she had a quick shower, dried herself, and put the little towel round her for modesty. There was Yianis waiting for her to get into bed. He kissed her goodnight and she thought he was going out of the door which was open behind him.

He had no intention of doing so, she found. He went to shower. Rose lay there with one eye on the shower door and out he came, sans modesty, naked as the day he was born and got into the other side of the bed.

Oh! Well! Rose thought. She had the strangest sensation that they'd been married for years! Whether it was because she was somewhat inebriated or whether it was that she had two marriages under her belt, she really couldn't say but there it was, with no problems and no flourish and much brief pleasure. She did finally manage a deep, if somewhat brief sleep!

Three hours later, Yianis woke her with a cup of tea and she found it was six thirty a.m. He was dressed and ready to take her back to her hotel. Hand in hand they walked down the road, Rose, self-conscious in her short black evening dress and high heeled black evening shoes, being greeted by all the old Greek women, out sweeping their steps in the early dawn sunlight. They stopped and stared at her. She smiled back, hoping nobody would pick up the first stone!

"Calimera sis." And her - "Calimera." Back from Yianis.

"Yiasou." - "Yiasou," from Rose, smiling and nodding, hoping that was expected from her. Yianis greeted them all. She supposed they all knew him. What they said to him, she couldn't say! He looked undisturbed, chatting to them probably about her being locked out of her hotel, which they probably knew already.

The fat old woman with a black shawl over her head was back behind the counter in the hotel, scowling at Rose. Yianis greeted her pleasantly and spoke to her for a bit. Maria told Rose that the old devil had heard the knocking and calling, but she wasn't going to get up for any stupid tourist. Yianis pressed Rose's fingers and said, "Eight o'clock!", turned on his heel and went. The old crone glared at her balefully, slid the key across as if it were contaminated, and she took off upstairs to her room for quick shower and changed into her top and trousers for the journey back to Athens. She lay down on her bed to try for a couple of hours sleep, but her mind was full of the music of the night.

Yianis, after his three hours sleep, was fresh as a daisy, driving for the next eight hours down the winding mountains, a coach full of tourists. Maria and Danai, too, were as fresh as if they'd had eight hours' sleep. The stamina of these Greeks was phenomenal. Rose dozed in the coach quite happily, as the flat land approaching Athens was uninteresting, just dotted with small hovels graced with enormous TV Antennae. Greeks struggled to make a living but even the poorest seemed to have a large TV., sometimes in a hovel no bigger than a henhouse.

They were dropped at the hotel and Maria said Yianis had asked her to tell Rose that he would call for her at eight and they would all go out to dinner. She showered and put on her short black evening dress again but chose her high heeled orange shoes an orange evening bag and her mother's three string amber necklace. She felt that Yianis would appreciate her effort. They made a group of six, Maria, Danae and their partners, Yianis and Rose, first going to the Plaka for drinks and snacks, then at nine, they wandered around the streets there, stopping at various places for another drink and at ten, they ended up in a large restaurant with tables around a centre stage and a bar further away. There, large as life, was the most famous bouzouki player in Greece. They applauded, and a singer stood up and sang for them. The bouzouki player launched into a popular tune that had Yianis leaping on the stage and dancing a Greek dance, a very agile one, twirling around, grabbing piles of plates that were handed to him and smashing them on the corner of the stage.

Maria told Rose that he was dancing for her. She said Yianis wasn't like this usually. He really liked her. He didn't do this normally! Everyone cheered and clapped and a some of the men joined him as the bouzouki player broke into the Zorba dance music. She bought a record of the Greek players to remind her and one for Yianis. When he came back to her side, Rose did her best to show her appreciation. "Efharisto, Yianis, thank you for dancing for me. Maria, tell him I loved it!" He smiled, pressed her hand and plied her with wine. So, the time passed again and, before she knew it, there was another Greek consultation and they were off, not to bed, oh, no! They were off to the beach to see the sunrise!

On a long wooden platform, jutting out onto the beach from a crowded restaurant, were extra tables and chairs. About fifty other people, some young, some ancient tiny, black-veiled widows with brown, wizened little faces peering out. Weaving amongst them was a beautiful little girl aged six or seven, with curly black hair and huge eyes, holding out single roses. Yianis bought one and gave it to Rose. They had cold drinks and some light snacks and watched the sun rise over the sea, first lilac and pink, changing to red and gold. Then, as a fight started, and a bottle was smashed, Yianis drew Rose up and ushered her out and they took her back to the hotel. She crept in, this time at nearly seven. Nobody saw her in her evening wear. All the other tourists were still in their rooms.

A quick shower and change, a bite of croissant and a swig of coffee to wake her up a bit and she was boarding the coach again, bound for the Acropolis. Dear God, she thought, give me strength! There was Yianis, as strong and suave as usual, sitting at the wheel as Danae counted heads and saw them onto the coach. It was her day to be guide and recount the history of the Acropolis when the Turks invaded.

It was magical to see Danae against the pillars, totally unaware as she talked, of the picture she made with her beautiful face framed with long, honey-coloured hair blowing in the wind. Rose itched to paint her. Even her skin was honey coloured and she needed no makeup. She was timeless, like everything Greek seemed to be. That evening, after a short time with Yianis, who took her to the Plaka again, she said she must have an early night. She needed her sleep – just that! She thought he probably needed his as well and was being gallant.

The next day was a full day on the small ship, belonging

to Yianis and the captain, calling at three islands. Only Maria came with them to herd the 52 tourists and see no one was left behind on one of the Islands. Yianis and Danae had another coachful to take to the Acropolis. It was a very restful, pleasant day and Rose wore her big sun hat like Maria's and swam in a cove on one island, all alone in the emerald and sapphire sea that lapped gently on the black rocks. The other tourists had gone to see a ruin somewhere out of sight and Maria had shown Rose the little private cove she used. The sand sloped gently between black rocks and suddenly fell away so that she could dive off the rocks or walk into the water. It was perfect, and Rose did a hasty sketch in her diary, as she had drawn Yianis, Maria and Danae. She intended to paint them when she went home.

The ship returned at five and they were dropped back at the hotel for a shower. Yianis again desired her company, Maria said, at eight he'd come for her. Together with his best friend, who spoke English, they went to a taverna in the Plaka and his friend told Rose what Yianis wanted to say to her, and she to him. It was strange communicating this way but rather touching, in its way. He was an old man and was at pains to tell her when they were alone, that Yianis was married but hadn't Lived with his wife for years. He, himself, was single and available if she preferred him! She thanked him and said alas no, she didn't!

Yianis came back from wherever he'd gone, said goodbye to his friend and ushered her into a small hotel where he had been booking a room, she realised. The room was a luxurious one, all marble, with a large shower room and a king size bed. There, she was to experience the most extraordinary feats of strength and manipulation she could have ever imagined! Smiling, Yianis led her into the shower, having taken off her clothes and his, and kissed and fondled her. Then he proceeded to soap her and himself and wash her gently as if she were a little child. It was charming and extremely arousing.

Yianis had a tanned, muscular body and the feeling of his wiry strength against her body made her relax her inhibitions and become as wild as it seemed the showering was becoming. This was no child being washed now and she was splashed in the face so much she feared she would drown.

"No Yianis, NO!" she gasped when she surfaced – not realising that "Ne" was Greek for "Yes"! Finally, he got the message and turned off the water. He dried her and himself, threw her down on the bed and began making love with such expertise that Rose was carried into a previously unknown erotic realm. Talk about gymnastics! Rose hadn't realised what could transpire whilst practically standing on one's head! Yianis gripped her hands and pulled her up as if she were light as a feather, swung her round to the bed and there they slept together.

Rose knew she had experienced a strange metamorphosis for a little while. She had to get back to the reality of living normally. She didn't really want a repeat performance; it was too Bacchanalian! There was no future in this frenetic storybook existence. It had been very different yet the same in a way, with the short week in Holland. In plain reality, never could she have stayed in Holland. She would have always felt afraid of another breakdown. Poor, dear Ben! She would never tell Ben about Yianis! It would be too cruel.

Yianis had kindly arranged for her to spend the next day on a trip to the islands. She had a stateroom and meals with the captain. Yianis had to drive the other tourists to another venue in the coach. She, on the other hand, couldn't face a day with the others, touring to another place of interest – not after that experience! She had felt worn out, physically and emotionally. Rose enjoyed the day but found it a little boring being on the calm, still Mediterranean nearly all the time. She had plenty to recall, however, but her thoughts were rudely interrupted as the captain came in and questioned her about Rhodesia for a long time. Yianis met her back in Piraeus when the ship docked. They ate fresh fish there and went on to the Plaka, sitting close together drinking wine and holding hands.

This was goodbye. They were rather subdued and when they returned to Omonia Square and the hotel they met up with Maria and Danae and all went for a farewell drink together. They promised to write to her. Danae said she had arranged with Yianis to write for him. Rose promised to answer through her. She loved all of them and Greece and was seriously thinking of living there. They all clamoured for her to come back for good.

In the morning, the touring party boarded the coach and were taken by Yianis and Maria to the airport for the flight to Luton. Rose stood with Yianis until she was called and then she was away. It was over. She thought of Greece and the heady atmosphere there you could drink in. She recalled the strange events in Delphi when she was literally thrown into the arms of a stranger. Surely, she thought, rubbing that lump of stone must have summoned the shade of the Oracle who was in a mischievous mood at the time. She felt changed forever, and so sad about leaving Yianis.

She fully believed that Maria and Danae were truthful about their friend Yianis who reminded her of the famous Greek charioteer in profile. They said he had left his wife years before and never divorced or given her grounds because Yianis wasn't 'like that'. He still supported his wife financially and always would. Only now was he 'like that' over Rose! She found and brought home a small metal copy of the charioteer in his chariot just as a reminder. Then she found a small booklet on the Delphic oracle in Greek for Yianis and got Danai to tell her how to write in it 'The oracle predicted, Yianis!'

Yianis gave her a beautiful Greek turquoise brooch – a large, round stone set in gold. She pinned it on the lapel of her special white coat, worn for her departure for England.

She knew she could never come down to earth and be an ordinary Greek housewife, sweeping and scrubbing the front steps! She thought of the little, shrewd, narrow minded old gossips in Delphi, picturesque though they were, and she had no way of fitting in – any more than Yianis would have fitted in her home environment. He must have known that too, she felt.

Husbands and lovers, and one or two others - but no Vermin

A few hours later they landed in England once more. Before Tour No 3 to Malaga and Southern Spain, there was a ten-day gap she had to fill, so she paid ninety-nine pounds for a week in London with two shows, a special dinner and a choice of one of the best hotels. The hotels offered bed and breakfast. This week would cost her the same as the tours, but she thought she would be lost trying to find her way around London otherwise. She had never been there before, and she still had to master the intricacies of the tubes, let alone find her way to anything she wanted to see, like the Tower of London or London Bridge or the Royal Academy where her mother had studied the piano she played so beautifully.

She thought she'd have a big English breakfast and little else to eat all day. That would fit her budget which was stretched to the limit. She chose the Cumberland Hotel. Why? Because it was near the Park and Marble Arch and the Speaker's Corner. These places rang in her ears for some reason – babies in big prams being pushed by nannies – the Serpentine (whatever that was!)

So, Rose packed her best long dress and fur stole for the theatre. She almost bought a tiara, thinking she had better match up with Londoners sweeping into the wonderful theatres in London – the men in tails, the women in their real diamonds and pearls. She had seen the film My Fair Lady! She added her best clothes, bought with the Riviera in mind, her leopard skin cap and leather boots, her great aunt's real gold bracelet with the turquoise stones and tiny pearls on it; oh! also her real pearl necklace with knots between the pearls and her little folding opera glasses.

She lugged the suitcase into the underground and spent

a long time contemplating the escalator before leaping blindly on. She made it and nearly fell flat on her face getting off plus suitcase. They were so long and so fast and there was nothing like that in Rhodesia or South Africa.

Of course, soon she was as agile as everyone else jumping on and off escalators and into tube trains and she began to enjoy it. She made it to the Cumberland Hotel! She walked in with a liveried doorman taking her case, feeling as if passers-by would be standing back watching her. Only the rich and famous would be staying there and she was amongst them. Lights? Cameras? Fat chance! Such was her illusion about the Cumberland Hotel. She had based her assumptions on a vastly different era!

Her key was handed to her by a bell boy from the central desk who showed her to the lift and up to the sixth floor, a good way along a thick carpet and around a corner to her room. Opening the door, he deposited her cases on a luggage rack and stood for a while until she woke up to the fact that he expected something. She obliged, hoping her coin was enough. He refrained from commenting and left.

Well, this was just what she had expected! This huge bedroom, full bathroom and shower, plus all sorts of little bottles in a row and mirrors everywhere. She had never really stayed in any five-star hotels before, so this was a different experience. In the morning, after luxuriating in a second bath full of provided bubbles and perfume, she descended for breakfast, expecting to be seated immediately. To her surprise, there was a long queue standing waiting. Of course, she sounded off to all and sundry and all the sheep in the queue looked down their noses at her. This was England, don' cha know? The English don't deign to talk to strangers! Its bad form. Men buried their heads in their papers and women studied the ceiling.

Only a tall black man behind her used his vocal chords to say this was normal. Someone would come out and select people when tables were free. She resigned herself to this indignity and edged forward, reading the newspaper over the shoulder of a mild little man in front of her. By the time they approached the door, with a tall, effeminate man dancing about on the step from time to time, pointing a finger and calling "Three…table for three?" then "Four?", her little neighbour was on speaking terms with her and they were right near the front.

Dance, dance, out he pranced, with his little pencil moustache twitching and his eyebrows up high, "Two? - Two?" Quickly, the little man asked under his breath, did she mind sitting with him and she immediately called "Here! Here! We are two." Pointing at her neighbour. The dancing queen turned to her little man "Are you with this lady sir?" "No, but we don't mind sitting together" said he, weakly, instead of just "Yes!" It was humiliating to hear.

"OH! I'm sorry sir, but only couples who ARE together can be considered! ….. Two?" Looking over their heads, he called again "TWO?"

Rose was livid, absolutely seething! Her neighbour laughed and told her it was a rule in the Cumberland to avoid prostitutes getting in. Prostitutes attached themselves to likely single men in the queue. That only fueled her aggravation! Did she look like a prostitute to that individual? How dared he! She fumed in silence. Suddenly she was singled out for special favour.

"Madam, there's a lady on her own who doesn't mind sharing. Would you like that seat?"

It came to Rose in a flash! She moved forward, saying

loudly for the audience behind her, "well! I don't mind - as long as you are sure she's not a LESBIAN!"

The usher looked suitably flattened! Thus, and rather smugly, she got her revenge!

Seated, she found herself at a table near the tall black man. He was impeccably dressed and spoke English perfectly. His face had Caucasian features with a large, straight nose and thin lips, He didn't look like the Africans in Southern Africa. Rose thanked him for assisting her outside. He asked her if she was on holiday and she told him she was Rhodesian. He wanted to know the political situation there and told her he was a diplomat from Nigeria. He was so interesting that she couldn't get enough information. His name was Michael Phillips, which seemed very strange to her.

It turned out that he'd been at the Coronation of the Queen, and the wedding of Princess Margaret by invitation. They were still discussing Rhodesian politics when they reached the foyer near the entrance. Suddenly, he looked at his watch, "You've made me late for the choir stalls in the Abbey!" He was going to Westminster Abbey Sunday morning service. "Would you like to join me?" Did she ever! She dearly wanted to see Westminster Abbey.

Here was Colonial Rose, standing on the steps of a hotel with a black man, of all people, as he hailed a taxi. All she could think of was her farming brother, Michael. She thought if he walked along the pavement and saw her about to leave the Cumberland and get in a taxi with a black man, he might pull out a gun and shoot her!

They travelled through London in the taxi and the African gentleman, whose name was so strangely English, ushered her into the wonderful Cathedral and chose seats that he considered suitable. The service was superb, and the choir sang the full communion service. Rose felt pleased to be in this man's company. Afterwards, he looked at his watch again, asked if she could find her way to the places she wanted to see. He pointed out the way to go and said he wouldn't see her again. He had to be at the airport to welcome General Gowan who had been spirited out of Nigeria diplomatically after he was deposed. Michael Phillips was protecting him and taking him to a safe house. This was news to Rose. She hadn't followed the fate of any Nigerians or any leaders of African countries except those in the Congo and Zambia and perhaps Angola, countries adjoining Rhodesia.

But Africa was always in a state of turmoil, with power wars erupting on all sides and murder and mayhem rife. Guns had replaced the spears and bows and arrows – that was all. Witchdoctor "muti" and Christianity were mixed in the muddled minds still, and occasional lumps of 'long pig' were rumoured to come out of the cooking pots in remote places!

Rose wandered down and came to the British Museum. Needing a visit, she found the public toilets and was fascinated to see that the paper was that nasty slippery small sheet variety. Each little piece had printed on it "This is the property of the British Government". She just had to save a few bits to show people at home. She felt like smearing a little brown paint on a piece, folding it up and returning it to the Home Office with her thanks for the loan, but she managed to restrain herself. She didn't think their sense of humour quite stretched that far!

So out she went and along her way until she reached the Victoria and Albert Memorial, a fantastic Victorian edifice reflecting one woman's loss. Old Queen Victoria really knew how to grieve and how to make millions grieve with her. Her Albert, dying so young, left her totally immersed in grief in her forties, even though he also left her with about eight offspring to remind her of him.

Rose found herself at the bottom of Hyde park, at the Serpentine, not very sure of her bearings but aware, after enjoying the scenery there and sitting under the trees at the edge of the little lake, that she needed to make her way up the vast expanse of grass to the top of the rise where, according to her tiny map, she'd find the Cumberland and see Rotten Row. She set off at a smart pace which slowed after a while to a trudge, up the sea of grass. After about half an hour she suddenly found herself heading downhill for the Serpentine again. She had gone in a complete circle! She couldn't believe it! That park was enormous! She'd read of people doing this in the desert, but surely not in the centre of London?

She could have taken a bus or tube, but she decided to set her sights firmly on a group of trees up to the left and keep them in her mind. Finally, she saw the upper exit and was out on the famous Rotten Row. Up to the left was the Cumberland, she knew, so off she set. Suddenly, a black Jaguar slid to a halt beside her, facing the way she had come. An extremely handsome man leaned across from the driving seat to ask her politely if he could give her a lift? How kind, she thought. Dammit! A, there's my hotel one block away and B, he's going the wrong way! She went up to the car and thanked him, telling him that. He gave her a long look and said 'Oh!' Rose gave him her most charming smile and thanked him again for stopping. He seemed nonplussed and went. Later, various friends put her wise to the fact that Rotten Row was where the hopeful rich trawled for company for the night. Rose felt very green, and thankful that she hadn't gone so far as to accept the lift. That would have made for an interesting situation! She had lots to learn about London and about herself.

She carried on towards the Cumberland and was about to cross the road where it was safe, when she heard a shouting commotion a little way down from the corner. She hurried along to see why a crowd had gathered and whether anyone was injured, passing two nuns kneeling on the grass facing her with their eyes shut and hands folded in prayer. An accident? she thought. Somebody dead?

The crowd surrounded a man shouting on a raised box. This, she realised, was Speaker's Corner! What luck! She'd read about it. She moved into the mob to listen. He ranted on and on about atheism. There was no God. Nothing! The nuns crossed themselves and prayed. Rose felt she had to put in a word. She piped up loudly;

"Surely you believe in a force of Good and Evil?"

There was a deathly hush! A little space was suddenly made around her as he leaned over his railing, pointing at her.

"Aaah! An intellectual, I believe!"

"No. But I do believe in a force of good and evil."

"Ah! - An American?"

"No."

"Canadian?" "No." "South African!" "No."

Keep going, she thought, you'll never get there!

"RHODESIAN!"

She said yes, like a fool! She didn't dream this would fall on the air like manna. From all sides, she was pounced on verbally. Men were picking her out as if she were responsible for some horrific crime.

What was she doing to the poor, down trodden black slaves? She should have climbed on the box from which the atheist had disappeared. For her, it was as if she was being plucked at by the fiends of hell. She was being mobbed, literally. Suddenly, leaning over her, threateningly, was one of the most revolting men she had ever seen. She felt afraid. He had a cropped head, a dirty stubbly face, staring eyes and a slobbering mouth with all top teeth missing. The bottom teeth had grown long, like fangs. He almost prodded her with his bony finger, shouting at the top of his voice and spitting on her as he screeched in rage.

"KILL the WHITES! All the whites must F—KING – WELL - DIE!" The rest quietened to absorb the latest drama. Rose tried waving away the rude word for their benefit, trying to belittle him.

Some people said "Leave her alone. She's just defending her country." She was afraid by then. He looked demented.

"You should ALL DIE! ALL THE F...ING WHITES must F——. Suddenly, two London bobbies in their lovely helmets appeared at his side, took him by the arms and dragged him away. Rose thanked them profusely, but they just disappeared with him. She was told later that the policemen had not dragged him away to protect her. It was forbidden for the F word to be used anywhere in, or near Hyde Park.

However, the crowd had not diminished, they continued heckling her and she was saying "No! No! It's not like that. Nearly all the Africans are on our side. They are not all Communists! No! No! You've got it WRONG! OUR AFRICANS ARE NOT LIKE THAT!"

A man stepped forward and grabbed her hands, "What

do you mean? YOUR Africans? Do you think they are YOUR PROPERTY or something?"

Everyone was silent, waiting for an answer. Rose thought for a moment.

"NO. They are OUR AFRICANS and WE are THEIR EUROPEANS!" which was a fact. It was the first time she had realised the truth of it.

They continued to shout her down and the big man who had asked her and grabbed her hands, held them still. He turned to the crowd.

"Leave her alone, she's just trying to defend her country." The whole mob was silenced by this and started drifting away. Her hands were still held, and he said "I'm Bernie Brown. Sorry about all that! Look, I'm off to the Albert Hall to hear Tchaikovsky's 1812 and I can only just make it. Where are you staying? If its close, I'll see you back safely – unless you'd like to come with me?"

Rose made a snap decision. He was a good-looking man and seemed a decent one, so she agreed to go with him! She judged him to be about ten years younger than she, and was probably Jewish, with his big brown eyes, well-formed nose and his love of music. He grabbed her hand and they ran across the street to catch the right bus. He helped her on just as it took off. He asked her about herself but didn't tell her anything about his life. He stopped the bus and as they got off, Bernie grabbed her hand and said run, or we'll be late. She felt very young and happy. Here was Rose, moving towards her fiftieth birthday and feeling about half her age.

They were early enough to wait at the back entrance where Bernie went to get tickets. He finally returned, grabbed her hand again, flourishing two tickets he'd acquired on the cheap and went bounding up God knows how many stairs until she thought she'd collapse. Then he ushered her round to the very middle of the top gallery, way up in the Gods. "Come here!" he said. He put his hands firmly on her waist and told her to jump!

As she did, she had a fleeting moment when she thought he might let go and send her plummeting down into the stalls to her death. It was way down below, with the full orchestra tuning up and the music about to begin. Instead, she was comfortably perched on the handrail but glad that he insisted on keeping his arms round her 'in case.' At the end, real cannons were fired right next to them and she nearly jumped out of her skin. In the tight embrace of one Bernie Brown, she realised that he had planned it quite deliberately!

When they came out, it was evening but still daylight and he suggested a Chinese Restaurant in Soho that he liked. Would she like to come? Had she been to Soho? Of course, she hadn't been to Soho and she wouldn't have dared go there alone in any case, from what she'd read about it. She went, feeling that Bernie Brown would protect her, which was rather idiotic as she hardly knew him. Bernie spoke about the red-light area and the streets he didn't go to and wouldn't take her near. He seemed fascinated over her naiveté. He couldn't believe she didn't know what it meant, when she read the little adverts posted behind glass on the walls of some buildings: "I work in leather and lace." That honestly meant nothing to her! She thought that like Mimi in 'La Boheme', it meant they did embroidery and tooled leatherwork!

They went down a couple of steps into a dark and dingy little room with Chinese pictures on the walls and Chinamen serving at tables. There he ordered some dishes when she asked him to choose. Everything was delicious, and she drank a potent little glass of rice wine, hoping it wasn't doped. Ending up with some lychees, it was time to leave there and head for the hotel. They went on the underground and when they got back to the corner where they had first met, he suggested a stroll down the Row and into Hyde Park for a little while before they parted.

This was pleasant. It was a lovely evening and they settled down on a bench to watch people strolling by and Bernie became amorous as Rose had expected he would. It was perfectly in keeping with the strange day and people were passing, so she didn't think he would drag her into the bushes and rape or kill her. She felt she owed him for the Albert Hall and dinner in Soho and after a suitable farewell smooch, she could say goodnight. He unbuttoned his shirt to the waist, saying he was hot, and Rose was surprised to see that Bernie Brown was as fuzzy as a baby bear! He was covered in brown fur from neck down. She couldn't help running her hand over it and cuddling up to him. But the night had more to offer!

Two or three couples were looming out of the gloom when Bernie suddenly unzipped his trousers and stood up, moving a little closer to the path. Good God! she thought, he's a flasher! And he was! She felt quite revolted. Let me get out of here, she thought. He turned and came back. She said, "That wasn't very nice, was it!" Bernie just laughed, buttoning away his hairy chest and zipping up his crown jewels with an unexpected show of modesty. She said she really must go to the hotel. He walked her back and suggested they meet again next night. It was her night for a dinner out and a floor show, included in her special London week. She thought that would let him down lightly. She was still in the confines of the park and needed the open street and lights and the Hotel doorman in sight before she said anything.

He said he'd come to the hotel and ask for her at ten p.m. the next evening, and so they parted. Forever, as it happened, because her 'special dinner show' lasted a long time and she dawdled over a cup of coffee until as late as she could. The underground trip was long, and it was past eleven p.m. as she reached the hotel. If Bernie came to the hotel at ten, he was out of luck! So, Rose never found out the truth about Bernie Brown.

That day, she had made her way to Oxford St. and found Harrods and Fortnum & Masons and seen the wonders of the East End. She'd walked down to Green Park and seen Buckingham Palace and even found the Royal Academy where her mother had studied and become a concert pianist. She slept late and was one of the last in for breakfast so there was no drama. This was a day of investigating all the bridges over the Thames and seeing the Tower of London and Madame Tussauds; seeing as much of London as she remembered hearing about, and going to Covent Garden, shopping a little because little was all she had to spend and just soaking up the atmosphere of London.

Being an evening performance, Rose dressed in her full long evening dress, stole, pearls and all. She set off early to reach the right part of London on the underground. The long dress was a hazard but thankfully she didn't get jammed up in the tube doors or anything. She stuck grimly to her plan to enter in state even though she was on her own. She was living in the past of course, and realised the truth about London 1975 when she took her seat in the gallery. She cannot recall the show or the theatre. It was a musical and worth seeing but nobody was dressed the way she was. The large woman next to her was wearing a short, tight summer dress and sandshoes. Her children, who didn't stop eating sweets and crackling paper bags, jumping up and down and talking all through the performance, were enough to shake Rose out of her delusion.

She left the theatre well into the night in a mood to murder. Back in the hotel, she ordered sandwiches and coffee in the resident's lounge. As she walked in, she passed a dark little man sitting alone there. He seemed foreign, probably dark Italian, and he stared at her with a concentrated, goggle-eyed leer. She looked the other way quickly and sat on the far side of the room. To pass the time, she took out her diary and recorded a few of the day's happenings. Every time she looked up, he was leaning over the side of his armchair ogling her. Her coffee arrived, and she drank it quickly and made her way out to the central desk to ask for her key.

To her surprise, there was the little man, suddenly at her elbow, asking for his. She turned away and took the key, heading for the lift. The lift opened and in she walked. To her horror, the little man skidded in beside her, talking volubly in what she guessed was Italian. Quickly, she pressed six and the lift closed. "Madame," said the man, brandishing his key, "My room?" Then a flow of Italian spouted forth, heavily spiced with garlic. He crept closer to her and nudged her. He was a good six inches shorter than Rose, skinny and bent over, with a face like a brown, crinkled prune. He smirked, as he thought, engagingly, "My room, Madame? What on earth! she thought. Can you credit it? She tried "Non! Non!" and gave him a shove with one finger. Hard! "Please, please, Madame, Forty

321

pounds! For you?" He brandished some notes. My God! She was being propositioned!!! In the Cumberland, of all places! The lift arrived at the sixth floor. The door slid open and she hopped out quickly. Whew! Thank goodness! But that wasn't the end of it. He hopped out too, repeating the "Forty pounds!" and flourishing money.

This was so ridiculous that Rose felt like striking a theatrical pose, hand on heart and saying, No, no, a thousand times no! However, he seemed to be intent on following her to her room. The burning question was how on earth was she to get rid of this ghastly little toad! Inspiration came to her.

"Oh! Non! Monsignor - MONSIGNOR! - IN MIA CASA!" she pointed dramatically down the passage.

This was her best Italian, or so she thought. Well, it was the best she could do, anyhow and most Italians understand gestures anyway! She pointed down the corridor, stabbing at the air again. "OH! Sorry Madame! Sorry!" He turned and slid into the lift, much to her relief, as she ran to her room and shut herself in quickly in case he slid in. Only then could she reflect on the whole episode. Should she call for the manager? Too late.

Better just get to bed and think about it. The funny side hit her and suddenly she found it unbelievable! Added to that was the idea of forty pounds! That made her think she would make a good profit in one line of business! She shuddered at the thought of having to bear a little toad like that crawling all over her! Fancy this! In the five-star Cumberland! She drifted off. Cautiously descending for breakfast, in case he slid into the lift again, she handed in her key and asked whether they recalled the little creep the night before? They said he had checked out, so she didn't voice her complaint.

She had breakfast and then decided to visit the cloakroom down a few stairs for a last wash and brush up. Next to her were at least four young beauties, applying makeup and chatting. They greeted her, and she suddenly thought she should give them a word of warning about her experience. She thought the offer of forty pounds would shock them. No such thing! They laughed and discussed the going price of their favours. It appeared to be a hundred pounds for a night of delight for occupants of the Cumberland. Rose realised that she was talking to a bunch of prostitutes! She quickly left in case anyone saw her in their company. Apparently, as she was told by others in the know, the Cumberland was a literal hotbed of hot little devils making a fortune. That was why the rule, only genuine couples were to sit together in the breakfast room. The poor man was trying to keep out the ladies of the night who tried to attach themselves to likely males in the breakfast queue. She lost sympathy when she recalled his attitude towards her! Surely, he didn't think that at her age she was a tart?

Well, goodbye London! She boarded the train for Folkestone again and went to sort out clothes for the Tour No.3 in Spain. Billie and Dorrie were highly entertained by her revelations about London and could hardly wait for the next tour to produce more. They didn't have a very interesting life of their own in the Metropole.

This time, Rose stayed in the Rhodesia Hotel, of all places! Walking up the Leas, she had suddenly come across the Hotel Rhodesia and the Salisbury Hotel opposite it. Delighted, she went in and was told that two wealthy old Portuguese men from Rhodesia had retired there in about 1910 and built hotels with the money they made on gold mines. They were Baron de Rezende and Count Penhalonga. Rose was born on the Rezende Mine in Penhalonga Village, in Southern Rhodesia, right near the Portuguese Border. The two Portuguese dignitaries had sold the claims to Lonrho Mining and Land Co. Her father was one of Lonrho's Managers. Also, Rose spent a good part of her later life in Salisbury, the Capital. To come across these hotels in Folkestone was incredible.

The only single rooms at the Rhodesia Hotel were originally maid's rooms on the fourth floor. These were tiny, with dormer windows leading out to the steep, tiled roof. Early in the dawn light, there was a screeching chorus from countless huge seagulls, perched precariously outside, flapping and quarrelling with each other as they slid down the slippery roof. It was entertaining watching them. Leaning out, she could see the sea change colour and watch the splendour of a large, red sun rising out of the water and painting a glittering trail across it. Nothing could have improved the picture. She revelled in the glory of it regardless of the ungodly hour of five a.m. Summertime.

One night they had a raging storm pounding at the windows and Rose had to keep them firmly closed. It didn't let up and was equally dramatic in the morning. The black clouds scudded across the sky, with thunder and lightning showing the sea churned up and waves crashing over the barriers. On some mornings, the wind howled, and rain lashed the window. Even that was riveting, with the sea churned to a foaming fury and wild breakers hitting the rocks and spraying the road along the seafront. The gulls would scream and soar at the water's edge, swooping downwards to harvest some invisible catch. That was exhilarating to watch, before she went for her morning shower.

She had her fashionable, brown mackintosh and hood and her brown boots to protect her, so the English weather didn't hamper her. She sorted out her choice of wear for the Spanish Tour No.3, then travelled by rail to Heathrow, joined the Cosmos guide and, together with different tourists, boarded the plane to Andalusia.

Nothing prepared her for the types of hotels and the Spanish towns. She had expected charm, but they were stuck in the concrete jungle of progress and development. Squashed between the ugly, high rise blocks of apartments and charmless hotels, were tiny remnants of the old, Spanish homes but they seemed sadly out of place. Only when they boarded the coach, did they see, in passing, a few interesting spots like those on the picture post cards one could buy. Spain was a failure for her and she made a mental note that if ever she returned, it would not be on a tourist coach.

However, sitting next to her on the coach was a burly Australian man, so brawny that he kept his arms crossed to keep them off her side arm rest, so she had both arm rests to herself. She couldn't see over him, but she had the window seat and an uninterrupted view of the scenery. His name was Ray. Grenada was one of their ports of call and she hummed the song which he encouraged her to sing quietly. The words she had forgotten he supplied and she wrote them down, surprised that he knew them all. Thus, she found a pleasant travelling companion and they had a chance to criticize and share their irritation over the senseless development of ugly blemishes on the landscape. All the concrete monstrosities seemed like a scaly disease covering the place. If this were progress, then for God's sake, let us retrogress thought Rose! Ray had much to tell her about himself, He was leaving London after this tour to go to Las Vegas and play tennis in the Celebrity Contest. He loved Las Vegas and had won $63,000 over there gambling. He wanted to see 'Shampoo' in London when they returned and if she was free, would she like to go with him? She said yes, she would.

Here and there, they saw prepared shows for tourists, like a trip to a cave in the hills with Flamenco dancers strutting their stuff to the thrumming beat of qualified guitar players, dressed as if they were about to stab a bull. There, they ate bits of barbecued meat and pimentos etc. and felt quite Spanish. The passing scenery showed vast expanses covered with either sunflowers, which presented a glorious spectacle. Some of the hillsides were dotted with little trees in a uniform pattern. They turned out to be olive trees – not with the ancient, twisted charm of the olive trees in Greece, but with the view of polka dotted mountains receding on all sides to the horizon, sand coloured with grey green dots. The scenery was vast and seemed endless.

Interest flags after a while, and seeing there was a long journey ahead, Rose was glad to have Ray at her side. Had he not reminded her of her second husband, with the same massive shoulders and general largeness, she'd have been more interested in him. Strangely, he was also an Aquarian, like Tom. He was unaware of the cloud he lived under as she considered that he may be a violent man as well. He flattered her, of course, by taking photos of her at every view point. She realised that he was attracted to her. She still has the photos he sent from Australia later. Rose, perched on a camel in Morocco, Rose, with a huge snake draped around her neck in Tangier, Rose, draped in front of a large grey Mercedes in one street, because it was the same as his at home. Rose, crouched at the fountain edge in the Alhambra, showing the fretted wooden screens the concubines had looked through behind her and one of her sitting on the seat they occupied near the sunken bath, looking out through the screens.

The Alhambra was a highlight of the tour. They spent a full day in it, walking in the gardens and taking in the atmosphere of the past splendour of the Sultan's exotic life there. They sat in the private apartments of the concubines and the guide told them about the eunuchs guarding them in their sunken baths and preparing the chosen ones for their night with their lord, by oiling and perfuming them and plucking every hair out – not from their heads, of course! She suddenly though of one of her father's old ditties, not understood at the time of course!

T'was Christmas Day in the harem,
The Eunuchs stood on the stairs
Watching the Sultan's ladies
Combing their short curly hairs
When in walked the Sultan boldly
And his voice rang out through the halls
"What would you like for Christmas?"
And the Eunuchs answered
"What do you think!"

She decided to keep that one to herself!
They travelled over the vast distances, Rose had time

to think back to their first night in Malaga. There, after an afternoon of comparative boredom in the concrete jungle, the most interesting thing she found were some castor oil bushes over a wall, covered with small snails. They had flat, cream coloured shells spiralled in the opposite way to theirs at home. Were these the edible snails? Rose meant to ask but never did.

That evening, at dinner, a good looking young waiter leapt about putting plates in front of her and asking her where she came from. He spoke English well and she asked him where he learned it. He turned out to be a University student from Madrid on a working holiday. He said he was off duty in a few minutes and would she care to come with him to the night club?

She was intrigued. He was half her age but even so, it would be better than mooching about disliking the place. Rose said yes, in half an hour she'd meet him in the foyer. She showered, and as it was so hot, changed into a light nylon blouse and widely flared skirt. They walked a few blocks to the club and he turned out to be a good dancer. He kept buying bottles of wine and she found she was having a good time with him. It was fun dancing there with such a good looking young man, until, at midnight, they dimmed the lights to ultra violet light. After another hour, she noticed that her young partner kept looking at her chest. She looked down to see if she had dropped food on it and saw to her embarrassment, that her nylon blouse had practically disappeared, and she seemed to be dancing there in her bra only!

She left the floor quickly, telling her young partner she must go back. He was highly amused and assured her that she looked super as she was, but she insisted and off they went. In the morning, they boarded the coach were off. They returned to the coast and caught a ship for the crossing to Morocco, in Africa. There, they boarded the coach again and ended up in Tangier in a hotel with a manager who was dark grey and at least seven feet tall. He was enormous and broad with it. They were told not to go walking about after dark in any of the side streets and were marshalled and heads counted wherever they went. It was interesting and quite exciting. Rose kept thinking of Casablanca, the film. She was glad of the company of Ray wherever she went. This was Tangier, a new experience of a wild, dangerous and evil city.

In the morning they were off again, travelling in the Riff mountains, stopping to view various places and soaking up the atmosphere of the land of the Riffs. She had a feeling of acting in a film somewhere. There, she rode a camel and held a large snake draped round her neck and Ray took his pictures. The snake was about ten feet long and had just finished rearing wearily out of a basket to the plaintive piping of a scruffy Arab in a dirty turban. The Arab stood and offered the snake to the onlookers. Rose was the only volunteer. He settled the snake on her and whipped off his turban, offering to put it on her head for extra effect and Rose hastily declined, thinking of the number of willing lice she'd gather.

They spent four days there before sailing back via Gibraltar to the Spanish coast again. At Gibraltar, they couldn't disembark for a couple of hours. It was some political stand-off between Spain and Gibraltar, and they were stuck in the middle of it. The police were brandishing guns. After two hours in the hot sun, Rose made a move forward but thought better of it when a soldier pointed a gun straight at her. Finally, they set off and the ship docked in Spain.

They hastened aboard the air-conditioned coach and at the Hotel, they were treated to the cook's specialty paella dinner. They left early for the airport in the morning. In London, they had been booked into a hotel by Cosmos, so Rose decided to accept Ray's offer of dinner at an Aberdeen Angus steak house and the cinema afterwards. After the film, which Rose didn't really enjoy, Ray saw her to her room and came in for some coffee and a cuddle and a few kisses – nothing spectacular. He was flying to Las Vegas the next morning. There was a somewhat tame amorous interlude but nothing much to recall, in fact she found him rather boring. She promised to write and that was that.

She contemplated arranging the fourth tour of Russia which was very tempting, but realised she was travel weary, so she settled in the Rhodesia Hotel in Folkestone for the last three weeks until she was due to fly back home. There was a South African man named Gerald Jennings amongst the residents at the hotel. He was quite old and rather portly, and he sat at her table at breakfast. He asked if he could take her to see Dover Castle and she jumped at the opportunity. He drove a small red hired car and they set off. It was a beautiful day and the Castle was all you could expect, drawbridge and all! The queen was going to arrive shortly to see her regiment and present the new colours. Rose wasn't sure of the facts, but she took off, running down the grassy hill to the road to see the queen in person as she went past. As the queen drove by Rose waved frantically and had the pleasure of getting a wave back. It was rewarding because of the war in Rhodesia. Having declared U.D.I.in 1964, eleven years before meant that she was no longer the queen of Rhodesia, but some refused to even acknowledge this, including Rose.

Gerald took her to several places of interest before he left the hotel. A week later, she was surprised to get a phone call from him. He had tickets for an opera at Glyndebourne and said if she would catch the train to where he was, she could join him. Unfortunately, the name Glyndebourne meant nothing to her. She couldn't really face the business of getting clothes packed, her hair done and catching trains at such short notice, so she called him and said she couldn't make it. People told her she was mad not to have jumped at the opportunity. Apparently, the tickets were gold plated and she should have realised how lucky she was. He had given her his address in Capetown and asked her to write but she didn't.

The next time she went to England, she called in to see Pat Carillon, the Hotel manager, who said that he stayed there each time he came overseas. Apparently, he'd had his leg off. He was diabetic and had suffered from gangrene. Rose felt sorry for him. She really liked him and asked the proprietor to remember her to him. He was still driving a hired car and making the most of his holidays as best he could with one artificial leg.

Rose spent quite a few evenings with Billy and Dorrie and used the weeks just enjoying England; sitting on the benches on the leas, enjoying the sea view over the cliffs and the hazy outline of France with seagulls wheeling and mewing, reminding her of war films she had seen. Then there were performances in the little theatre and the brass band playing on Sundays. She walked down the side of the cliff where there was a paved path and sat on the cobble beach, collecting little stones to take home. She walked over to the wharf where there was a sandy beach and shops selling cooked shrimp, cockles and other fish in packets and sat on the sea wall eating them with chips, feeding the greedy gulls that swooped around her. Having a little holiday money left, she managed to stand Billy and Dorrie to a dinner at the hotel where they had first booked her in and she finally collected her massive case and returned Billy's small one.

The train took her to Victoria Station and right to Heathrow where she stepped into the T.A.P. plane for home. They landed in Lisbon as before and, to her surprise, they were whisked out of the city to a new hotel where she was to stay for a night or longer, waiting for a plane to Luanda and Salisbury. This hadn't been planned. Apparently, there was drama in Africa again. There were hundreds of Americans stranded at Luanda, in Angola. All planes were evacuating them first, and then collecting the Americans stranded at the Hotel for two days, waiting for a plane from Luanda bound for New York. Some were desperate and kept complaining loudly to the hotel staff who stared at them blankly, making out that they couldn't speak English.

Rose found herself in a huge double room with a large balcony and a fantastic marble bathroom full of mirrors and chrome. There was even a bidet! The bed was giant size and she sank into a cloud of comfort. She only wished she had someone to share it with, preferably, a husband! Or, perhaps not! Husbands seemed to come with unpleasant side effects. The ties that bound you to a husband were difficult to untie without unforeseen hazards arising.

Rose had plenty of free time to consider the alternatives. Yianis? Now that was a tempting thought. But could she bear all the physical energy required for a repeat performance from him? Then there was Ben. Could she chance it? No, she couldn't. Ray? She couldn't see herself really enjoying his company to that extent. She decided to luxuriate alone! Next time she went on holiday, if there ever was a next time, she'd go with a daughter, she hoped.

Apparently, the Americans were all being evacuated from Angola because of the fighting there. Finally, they were called and left. Then, suddenly, it was Rose's turn to be taken to the airport again and their plane left Lisbon to land in Luanda some hours later. Again, the shutters were closed, the lights put out for landing, and they were shepherded quickly into the lounge and locked in! This was unexpected and rather unnerving. The passengers wondered what on earth they were doing. Two hours later, they were hustled back to the plane and they prepared for take-off. All lights were off again, and all shutters closed. As they took off in darkness, Rose peeped under the window shutter and saw a jeep racing across the runway in front of the plane with another in full pursuit. She could see red flashes of what seemed like tracer bullets spitting out of the back jeep. Suddenly, the front jeep exploded in a ball of fire and the plane dipped dangerously to one side. Thankfully, they were airborne and climbing swiftly and steeply, banking sideways to change course.

Finally, the lights came on again and they relaxed their nervous tension by talking about dinner because it was late, nearly ten at night, and they were starving. The pilot came on the air and welcomed them, hoping they would enjoy the flight. He hesitated, laughed a little and dropped his bombshell. There was no food on board, he regretted, it had been stolen at the airport!

Their plane was the second last to leave Luanda before a total closure and he said they were fortunate to have got away safely. The war was being fought on and around the airport. They could order any drinks they liked. They were free, at least. Rose immediately ordered wine and a Bloody Mary or two. The flight attendants even scraped up small packets of nuts and biscuits. They had cheered the pilot, jeered, clapped and laughed over the food disaster and they settled down to drown their sorrows, glad that they hadn't been blown up on the runway. They would have been more afraid had the Viscount disasters already happened in Rhodesia. Heat missiles were unknown to them then. One after the other, two Viscounts were blown out of the sky up at the Zambian border, and surviving, wounded passengers were raped, mutilated and bayonetted. One of the greatest tragedies of the Rhodesian war.

At last they arrived in Salisbury and it was wonderful to see 'their' African's faces smiling and have them greet white people as if they really meant it. Yes, she thought, we were 'their' Europeans and they were 'our' Africans. A very non-PC thought, but there was genuine affection in that relationship. It was something that the rabble-rousers at speaker's corner hadn't experienced and couldn't hope to understand.

SIXTEEN

SURVIVAL TACTICS

After the holiday, Rose had to get down to finishing the house and furniture moved into the new lounge and dining room. The kitchen had to be kitted out. The only problem was the strange twitching of curtains at night and, sometimes, footsteps on the roof. She felt a bit nervous and often crept out of her bedroom in the early hours with her gun on safety and the little cat, Cindy, creeping along, tail lashing and growling like a dog She also sensed that there was somebody up there.

Rose shone the torch up above the telephone vestibule to see if the iron sheets had been disturbed and lifted. It was the most vulnerable spot in the house, old and about to be replaced. Being just a few steps from her bedroom, she felt nervous about black bodies creeping in during the black of night. She had a feeling that the vestibule needed to be completed first – after the case was heard. In the light of day, these fears vanished. Rose was resilient to the point of foolhardiness, never really heeding her inner warnings about the strong possibility of some disaster befalling any woman living alone in such a secluded place.

She went to Johannesburg to see Jenny who took her

backstage to meet the cast of The Great Waltz, in which she was singing and arranged for her to see it from the best seat in the auditorium. It was a wonderful production at the Civic, which had the Mechanization to bring the whole orchestra out of the pit on a platform when the young Strauss played his father's masterpiece, the Blue Danube, and move it to the back of the stage for the ballroom scene. The following evening, she arranged for Rose to sit in the orchestra pit and see everything from there. Rose had to remember to get off the platform before they moved it so that she didn't go up on stage with the musicians!

Before she left, they went to the Little Chelsea Theatre and saw the Jacques Brel Show, cleverly done by two men and two women wearing black polo necked sweaters. Just a black curtain behind and café chairs and tables where they sat drinking. The small orchestra was placed behind the curtain and in front of that was a frame with hats and a posy of flowers. Those were their only props and singly or in twos or all together they stood in the spotlight and sang Jacques Brels songs, clever, haunting and funny. It was a delightful performance.

Then she flew to Capetown to stay with Christopher and Shirley. She went by train to Simonstown where the navy had a training ship in the docks. Shirley accompanied her, and they walked up the hill to see the cemetery. There were gravestones dating back three hundred years, with the names mostly obliterated by time, where the original settlers were buried. The train tracks ran along the side of the mountains, almost in the sea in some places. On the Sunday, Christopher drove them to Franshoek, through the grape growing estates and wineries. It was called the fairest Cape; the Cape of Good

Hope and Rose wanted to live there and paint many scenes. There was a beautiful view round every bend. She went into the city, to Barclay's Bank and who did she bump into but Gerald Jennings, last seen in the Rhodesia Hotel in Folkestone. He was changing money to go to England again that afternoon There was little time for catching up, as both were in a hurry, so after a brief chat they went their own ways.

Kit couldn't wait to get Rose up to meet their Lebanese friends. These fabulously rich people owned a mansion with tennis courts and a huge chestnut tree on two or three acres of lawn, perched up the mountainside overlooking the sea. The women were fortyish and quite beautiful, and their conversation was about their young lovers. Champagne flowed, and a huge bowl of roast chestnuts and other delicacies graced the table on the patio.

Passed round for all to enjoy, were grass cookies. Rose had no idea what they were which amused her son and everyone else. "Go on. Try one!" they said, but Rose held back. "What's in them? Grass?! Everyone laughed. "You'll get on a high! Have one." Rose was shaken. It was totally illegal in South Africa - gaol sentence if caught. Everyone except Kit, Shirley and herself, ate them. Rose was glad to see her son and Shirley did not. Later, the host decided to go on to the Heerengracht Hotel Night Club, paying for everyone to go in. There, in the basement, huge pillars supported the ten-storey building above it. Behind one pillar was a lad of about seventeen, darting back and forth, giving one of the wives long, smouldering looks as she whispered and giggled with her friends. Apparently, he was that wife's lover. The husband ignored them, chatting up one of the other wives. Rose had had enough by then and was glad when they went home to bed as her plane left for Rhodesia early the next morning.

In June, Rose had a phone call from an African at nine at night. He said he was Raphael the well digger. "Remember me, madam? I put the slate on your verandas." Rose did recall him and wondered if he was wanting another job. He said he was a police informer and he had seen Tom's cook, Tickey gambling at a place in the next suburb and selling clothes He remembered when he was working on her verandas that some clothes had gone from the line. Two policemen were there, and he had been asked to phone Rose to come and identify clothes. He was helping the police and they had Tickey in custody. Please meet him on the main road near the racecourse and he'd lead her to the house. The policemen were waiting there.

Rose had lost some clothes and other items and the police had been told about it. They had gone off the line, she thought. Raphael had seemed a pleasant young African who worked hard on her verandas. She agreed to drive along the road but took the precaution of calling the main Police Station number. They agreed to come out on the road and meet her and Raphael, so she drove along until she saw a man waving her down. She shone her torch at him but didn't really recognise him. He said he'd get in the back and direct her. There was a track over the field they could take that would go right to the place.

In he got, behind her, and pointed to a rough path. Rose looked down the road, but still no sign of a police car so she started to go into the long grass along the bumpy pathway. She was uneasy about it. It was no road for a car – too stony and rough, so she braked and reversed quickly, saying to Raphael that he must run along that way and she'd drive round on the road. She was relieved when he agreed and got out. Then she drove round on the main roads to the house he pointed out but there was no sign of anybody there. Puzzled, she went home and phoned the police again. They said they'd go and look but she must not go there again, ever. It was probably a hoax call. Because Raphael had said he was a Police informer, Rose expected him to turn up at the house to explain, but he didn't.

In July, there was a Celebrity concert at the theatre and as her acquaintance Steve was singing in the male voice choir, Rose decide to go to it. She dressed in a long skirt and top, wore her woolen stole for warmth and set out, making sure she had her F.N. pistol on safety in her evening bag. She would be late coming back.

There had been the noises on the roof and prowlers about the house and she needed the security of her gun. At eleven p.m., she drove into her gates and, looking at the house as the lights swept round the drive she thought she saw an odd sight at the back. What looked like an enormous puffball moved away from the house and faded in the blackness. Rose thought she had imagined it. It was so ridiculous! She drove round to the side door of the temporary kitchen and parked the car, careful to check the surroundings and the roof, in case anyone was up there.

Uneasy, she took the gun out of her beaded bag and made sure it was loaded, ready to fire but with the safety catch on. Then, with the door key ready, she got out and locked the car quickly. She unlocked the door, fearful of the roof that sloped down to just over her head. Hastily, she opened the door to go in and blocking it was Jenny's little cat, Cindy, with her hair standing on end like a dinosaur, stopping her quick entry.

"Go in, Cindy, quickly!" said Rose. She pushed past and shut the door, but Cindy had disappeared. The light was on as she had left it and she felt safer. Normally, she'd have boiled the kettle and made coffee, disarming the gun and putting it back in her bag before going to bed, but, because of Cindy's greeting, she kept it in her left hand as she unlocked the iron door to the bedroom section and pushed the door open. Strangely, there was something stopping the door from opening fully. Rose pushed harder and felt a sliding movement behind it.

"Oh! My God! There's someone there!" She just had time to grab the gun from her left hand, letting go the door as a huge black man slid out with his hand up pointing a knife at her. Rose let out the loudest shriek she could. It stopped him dead still for a moment; enough for her to get the safety catch off and start firing.

"Aim round the door!" thought Rose "The bullets may ricochet into you, if you hit it." a lightning shift of aim that made her miss her target and hit the newly plastered wall of the passage. They ricocheted with a loud whang behind him, and she finally realised her error and tried to aim closer but, in that split second, he grabbed her and dragged her into the dark passage with her struggling to turn away and clutch the gun close to her body. She counted four shots, so the gun still had two bullets in it.

Down she went, face forward, on her knees and then flat on her face with him on her back. That winded her for a moment but the scuffle went on as he pulled her around and she saw something moving next to her as he tried to haul her over. It was a khaki clad mass of body and she had the gun still in her hand, free, right there so she fired at it – one – two? There was a click. No sixth bullet! Then she recalled that her brother had fired one at a tin out at the farm. She put on the safety catch anyhow and felt the body slide back on her back and his knife at her throat, pressing it.

"I'm going to kill you now!" he said.

"Oh! my God!" thought Rose, "I'm going to get my throat slit and die in a pool of blood and that's what my children will find if they get here." She felt a deep sense of pity for them. Then she rallied and thought what to say. Out poured the strangest words Rose had ever used.

"Oh, please don't kill me! Killing's a terrible thing! I wasn't trying to kill you. I only shot you because I was frightened, I wasn't trying to KILL you!!!" she gabbled on, thinking she was being a bit senseless!

To her surprise, his hand went down. The knife was no longer at her throat. She thought she'd charmed him. Actually, she hadn't. One of the bullets had lodged in his shoulder! She raised herself up on her elbows and turned her head, straining to see his face. She thought "I've had my first reprieve. If I get out of this alive, I want to be able to identify this bugger!" She tried another tack.

"Who are you?" - answer - "You don't know me!" Try another stupid question, thought Rose – buy time! Where was everybody? Surely, they had heard the shots?!

"What do you want?" Probably money, she thought.

"I want you!"

Oh my God! I've got a rapist! Don't struggle. Don't scream. It makes them worse. Try a casual approach. Don't panic!

"Oh, that's alright! — but I have money – LOTS of money!" Silence. He was thinking! Good!

"Where is it?"

Oh, no, my boy! I'm not telling you that. You'll kill me.

"I'll get it for you!!' she said. She didn't have a bean in the house. Silence.

"Give me your gun." … Check the safety catch is on. Empty, surely. Hopefully!

"Here you are, you see I'm not shooting you any longer." She handed it over her shoulder. Damn! He might bash me over the head with it.

She felt him getting off her back! It was her second reprieve.

"You get up." he said. Rose sat up slowly and turned her body to see him.

In the light from the kitchen, she saw him standing there, gun in one hand pointing at her and knife in the other. With his knees sagging in his khaki trousers, he looked for all the world like a cowboy! She had a fleeting ridiculous memory of the film "High Noon".

Creep up as slowly as possible! There's no money! Where is everybody! She was half up when suddenly he fell backwards flat on the floor.

"Custer's last stand" - the end of a rapacious career for *Rafael the Well Digger*

Rose leapt up! What to do? Run past him to the phone. Phone the police? NO! He might wake up and grab her ankle. Run for it!

She ran to the back door. The key was still in her left hand, together with her bag. Her stole was still round her shoulders. She began to go into shock and was shaking so violently, she couldn't get the key into the hole. Every moment she expected to be grabbed again from behind. Finally, she had the door open and she ran up the bank to the road, glad that the wire fence hadn't yet been put between the brick pillars. She screamed out:

"Betty Ann! Bobby! Help me! Help me!"

Then she saw Bobby, her neighbour, running over the road to grab her. He rushed her to their house and by then she was urgently needing the toilet, so Betty Ann took her to it and she sat there, safe at last. It was then that reaction set in. She had a blinding pain in her head and a tight band of pain in her chest. Her chest heaved, and every breath was drawn in with a loud wail. Betty Ann said she'd never forget the sound. Rose thought she was going to die. Finally, she calmed down and the pain went.

Outside three police cars had arrived, one of them the dog section, and two ambulances. Ballantyne Park was certainly awake now! This was something the whole neighborhood was out to see at midnight. Betty Ann gave Rose hot, sweet tea and Bobby brought in a high-ranking police officer who sat on the sofa with her and questioned her. Out came the story indelibly engraved on her memory forever. He took her hand and smiled. She wanted to grab him and kiss him, she was so glad to have him there. "We'll have to teach you to shoot!" he said. She wondered why? "Can you come over with me to the house?" Rose wasn't keen to do so but agreed. He had to support her because her knees were buckling but they made it. There were policemen everywhere, lights flashing, and ambulances at the ready. On the floor of the passage was a chalked outline of a body – no body! That puzzled her. The gun was next to one hand and the knife next to the other – still there. Odd! Then the police inspector told her the body was missing. That's why he had said he'd have to teach her to shoot!

The dogs found the body – still alive, down near the corner of her three acres, in the grass at the side road edge. The dogs lost the trail at the road itself and the police surmised that a gang had carried the rapist out, then left him for dead as they escaped with their haul in a car. Betty Anne said she had a guest room for Rose and she need not go to hospital, so the one ambulance went off, also the police cars, except one for the policemen waking the rapist. They were trying to get the names of the accomplices with the car and stolen goods however he remained silent and they sent him in the other ambulance to the prison hospital for attention. There, the doctor dug a bullet out of his shoulder and delved in his lower abdomen for another, where it was established that the shot under Rose's arm at the khaki mass had ricocheted round his bladder. They made sure to inform her that he would never be able to rape again.

In the morning, Wally, Gillian's husband went in to work at C.I.D. Headquarters to be told the news of the day – the Ballantyne shooting – and he said immediately, "I bet that's my bloody mother-in-law!" and it was! At least, she had been a couple of years before, when married to Tom. She was his step mother- in- law for the two years of the short marriage, but he claimed the relationship for the occasion. As head of fingerprints department, he had the pleasure of telling Rose that the rapist was none other than Raphael the Well Digger!

After a long and protected sleep in Bobby and Betty Ann's house, Rose went over with Betty to check the house and look for Cindy. There she found that the gang had made off with nearly all her beautiful clothes gathered for the holiday, including her lovely turquoise brooch from Yianis. Also, her box of silver cutlery and many pieces of jewelry. However, Rose was grateful for her life – nothing else mattered. She found little Cindy eventually, in the shed and Joel was still there. He was a young African gardener who had replaced Joseph. When Tickey came to Salisbury with Tom, Joseph came and told her he had to go to his home in the reserve. She knew that he didn't get along with Tickey but that wasn't mentioned. Africans were like that. They skirted round the reason. Rose just gave him a hefty bonus and said go well.

Joel was an odd little chap. She found he could make radios out of a tin can and a box. They worked! He sold a good number of them, only buying small crystals for them, to pick up the waves. Clever! Without an education, he had found a way to better his life and had the makings of a businessman. Joel remained the caretaker and Rose spent the days organising her move out of the place, packing up all her possessions again. She plastered the holes in the passage where the bullets had hit and gave the place to Steve to sell 'voetstoots' – the lovely Dutch word meaning "as it stands, without comebacks."

Rose was nomadic for some time, kindly protected by her daughter and son in law for some months in their flat and then in their house. Finally, she managed to rent a penthouse flat in the upper avenues of the city. There, she felt safe, as it was on the sixth floor in a protected block. The gates were locked at night. Rose had a garage in which to store her furniture and a carport. The huge glass doors opened onto a large private patio area that the American doctor renting it had graced with a rockery and long awning with coloured lights running down it. On the high walls were sconces holding aluminium cones containing paraffin and a wick.

There, he said he entertained as many as 150 people. To secure the flat from the walkway outside, there was an eight-foot wall in face brick. He had installed dimming switches and put in full length Belgian linen curtains that were fantastic. These embellishments, Rose had to purchase to acquire the leasehold, but she jumped at it, for the security alone. Apart from that, the whole penthouse with its luxuriant curtains and dimming lights and the doors open to the patio, was a feast for the eyes.

She had joined the Operatic Society as well. That meant having to take lessons from Greta Muir who was president. They had closed their doors and that was the only way, according to her friend Steve, that one could get a foot in. Once she heard Rose sing, she made her a member. In Greta's house, Rose was surprised to see a beautiful boudoir grand piano in perfect condition, with such extraordinary features that Rose couldn't take her eyes off it. The legs were bulbous, raised on brass castors and the keys were real ivory and ebony. It was a delight to behold. Greta said it belonged to some old man who was leaving the country and wasn't taking it with him. It was selling for 700 dollars. Rose didn't hesitate. She bought it there and then, before anyone else snapped it up. Apparently, it was nearly a hundred years old and had come from the bogs of Ireland without the soundboard cracking. It was a John Broadwood and Son and a rare find.

The matter of getting it up to the penthouse was a worry. They thought it would have to be hoisted up the side with a crane, all six stories, onto her patio. Steve said he was going to bring a chair and sit in the garden below to watch! By great good fortune, it was brought up in the lift with a finger's breadth to spare each side and parked in the middle of the lounge/dining area, taking up half the space. Rose didn't care. This was her new baby and it simply graced any room it was in, totally. She moved it to the back corner and there it stood, increasing the luxury of the penthouse, to be admired by all who came into the place.

Every place has a character of its own and there, Rose felt comfortable enough to walk about in the nude. Never had she had that inclination before, but it was six stories up and out of the windows that stretched from floor to ceiling, there were the tops of the huge Jacaranda trees. It was sybaritic and secluded, so there she wandered, into the lounge and main bedroom or fetching her breakfast and eating it facing the patio, without a stitch on!

The months passed, and Rose enjoyed her seclusion, occasionally inviting people in and feeling richly rewarded for staying alive. She realised that she didn't miss the beautiful Ballantyne Park and her achievement in building up Seven Springs. She had a feeling of dread about going there to check on the woman who had bought it but this she had to do. To get it sold quickly, Rose agreed to let it go to a woman named Cindy, on terms of payment – no deposit and full amount within three months; this, on the assurance of her lawyer, Tim Tanser. A couple of weeks later, Rose rang Cindy and drove out to meet her and explain what she envisaged for the veranda room.

The first thing she saw was that the new patios had been removed! She was appalled but the stranger named Cindy welcomed her effusively, calling her darling and inviting her in for tea. Would she like Lapsang Souchon or Rooibos? Rose said either would do fine.

There, on the wall of the veranda room was a huge picture of a woman with writhing snakes for hair, a third eye in the middle of her forehead and a very evil look. It was some Indian god or other. Along came Cindy with tea and an evil looking Shiatsu.

The dog sat growling at Rose and then jumped up and sat growling at its mistress as well. All was darling this and darling that until Rose drew the agreement copy out and pointed out that Cindy shouldn't really be destroying the verandas until she had paid something and asked Rose for permission.

The woman's face changed instantly, and she snatched up the agreement and brandished it in front of Rose's face snarling;

"This is what I fucking-well signed!"

Rose had no words! She got up, hastily collecting her things and said she must go. Off she went to ring Tim Tanser. The woman had paid nothing and was destroying the property. She was very uneasy. Tim still assured her that the money would be forthcoming. This was the ex-wife of a tycoon in Johannesburg. She was loaded – don't worry! She'd just returned from India where she had been visiting her Guru. She was Rhodesian and bound to have a massive settlement from her ex. He was one of the wealthiest men in South Africa. Tim promised to have a word with her but not about the 'effing' expletive!

A week later Cindy phoned Rose and asked her to come along for tea again, darling, that afternoon at three. Rose thanked her and said she would love to see her but couldn't stay for tea! She had to be elsewhere in an hour. she arrived, she was greeted by Cindy with plenty of darlings and they were about to go in when another car driven by a chauffeur rolled in. A small blonde woman, sitting in front with the chauffeur, got out and they embraced effusively. Cindy introduced her to Rose as Mrs. Fowler, who said she had to go but she just had to drop off these, darling, for Baba.

The chauffeur opened the back door of the car and brought out an enormous arrangement of flowers taking up the whole back seat. This was carried into the bedroom section of the house and deposited on the floor in the end room. That room, Cindy said, was where she meditated and communed with Baba by E.S.P., because he was in India. She said he had advised her by E.S.P., that Seven Springs was the house she should buy. Rose felt she should send Baba some message by Morse code, thanking him. Cindy's was the only offer Rose had, and she had accepted it.

The flowers were placed at the top of the bare room near some lighted candles, behind a prayer rug of sorts. Mrs. Fowler and the chauffeur departed, and Rose had a chance to ask Cindy the burning question that had been bothering her.

"Where are the new roof tiles?"

The whole new roof of the cottage section had been stripped bare of the dark grey tiles and it had only the latticework of wood left. Cindy assured Rose that the new tiles would be on in a day or two. She didn't like the colour and was changing it to orange. Rose thought that the orange would clash with the lilac of the bougainvillea, but she didn't say so. She hastened to find out from Tim that the building was totally covered by insurance in the event of rain. The place was embellished by Arthur Azevedo wrought iron gates and sash windows from the demolished hospital building in the avenues. Rose was paid in full and never could bring herself to go there again to see it.

Cindy soon waltzed out of it, letting it for two years to the Fowlers who, as it happened, were the proprietors of the Chicken Inn, which amused Rose. Two years later, when Cindy returned from her sojourn with Baba and travels around America, she couldn't winkle the tenants out of her house because they exercised their 'option to purchase for ninety thousand pounds', a special clause written in the lease agreement. They fought it out in court and the Fowlers won. The house, then, was worth about two million! Only a few years later, Mr. Fowler died suddenly in his early fifties, of a heart attack. Rose felt that the place itself, although it was so beautiful, was cursed in some way.

Rose spent a year in the penthouse flat and it was conveniently close to the Reps Theatre where she was singing and designing sets for the big musicals. There, she met a man who was divorced and who interested her. He had several degrees, honours in English literature and English, Economics and Politics and was at present with a law firm in the city, about to take a degree in Law. Rose found him so clever and amusing when he described some of the cases he was defending in court. He could sing and had a deep bass voice. He had been a theatre critic and had written two books – not everybody's taste in literature but, as Rose was interested in Politics, he gave her a copy of 'A Portrait of an Economy under Sanctions' and 'The Real Case for Rhodesia', both clever efforts to convince the rest of the world that the Communist threat was real in Africa and that the bringing down of the white government in Rhodesia would be a disaster for both black and white.

His name was John. He played tennis at the Avondale Club and cricket with the famous Ron Coventry's veterans at the Royal Salisbury Golf Club. Rose asked him to come to her penthouse and sing for him. She wanted to hear him sing Old Man River and she could play for him.   When she went to Greta for a singing lesson she mentioned him for the Operatic Society and was surprised at the horror Greta expressed. "Rosemary! For God's sake don't get mixed up with that man!" said Greta and she proceeded to tell Rose all about him. Apparently, he used to lock his wife in the house and neighbours heard screams in the night. He had been in the Operatic Society and had a good voice but suddenly changed key, so she had asked him to leave. He had lost his temper and threatened her, and she had been quite afraid. Rose wondered whether this was a personal quarrel and Greta was exaggerating.

She continued to go out with him and was invited to his house in Arundel, one of the best suburbs in Salisbury. He was charming to her and set out to attract her. Always, Rose refused to take advice and condemn anyone out of hand, and she really wanted to marry this man, which seemed to be his intention. He couldn't have been nicer to her and finally he asked her to marry him.

Rose held back, sensing his odd behaviour. He took her

out in his Mercedes and she found that he didn't change gear; just travelled along revving up in second at a high speed and ignoring her when she tried to remind him, annoyed because he was talking and what he was saying was far more important than the irrelevance of gears and pistons! He had an extra room built on his veranda, opening his lounge exclusively for her grand piano, even though she hadn't agreed to marry.

He insisted that she must come up to his house to help him understand the trust account, part of his final exams in law. She wasn't sure she was qualified with her small knowledge of accounts, but she went to do her best. It was simple to answer the questions on previous exam papers and soon he understood the trust account. He only needed an audience when he expounded on every subject. He was a bitter man who kept going on about his past. Even his childhood was explained in detail. When he was born, he had eczema, asthma and ear trouble, so badly that the doctor leaned over the cot and said, "Poor child!" He was a year in bed with a dangerous mastoid infection when he was fourteen and still studied for his matric, passing with flying colours. He took his first degrees in London University, Honours in English, English Literature and Politics.

Later, in South Africa he got degrees in Economics and History. He had recently returned from Pretoria where he had been employed by the Americans as Economics Advisor on Rhodesia in the American Embassy for seventeen years. He had joined a legal firm to take a degree in Law at the age of fifty-four. Rose gathered when she knew him better, that he couldn't hold a job down in any case. The Americans had put up with him for seventeen years, which was a record. He was a true eccentric. People who had known him for years told her that he had started with one law firm and had to leave after a few months and apply to another. In the end, none of them would take him on to finish his articles. Finally, one lawyer who had spent some time in a mental hospital and who also wrote books and had his own law firm, recognised the problem and took him on. It wasn't long before they were no longer on speaking terms and Tony told him he could stay and finish his articles and once he had sat for his final exams he would have to leave.

This he did, and as there was an election coming up, he decided to switch from the Rhodesian Front to the Rhodesian Action Party. They used all his writing for their flyers and posters and he gave talks which Rose attended, hoping he would get into parliament. However, seeing how the Rhodesia Front bussed all the ancients from the old people's homes to vote for Smithy, because Smithy would get them through, Rose felt that the R.A.P. might not win. The left wing N.U.F. was the third contender. The result was 13.5 % R.A.P. and 13 % N.U.F., the balance going to the R.F.

For some time, he was out of work and then one lawyer died, and John manage to fill that position, working for a black lawyer named Hudson. John had an extraordinary experience there one morning and Rose was entertained by his story of what happened. It wasn't only the event that fascinated her, it was John's part in it. She already knew that he had a way of suddenly changing his voice as he spoke, and this was no exception. He called her to explain why he hadn't turned up where he had said he'd meet her. As he began his story, his voice dropped an octave and he intoned:

"I was on the telephone to a client, when I heard a commotion coming from the next office, and Hudson calling out "Help! Help! Murder! Quick!" – So, I finished my conversation as quickly as I could and went to investigate. There was Hudson, on the floor, unconscious, with blood spurting out of his neck. There was nobody else there to do it and I had to drag him downstairs and get him to hospital in my car. When I got there, he seemed dead and there was a pool of blood an inch deep on the floor of my car, at the back. What a mess. I don't think I will ever get the smell out of it." His voice had gone back to normal. He wasn't concerned about the fate of Hudson, just his precious Mercedes.

"So is Hudson dead." "No, he's alright. It's my car that's not, and I don't suppose he will pay for it, either."

Apparently, Hudson had repossessed a car from an African who had come to the office and stabbed him. He didn't offer to pay for the Mercedes and John shouted at him. Hudson then paid for the cleaning of John's car and dispensed with John's services.

John was eccentric in the extreme. One of his best friends was another John. He was and alderman in the city council and Rose and John were invited to a party at their house one Christmas. John didn't want to go. He said that the house smelt unpleasant and he couldn't stand it. Finally, he changed his mind and they went. Alderman John's wife, Elsie, was in a wheel chair. She was huge and looked on her last legs, but for a while she sat with them. John chose a seat next to the open French door. He said he had to sit on a high straight chair because of his back trouble. Everyone drank wine or spirits, but John asked for coca cola. Rose wondered why, because he usually had wine.

There were several other couples there, including two lawyers and their wives and the conversation was lively. John joined in with his nose buried in his big glass of coke and kept it there all evening. He looked like a black gnome on a toadstool. There were two dogs in the room, one very old, blind one and one fat one, both with bald pink patches. Rose realised that the smell came from them. They both had bad mange. As soon as possible, John got up to leave. Rose asked him as soon as they were out of the gate, why the Coca Cola? He said it had a strong fragrance and that was the only way he could bear the stench.

Alderman John had shares in a company that Rose also had invested in. One morning, he came to collect her to go to the general meeting. He said, "Sorry I'm late, I've just dropped Jean."

"Where?" asked Rose. "In the driveway." Said John.

Rose was confused. It turned out that he had been helping her out of the wheelchair, into the car and he had literally dropped her on the ground. It took a long time for him and the houseboy to pick her up and get her back in the house.

John was still on "bread and cheese", as he called it, but that didn't stop him from getting the room finished for the piano. He had a new goal. He was going to have a party! He hadn't had a party for all the influential friends of his who had asked him to their homes and this would be the answer. He'd spend his last dollar if necessary and invite the lawyers and statesmen and others he knew and that way, once they saw him in his home, at least one or two would have a position for him. She could play Old Man River and he would sing. In his mind, this was the answer and she must help him plan it.

Rose was aghast! She was quite sure that it wouldn't work. She wondered why he had never had a party in all the years he was married and lived in the house and she recalled Greta's warnings. She tried to think what she could do to help him meanwhile. There was this constant clamour for her attention and if she didn't contact him and be with him, he was ringing her demanding that she come there, or he'd be at her door, knocking. He was threatening to commit suicide, shouting that he was going mad and why wouldn't she see what she was doing to him. She was the only one he had who could help him and he needed her.

She took him baskets of groceries and cooked meals and sat for hours listening to him and reading what he had written. Thus, Rose was caught in the net of emotional blackmail. She had a life of her own, singing and acting at Reps, designing sets and painting them for Reps and W.V.S. shows, and trying to fit her own life into his demands on her time. Over it all, loomed the problem of John's poverty. What could be done? Rose was a typical Mrs. Fix-it. She had an urge to do so and it was a Mason compulsion – or, perhaps a woman's.

Suddenly, it came to her. She didn't need to marry the man. She was leaving the penthouse at the end of the year anyhow, so why look for a house to move into. She could rent the large extra room he had that was almost detached from the house and was a virtual Granny Flat, down a side passage, with its door opposite the bathroom. That was the only problem, she'd have no separate bathroom, but she saw a way to build one on at the back close to the plumbing. The room was set back and had a French door to what could be a private garden right next to the driveway. It was ideal, and being at least eight metres long and five wide, was ample for a bed sitter. Then, the piano could go where John was determined to have it and she could use his kitchen, dining room and lounge. She was prepared to pay him the same rent as the penthouse as well, and that would solve his problems. She suggested it and he jumped at it immediately, with one exception. She was not to pay rent!

Rose knew better than to argue. He was too proud for that and would have been offended, but she realised that she could pay half of the household bills and purchase a good deal of the groceries and work it out that way. As soon as the music room was finished, she had the piano moved there. John kept admiring it and it seemed to lift his spirits, so Rose was satisfied. He consulted her over the curtains for the new window and put in a French door on the veranda side of the music room, which was an excellent idea as it meant that, for entertaining and soirees he intended to have, he could throw open all the doors and combine lounge, piano extension, veranda and dining room and have room for about twenty or more guests. The dining room had a French door to the veranda too, so there could be a buffet dinner set there. Rose became more and more enthusiastic and charmed with John over all his ideas. When John went anywhere he moved in the highest circle and she would too if all this worked out, that she knew.

Rose had to pack up the penthouse and move out, including the garden rockery and the ton of earth the doctor had piled on the patio. She brought Joel along with her wheelbarrow, and he trundled it all down in the lift and spread it in the grounds, large rocks and all. Finally, the patio was bare, the sconces removed, and the curtains taken down and packed. Bert and Sherrell said the boxes and furniture she wasn't taking to John's could be stored in their shed and she called a removal company to take her bed and dressing table, small dining suite and occasional chairs to John's. By the time she had motored to the house, backwards and forwards, with as much as she could take in her car, carrying everything down in the lift and then into the room, she was exhausted. John made no effort to help her, he said he had to finish his book and as soon as she was free, he expected her to help him!

She drove up with her last load at eleven that night. She'd had no lunch or dinner and hadn't sat down all day. Her last job was to clean the flat and cart the last things, including her handbag and the car keys. Her feet were bruised and painful and she hobbled into her new room, knowing that she had a bed to make, but she was so exhausted that she flung the bedding on and a pillow and quietly opened the door to go to the toilet before she could sleep. Back she came and closed the door, locking it. At last! She didn't do more than loosen her bra and lie down with all her clothes on. Her feet were pounding with pain, making it difficult to sleep but as there was a knock at her door, that didn't matter. "Rosemary, what are you doing? I was expecting you to come through. Why are you so late?" Rose called out "I thought you were asleep, John. Why are you still awake? I have only just finished, and I crept in. Don't worry about me, I must sleep, I will see you in the morning."

"I'm working, I've such a lot to discuss with you, come here. I must talk to you." He knocked on the door, tried the handle and pounded on it. "Rosemary, I need you to help me, why have you locked yourself in?" He bashed on the door and rattled it and she thought he would break it open.

"John, I'm exhausted! I must sleep. Please go to bed, it's very late. Goodnight." He just continued bashing and rattling the door and screaming at her to bloody well open the door or he would bash it down. Rose pulled the pillow over her ears and curled up, but her heart was pounding, and she felt afraid. What a disaster, she thought, what the hell am I to do? She got her little gun out of her bag and put it under her pillow, not knowing whether he had a key for the French doors and would come in and throttle her or something. Finally, there was silence. Rose turned over and slept.

She woke early and got up to check the time by the grey light of dawn. It was five thirty, so, hoping that John was not awake, she gathered up her passport and handbag and unlocked the French door, went out and locked it again, crept quietly over the gravel to her car, got in and half closed the door. She started it, hoping John would not run out and stop her. She was relieved to be away. Now she had to decide where to go? She headed for Helena Road where Sherrell was now living. Sherrell agreed to phone him and arrange the removal of her furniture and piano. She didn't want to speak to him and be persuaded to come back.

He came out onto the lawn and was surprisingly quiet. He said she needn't take her things, they could stay there until she made up her mind. She could keep the key and come and go as she pleased. Then he turned away and walked back without another word. They went in, Rose collected a few things she needed, and they left. Rose was relieved and at the same time she was sad. John was a lonely man, yet he was unable to accept limitations. He bit the hand that fed him, literally. She didn't know how all the lawyers gave up or why his two ex-wives divorced him, but she knew that he frightened her as her second husband had done.

One day, a motorbike stopped at the gate and the garden boy brought in a cellophane wrapped, single red rosebud. This was for Rose and had no message on the card, but Rose knew it was from John. She guessed that he was trying to make amends and wanted to get her back, but she didn't phone and thank him. She recalled the way Tom had also sent her flowers, in his effort to mend the rift, a huge florist's bouquet. Her first husband had written reams of apologies and regrets, begging to return. She sensed that in a way, each of us are truly the masters of our own destiny. The choice we make and the way we behave, steers our future into uncharted territory.

Bert returned, and he and Sherrell went ahead with their wedding preparations. They had decided to hold the ceremony at the house and Pat's husband Mickey who was a magistrate, would marry them. A few months later, Christopher and Shirley married, and again Mickey officiated in Salisbury. The bridal party then returned to Mike and Arlines' farm for the reception.

It was an interesting wedding reception, out on the lawn in front of the farmhouse. With the threat of terrorist activity, all the men carried their rifles! It looked for all the world, like a shot-gun wedding!

Steve had been showing Rose houses in the avenues. She had no desire to live on anything more than half an acre with neighbours close on all sides. What she found was a bungalow in Milton Park with large double storied houses surrounding it, in a beautiful avenue shaded by huge Flamboyant trees. The owner had moved into a home and it was priced at only fourteen thousand dollars as it needed underpinning. There were cracks in the walls that needed fixing. Rose bought it. Finally, she had a place for the piano and her furniture, so she rang John to arrange a day for the removal van to collect her things. John wanted her to leave the piano with him, but she wanted it in her house.

It wasn't the safest place. Although there were burglar bars on the windows, they matched the big glass panes and, apparently, thieves could wriggle through. Once she had lost several items of clothing and linen, she realised this, and had extra bars put in. John soon began phoning and turning up at all hours. He was pestering her again and demanding to know who she was going out with and why.

SEVENTEEN

THE DEB'S DELIGHT

Rose went on holiday to stay with Jenny in Johannesburg for a week or two and when she returned, her friend Phyl Jolly phoned her, very distraught because she had nobody to do her set for a play that was going on in two weeks. It was just a drawing room in a London Flat and it had to be furnished tastefully as well, please could Rose do it. So that kept her busy immediately, painting and decorating the box set that had already been erected on stage. She had paintings to go on the walls and finally, it was a matter of choosing the furniture.

Phyl had arranged to advertise the name of a furniture shop in the city in the programme and she asked Rose to go and choose a suite, sideboard and occasional chairs. The leading man would be there to help her. Phyl was surprised that Rose had never met this man. His name was Tim, and he was tall and handsome and very upper crust – and, he was a widower. He had played the father in The Winslow Boy a couple of years before and he was a very good actor.

Phyl said that during that play, his wife suddenly died. She was only 36 and it had been a great shock. After she died, he used to bring his children to the theatre each night, but he didn't let the producer down, he went on stage and finished the run. She said he hadn't done anything since until she asked him to audition. Rose went to the warehouse where the furniture was stored and as she walked in, she was met by the man Phyl had told her about. Looking down at her was one of the handsomest men she had ever seen. He had blue eyes that she drowned in and the moment he spoke, Rose knew she was completely lost. She wanted to put her hand on his chest and remain touching him. She wanted him to take her in his arms and hold her close to his body and never let her go. All she could do was say, "Hello. You must be Tim. Phyl Jolly said you would be here."

What she wanted to say was "Here I am. I'm yours if you want me!" She could hardly concentrate on what he said about furniture, but she followed him around, agreeing with everything he said. Her mind was occupied with the sudden fear that he had another woman in his life. That seemed to be something she should ask him before any mundane conversation about furniture. Fortunately, she restrained herself and came down to earth. His taste was impeccable. She knew that the choices he made would be perfect and in no time, they had finished.

She couldn't think what to say to keep him there, but he sorted that out by saying he had some items at home he thought would fit and would she like to follow him to the house and have tea. He wasn't going back to the office. Rose was delighted. He saw her to her car and off they went. The house was in Highlands. It was an old Rhodesian bungalow set on two acres, well away from neighbours. Tim saw her into the sitting room and went off to tell his cook to take the tea outside, they would have it there. He showed her the small tables and bookcases he had mentioned.

They were beautiful, and she asked him where he had got them. Apparently, they came from England and some were inherited. His paintings were extraordinary. Two she particularly liked were of the Household Cavalry which he had been in. He had been a captain in the Blues when he was in his early twenties and went on to tell Rose how they had to attend the balls at Buckingham Palace in full dress uniform, because the King expected them to dance with any of the debutantes they saw sitting out without partners, the wallflowers. He was called a Debs' delight! Every word was absorbed by Rose and she couldn't take her eyes off him. His voice was extremely cultured, and pleasantly deep, and she felt herself minding her pronunciation and trying to speak perfect English in the same plummy way. Finally, she forgot her resolve and chattered away normally. There were a thousand things she wanted to ask him but, realizing that she had better drag herself away and go home, she thanked him and said she'd see him at the theatre, no doubt.

Of course, the phone was ringing as she walked in the door and it was John, demanding to know where she had been. She told him, and he seemed annoyed. Who was Tim? Would she like to go with him to the Blue Gardenia and have a light snack? He had a lot to talk to her about. Rose agreed although she didn't really feel like it. He told her that he was teaching Economics at Churchill School for the rest of the year which would bring him in an income. It was pleasant at the Blue Gardenia and Rose had a toasted sandwich and a glass of wine. She tried to concentrate on John's conversation for a short while and finally he said he must get back and prepare for the next day. The Churchill six-formers were writing their final exams and he needed to coach them and see that they all did well.

The days passed without a word from Tim and she began to feel that he probably had another woman in his life. It was two years since his wife died and Rose was convinced that by now he would have met some young and gorgeous looking female. Phyl phoned to thank her for the choice of furniture and asked her whether she would like to come to the next rehearsal. She then said that Tim had asked her if she thought Rose would go to the cinema with him and whether she thought he should ring her? Rose felt a surge of joy and relief. Of course, she would, she told Phyl. They discussed him and Phyl said he was something else, wasn't he? "Mind you, he had a bit of a temper and he didn't suffer fools gladly. Some people thought he was a name dropper, always talking about the important people he knew." Rose thought he moved in a circle of important people so who else would he refer to? Next day, Tim phoned and asked her to go to the after-show dinner-dance with him. She had a beautiful blue chiffon dress that was set to stun him if possible. Rose was determined to spend a lifetime with him.

Rose's set was runner up for the award. Some small item, a chair not sat in was criticised. Then came the after-show dinner dance. Tim was there to pick her up a little early and she was still stitching her petticoat hem that had suddenly come undone. He made himself at home, stretched out on the settee and chatted, telling her not to worry, as there was plenty of time. Rose, flustered, pinned and stitched furiously and Tim poured her a sherry and told her to relax. Rose couldn't, of course.

She had hoped to meet him at the door looking stunning in her lovely gown and here she was in her dressing gown with her hair all mussed! To make matters worse, the phone rang, and it was John demanding that she come up to his house and help him. That was all she needed - a long argument and John screeching down the phone. She said she was going to the after-show party and she must go, now! She gave Tim a hasty version of the problem.

They rushed out in case John turned up in his car.

It was a magical evening and dancing with him was all she could have wished. She was so proud to be there with him. To her, he was the most handsome and distinguished man in the ballroom. At midnight, they left the stragglers drinking and went out to the corner crossroads to run over to the car. There was no traffic. Right in the middle of the crossroads, Tim caught Rose up suddenly; high in the air he swung her, round and round in her floating ball gown and as she was lowered, he kissed her, really kissed her. That settled it!

Back they went to the house. The telephone was ringing while they unlocked the gate, the veranda grill and front door, a persistent ring. Rose apologised to Tim and said this was what she had to deal with. He simply said leave it to him, picked up the receiver and listened for a moment. Then he shouted, "GET OFF THE BLOODY PHONE!", banged down the receiver, and that was that! Rose couldn't believe it. She kept thinking the phone would ring again and it was silent.

Wonderful peace reigned. Tim said she had better come and sleep at his place in case, and she felt protected, cherished and more than delighted. It was a wonderful sensation of complete happiness and security. She spent the night in his queen size bed and he slept in the spare room. His children were asleep in their rooms and he settled her in his big room, kissed her and left her to sleep. In the morning, there was a bath ready for her and a dressing gown to wear and she was introduced to a pretty girl of fourteen and a good-looking boy of just eleven. They jumped on the bed and snuggled down beside her. They seemed to take her for granted and so did a large yellow Labrador called Hamlet and three cats that tried to jump up as well. "Down Hamlet!" said Tim and the dog jumped off. Tim brought in a tray with scrambled eggs and toast for all. Rose was drawn into the family as if she'd always been in it!

Of course, she had to go home afterwards, in her evening dress, and face the prospect of John pitching up or phoning to shout and howl about where she had been and who with? There was no sign of him. Tim stayed a while, had tea with her and invited her to lunch as soon as she was ready. Enoch, his cook, would be there. "Please, darling heart, join us at twelve or before." Darling heart! Never had she heard that said to anybody and he never used it for anyone else in all the years they were together. She stayed the afternoon and he came over in the evening.

They had so much to talk about to each other, entwined together and loth to be apart for a moment. Rose told him a short version of her life and was more than interested to hear all about him. He was over three years younger than she and his father had been a gynaecologist in Harley Street, London, so he was able to send his only son, Tim, to the same preparatory school that the little princes attended in London. After that, he went to Eton.

During the Second World War his father had served in North Africa as an army doctor and his mother drove army officers around London, while Tim, aged 14, was firefighting on the rooftops during his holidays. They had to climb on the roof through the maid's room windows at the top and that was where he learnt all the facts of life from the maids! Nobody knew more about how to make love than he, he claimed with a straight face. The more intimate they became, the more she believed it. He charmed her totally one night by calling her derriere a divine bottom!

He brought out albums with photos of his children and Tim's father in England, down in Kent, at Mersham. His father had a small estate with a Georgian house on it, near Lord Louis Mountbatten's large one. The family home was named Hammerwood, a mansion with tall columns in front and about forty rooms! After his father divorced, Tim lived with him in Mersham, Kent, where he had bought a farm. Tim's sister Shirley was married to an excellent lawyer who numbered Lord Mountbatten among his clients! They had a functional and lovely farm nearby, with a spectacular garden which Shirley had designed. Bobby and Shirley had four grown sons who were still living at home.

His sister Caroline was married to a miller and had three daughters and a son, and Jane, the eldest sister was widowed, and lived in a picturesque Cotswold village in a double storied Cotswold stone house, complete with a farmhouse next to it, cobbled roads and stables. She had two daughters.

Tim's three sisters had been sent away to Canada during the war. Tim spent his holidays with his mother in London, fighting fires on the roofs when the Germans dropped incendiary bombs during air raids, and nipping back through the windows into the maids' rooms when the all clear sounded. He had a great time, obviously! He said his mother had an equally great time too and there were always different 'uncles' turning up with her. Finally, his parents divorced after the war. Rose was looking forward to their holiday in Greece and then England to meet the family.

After Tim left Eton College he joined the Blues and Royals, the Household Cavalry. Although it was after the war, he did a tour of duty in Germany as a Captain, not on horseback but in armoured cars. Then he went to Northern Rhodesia and finally became a District Commissioner there, leaving at Independence when the country became Zambia. Then, after a spell in South Africa, he joined the Southern Rhodesian Government in the Department of Native Affairs.

Tim said he would soon be able to take leave from his government position as Adviser to Fanwell Mapurangwa, Executive Officer of Mashonaland Central Authority. The country was divided into eight provinces based on the tribal areas. The country had been fighting a civil war for four years and his work entailed going into the most dangerous areas alone, amongst hordes of African villagers. When he could, he wanted to take her to meet his family, particularly, his father who was still alive. He was sure his daughter Catriona wanted to go to her maternal aunt Helena's farm for the next school holiday and his son Adam would go too. They loved staying at the farm in the Midlands, near Selukwe and the Prime Minister, Sir Ian Smith's, farm.

Well, that was exciting for Rose as well as rather daunting. Would he be asking her to marry him before then? If not, how could she go with him? Where would she be expected to stay – in hotels or shacking up with him? They had passed that hurdle almost immediately in both homes in Rhodesia, but it wouldn't be the same over there! The feeling between them was so strong that they could hardly bear not to be physically touching when they were together. Rose made sure that his children were asleep or away when they were intimate at his house. She understood how fragile Catriona was, with her mother only two years dead. It was very difficult. Tim told her that he had been at work and Catriona, age twelve, had rung him in the afternoon and said, "I can't wake mummy." Apparently, resuscitation was tried, but they couldn't revive her – aged thirty-six. Poor little Jackie, thought Rose. Her heart went out to the whole family.

One evening, Tim, who was about to go home and didn't want to leave Rose, suddenly got down on his knees and put his arms around her, burying his head against her and asking "Darling heart! Will you marry me – please?" For a moment, a great joy enveloped her. He seemed overwrought, and she held his head, kissed him and stroked his hair. She suddenly couldn't say anything. She wanted to say yes so badly. This was what she had hoped for and needed. Something made her hesitate and she thought of Catriona and said the best thing she could think of. "Yes, of course I will, but not yet. I don't think the children are ready for it. Let's give them time, particularly Catriona." She couldn't understand herself! She wanted to be engaged to be married. Tim quietly agreed and went home. There was no great announcement and things continued as before.

Bert and his tough army friends called Tim "Victoria Av." for some strange reason and her Rhodesian farming brother and neighbours labelled him "Over Yonder"! He fascinated them. It was his Eton College accent and somewhat extraordinary turn of phrase when he brought his Labrador and his Purdy rifle to shoot in the bush on the farm. Mike and a large Afrikaans man called Koos sat in the truck as Tim strode ahead with Hamlet, the Labrador, flushing out birds. He suddenly turned and said "Partridge!"

"Where?" said Mike.

"Over yonder." said Tim, pointing and aiming quickly to fire. This was manna from heaven for the two in the truck, of course. They had never seen or heard anything like it before. They were rough Rhodesians, not English gentlemen. Tim aimed the famous Purdy, shot and missed. They seemed to think Tim was an effete milksop. Yet they liked him. They couldn't help it. He was popular with everyone and the women couldn't resist putting their hands on him and hanging around him.

On the other hand, Rose's brother who was incredible with a rifle, having countless trophies to show for it, aimed a two-two rifle way up in a high tree and shot the brains out of a snake without taking off the bottom jaw. He was a crack shot and served his time in the bush fighting insurgent terrorists nicknamed 'ters' He brought down one such "ter" and captured another fleeing from his compound on the farm when the boss boy (staff supervisor) came and alerted him. The war was still hotting up and the killers were shooting from the hills, killing people on the road and travellers on the main road to the border, had to stop before dark and join a convoy protected by soldiers in armed vehicles.

Outlying farms were attacked, and farmers and their families killed with no mercy shown, even once a six-month-old baby that they killed by bashing it's brains out against a wall. Tim was no milksop. He had to travel to outlying government projects each week. Once or twice he took Rose and they returned, travelling at a hundred miles an hour to dodge any bullets fired from the surrounding hills. He was unarmed and working amongst all sorts of black people in the bush and he was fearless. Soon, he stopped including Rose, it was too dangerous.

The holiday to Greece had been put off for various reasons, all to do with Catriona's availability from school. Two years passed and before they could go, Tim's father died. Rose was never to meet him after all. She and Tim had first met in June 1978 and Tim turned 48 in August. That Christmas the children were going to Knysna to their mother's parents. Tim wanted to be with Rose, but the children wanted him with them, so it was arranged that Rose would go with them as far as Johannesburg to stay with her son, see her little grandson, Dustin, and hand out Christmas presents, then go by overnight coach to Durban and spend Christmas with Sherrell and Bert and little Tamsin.

Still, she was being plagued by John's steady stream of emotional blackmail – he just wouldn't give up! What would he do at Christmas time? He was banking on having her there as he intended to give this party, he'd never had a party – surely to God she understood how lonely he was? How could she stand that stupid idiot she was attached to? Bloody bastard had nothing in his head, he probably had money - that was it! Rose had to be firm. She was going to Durban to be with Sherrell and Bert for Christmas and Tim was going to Knysna and that was that - get off the phone! With that bit of evasion, she managed to stem the tide. But he had his plans as she found out later.

The previous Christmas, Bert, Sherrell and Tamsin had spent three weeks with her before leaving the country, and

Rose recalled the performance then. They were sitting having sundowners in the lounge when John phoned and yelled at her, wanting her to come and help him. She said no, her family was there, and he slammed the phone down.

That was fine, she thought, and returned to her drink with the others. Next thing, there was knock at the door and there he was! Rose asked him to come in and he refused so she shut it again. Knock, knock... knock, knock...."Rosemary!" - knock, knock...!

Bert laughed and said "Let me deal with him. It is Christmas, after all. I'll go and ask him in for a drink."

John was out on the lawn, standing in the drizzle. After a while, in came Bert laughing. He was highly amused to think that John had grabbed him by the collar and started a fight! His collar was ripped. This was a special forces Rhodesian military man! Trained at Sandhurst, he could have dropped John in a moment! He found it funny. There was silence outside for a while.

Then, once again, knock, knock, "Rosemary, Rosemary ....!"

Rose groaned and went to the front door. No one there! She was mystified.

The call came again and the knocking. It was coming from her left, so she went through to her bedroom and there was John, standing in the flower garden and looking in. She tried to argue with him. He was invited in, why didn't he come in or go home? He went on insisting that she must come to his house and help him. Suddenly he looked past her and shouted, "JESUS BLOODY CHRIST!" - turned on his heel, crashed out of the garden and went!

Rose turned to see what on earth he had seen, and there

was Sherrell, right behind her with her eyes crossed and mouth wide open and tongue out. She had her thumbs in her ears and was waggling her fingers.

"Well! It got rid of him, didn't it? Now perhaps we can have dinner."

They laughed at John, but they tolerated him. A week later, they were off to Durban and now, a year later, Rose was arriving for Xmas in their home and Tim was motoring up alone from the Cape to be with them and take Rose away for a week, alone, all the way to the Drakensberg mountains and a lovely hotel perched up high in the clouds.

This he did, and it was a wonderful week. They motored back, arriving on the steep, winding descent down to Durban, with a huge, full, golden harvest moon rising over the sea below. It was incredibly romantic.

Tim speeded up and began sliding and slewing round the dangerous corners with a sheer drop on Rose's side. She was terrified. What was he doing? She asked him to slow down and he revved up.

Rose and Tim at Catriona's wedding

Tim in familiar stance at the Acropolis

Tim and Rose farewelling Sherrell early in the morning in Harare

Tim and Rose   Vangie and Chris

Rene and Ingrid

Rose said a silent prayer and hung on for dear life. She vowed not to motor back home with Tim and his children. She felt sick and alone again. Why? What was wrong suddenly? They survived the drive and she said nothing. After they went in the house, she was going to tell Sherrell about it privately but Sherrell got in first.

"Guess what? MARY'S here!" she said. "Mary?" queried Rose.

"Yes, MARY, and she's yelling her head off over the phone!" Rose suddenly understood – it was John! Tim had gone straight to the bedroom and shut the door. Sherrell explained that John had followed Rose to Durban by air and wanted to see her and take her out. He was down here 'on holiday'. Rose wondered how on earth she had managed to end up in this odd situation.

John had booked into a hotel and said he would wait to hear from Sherrell when Rose got there. Sherrell bent the truth, telling him Rose was still in Joburg and wouldn't arrive for another week and she'd call him.

Rose left it to Sherrell to fend him off, at which she was becoming an expert.

Rose realised she would have to scrub her idea of going home by air and travel with Tim after all. That settled it and the perpetual downpour assisted them to cut short their stay and motor back early. Catriona and Adam arrived by air and sulked in the bedroom Sherrell had given them to use. They hadn't wanted to leave Knysna and the foul weather kept them away from the beach in Durban. Rose was glad to say goodbye to her family and get them out of Bert's way as soon as possible. She and Sherrell were happy about it and she left her capable and willing daughter to break the sad news to John that mother had gone back to Rhodesia early and not come to Durban after all.

Poor Tim had a whispered row with his fractious children in the bedroom about their bad manners and it amused Sherrell and Rose and made them sorry for him, trying to cover up his children's rudeness that was embarrassing him so. Having dealt with her own teenagers, Rose knew what they were like and she pitied him. He had perfect manners and hated to see the way his children were behaving. Once they were on their way and the sun came out, the two changed their bratty behaviour and were full of chat, nonsense and fun.

Tim had a few treats in store. They stopped at the famous Rawdon's Hotel for lunch and took a detour down towards Capetown to see Matjiesfontein in its old-time glory; even the pub was timelessly preserved. They spent the night there and then they found themselves heading for Pilgrim's Rest right up in the Eastern Highlands. Tim had booked a cottage near the old South African hotel. The charm of the place even filled the children with the right spirit of adventure. Instead of criticizing and complaining they joined in the experience of a mining town of two hundred years ago. Even the waitresses in the hotel wore Boer dresses and the whole village reflected the past. The gold mine no longer pulsed with life, but the old picks and shovels and the barrows were there. Each cottage up the side of the road had a name and the furniture was period as well, with four poster beds and creaking noises as if they were haunted. It was suitably eerie. They had the mine manager's house. It was just as if they were visiting and staying with the manager and his wife; the ghosts of the past walked amongst them.

Two days later they crossed the border at Beit Bridge

and headed for the Lion and Elephant Hotel, on the way to Salisbury and home. They knew they were back in a far more dangerous country again, so Tim sped up to arrive well before sundown. They were protected with huge security lights on all night, and guards walking past the chalets at all hours as they were back amongst lurking terrorists with A.K. repeating rifles and mortars supplied by the Russians and Chinese. Most of the men brought rifles to the dining room and no longer did anyone sit out on the verandas in the evening cool, under the stars. The slightest rustle or snap of a twig alerted the soldiers keeping watch outside. Built on the banks of the dry Bubi river, there was the added danger that the killers could approach the chalets over the sand in dead silence. It was creepy and difficult to get to sleep. They were relieved when morning came, and they sped through the deserted bushveld to reach home safely. There weren't many travellers on the road in those years but still they made a point of staying at the Lion and Elephant to keep it from going bankrupt.

Later, there would be the convoy with armoured cars racing backwards and forwards, giving a measure of security. Still, there were deaths along the way, attacks on the convoy. Rose was caught once when returning alone from Johannesburg. Her small Alpha stalled and wouldn't start again, so she had to wait at the side of the road where the soldiers had pushed the car whilst they carried on with the cars behind her, to catch up with the rest of the convoy. They promised to return for her which they did. A push start and a speedy catch up and Rose became tail end Charlie. But that twenty-minute wait, alone, with the hills each side possibly crawling with killers, was an experience that still haunts Rose when she thinks back.

Tim was in another play and Rose was involved in 'The Merry Widow', singing in the chorus, so they spent a good deal of time at Reps Theatre. His children were back at school, Cat in Bulawayo and Adam happy to be on his own at their house, doing his homework or mostly watching T.V., then going to bed when Tim got home. On Tuesdays, Tim stayed at home and every weekend Rose spent most of the time at his house at the other end of the city. Faithfully, dear Enoch, Tim's wonderful Portuguese African cook, cleaner and gardener, worked miracles in the kitchen, house and garden, which covered two full acres. Everything was done meticulously for 'the master.' When Rose was there, she was 'the madam.' to be treated like royalty by this thin, frail looking little black man. Indeed, he was very lovable and loyal.

Finally, the overseas holiday with Tim came to the fore. The arrangement was that Tim and Rose would go to Greece for a week and then to England for a month or more. The children were going to Helena's farm. Rose bought her plane ticket herself and began planning her wardrobe – too much, of course, but it would be cold in England, hot in Greece, shows in London, good things to wear to meet the family and stay with them. Smaller suitcases, that was certain! What joy! This would be like a honeymoon, alone with Tim in Greece.

Then came the turn-around. Catriona had changed her mind and wanted to come too – she wanted to see Grandpa. She wanted to be with them in Greece, she had never seen Greece. She didn't want to stay any longer with Helena than two weeks and could stay at the house on her own if they didn't want her. She'd get back to school somehow – somebody could drive her to the station and she could get a taxi to the school.

The tickets had been bought. Tim was in a state, trying to figure out what to do. Catriona was feeling unloved and unwanted. Didn't Rose like her? She had hoped they wanted her too. Rose decided not to hold out for a holiday alone with Tim any longer. It was making Tim too unhappy, so she said she quite understood Catriona's needs in life and he must agree to take her. She had to put up with all the attention the girl demanded, hours of discussion about everything, all about herself and her wants.

Tim stood Catriona to a new perm and she chose the most expensive type and it was lovely. Catriona thought it was awful and she kept grumbling about it. Rose said it was lovely and was met with the fact that she would think so – it looked so old-fashioned with all those curls and waves. Rose had a cheap perm and that one was too tight and frizzy, but when she washed it, it curled up tight on her head and looked good to her. That's the way she wore it, she had to, the damage was done! Perms are not called permanent for nothing.

Off they went to Greece and she soon found that she and Catriona could get along well after all. The three of them sat in the Plaka having wine and special Greek dishes to eat and admiring the beautiful full moon. Afterwards, they went back along the road and Tim saw one street cafe selling slices of watermelon, so he ordered a plate and they sat and ate it. When he asked for the bill, it was an exorbitant price and Tim lost his temper and refused to pay. Then he turned on Rose and Catriona and told them to find their own way back to the hotel and he disappeared to have it out with the Greek proprietor. Rose recalled the name of the hotel, but not the street. Feeling a bit nervous, she hailed a taxi and fortunately, the driver took them straight there. Both went to Rose's room on the floor above Catriona's, with Tim's, a separate room next door. They had a cup of tea, wondering if he had been attacked and worrying.

There was no need to worry as he suddenly turned up in a rage and went for Rose, frightening her so much that she hid behind Cat and whispered to her to give her the door key. It was lying in the middle of the bed. The Greeks had a good way of ensuring that no guest walked off with it. They attached it to a large ball of brass! Rose thought it was a dangerous weapon and she had no intention of getting hit with it. Fear of Tom and John had made her wary and watchful. Catriona was afraid, too, but not for herself.

She wailed. "Dad! Dad! .... Mom! Mom!!" and Tim changed immediately. He put his arm around his daughter, leading her away downstairs to her room. Rose realised that Catriona must have witnessed this behaviour towards her mother.

Rose quickly locked her door, wondering what on earth she could do. She thought she must get out and try to get home – forget this holiday and get away. There was silence and she lay on her bed fully dressed, with tears trickling down her cheeks, feeling hopeless and heartsore. Why did this happen to her? What did she do to always attract the same sort of disaster? What did she do? It must be her fault.

Then she heard her name and thought Tim was at the door. She pretended to be asleep and the call came again and again. It was from the balcony and her door was open to that. She went out and couldn't see anyone until he spoke again, from the next balcony to his room.

"Darling, I'm so sorry. I won't hurt you. Can I come in, please?"

Rose couldn't help feeling overjoyed. This was Tim! This was the difference, of course. She realised she would forgive him, seventy-seven times seven, for his lapses into the 'bi-polar' – which he seemed to have. Knowing Ben, she knew the power of the tablets to calm the nerves and she was glad to hear that Tim took them too. She loved him too much not to feel sad for him. The idea of a marriage to Tim receded as she began to see the pattern of his mental disturbance.

It seemed to affect his behaviour when he was overtired or worried unduly. Then he'd begin mumbling to himself and throwing things about, usually ending in kicking his box containing the pots of vegetable along the passage floor of her house and out to the car. In a state, he'd rev his car as if he wanted to send the pistons through the bonnet, tear off to the gate and ram on the brakes and then get out to unlock it. Once opened he'd rev through, jam on anchors and get out again to lock the gate so that Rose was safe. She couldn't help feeling that it was all a bit histrionic – an act.

On one memorable occasion, he got out of the car and trod right in a large pile of dog poo, deposited at her gate by the Alsatian next door. She was delighted to hear of it the next morning as she felt it served him right! It was embarrassing to suffer his shouting and she worried about her neighbours hearing him, Rose kept out of the way as much as possible if he suddenly lost his temper in her house because she'd be grabbed by the hands and they would be twisted painfully. Sometimes, when nothing had upset the calm for a while, she'd feel secure. Then she'd broach the subject and suggest they tried to make a go of it and get married, but he'd just be evasive, and the moment would pass. Just as well, really, because it would have been disastrous. Once, he turned to her in tears and said he wasn't sane. Rose thought of Ben again and gave up. Not only the moments but also the months and years passed. She loved him, regardless.

Twenty-one years, in fact until he died, and never did a day go past that they didn't think of each other and yearn to be together. It was literally a cross they both had to bear. Well, that's love - with or without consecration; for better or for worse. It was amusing to look at her watch and see the moments go by to seven thirty in the evening, look up and see his car draw up at the gate. He was totally punctual, always. Rose remembers how they would come out of the theatre at interval and she'd go to the rest room. Coming back through the packed foyer, she'd see him up on the steps, searching for her. He'd move towards her through the crowd as if nobody else existed.

Then, after nineteen years, for the first time since she met him, Rose felt afraid – afraid of losing him. A woman appeared to have set her cap at him and she was living in his house with no sign of moving out. This was the fiancee of the now thirty-year-old Adam, who had brought her out from England with him. Adam had lost interest in her and had another woman in his sights. She stayed on, however, ostensibly looking for a job as a teacher for the deaf, and settled in the house, acting as if she was part of the family.

Rose had the instinctive feeling that she was after Tim. She said he reminded her of her father and she began running the house, cooking special meals and welcoming Rose in as though she were a visitor. It was obvious to Rose what she was scheming, particularly when she arrived at the house one Saturday morning at eleven, to find the female still in her shortie nightie, lying draped on the sofa with her legs up and apart and facing the door – reading a book. She didn't expect Rose to walk in, or Adam, for that matter. He wasn't even there. Rose knew she was waiting for Tim to come through that way, not her! She was thirty-six and attractive and the full-on view of her fanny in panties was inviting to any red-blooded male, to say the least! The fact that she leaped up immediately and went to her room to dress made Rose realise what she was up to and she'd been caught out. Rose experienced a surge of anger and dislike, also dismay; she, at sixty-eight years old, felt threatened.

After a nearly twenty years relationship between Tim and Rose, a predatory female was literally living there as if she owned him! If this was jealousy, then she was jealous. Rose wasn't fooled, and she wasn't going to let her make her move. Tim wasn't aware of it, Rose felt, but any man could be tempted. Rose had a word with Adam about it, saying she'd be glad if he asked the woman to leave the house and she told him her fears. Unfortunately, there were repercussions! Adam told Tim. The next evening Tim suddenly swerved into her drive and slammed on the brakes. There he stood, in the middle of the front lawn. As she went out towards him, he shouted:

"You bloody, fucking, jealous BITCH!!

She was shocked. She had no idea what to answer. He leapt into his car again, revved madly backwards and out, speeding up the road and away!

Rose was at a total loss until she recalled asking Adam

to get his ex-fiancee out of the house and on her way back to England or somewhere other than their house.

"Jealous"? Probably!

"Effing?" She could wear that!

"Bloody?" Well! It made a good emphatic adjective. It meant that Tim thought she was suspecting him of doing something he wasn't, perhaps.

"Bitch?" Hmmm - Tim had obviously realised that the female of the species 'hath a fury' exceeding that in hell. Suddenly, as Rose meditated, she heard a car. Tim was back! Why, she wondered? She switched the outside light on again and went outside. He had the headlights on and was standing in front of them. Rose asked what was wrong and he stood pointing at the car. His shoulders were heaving, and Rose saw he was sobbing. Rose shaded her eyes and looked at the car. One headlight was bashed in and the whole radiator and front were staved in and crumpled. Water was dripping out underneath. She felt horrified. He had been in an accident. She rushed to him and gathered him in her arms.

"Oh! Darling! What happened to you? Are you alright?" There was a predictable reply. "Look what you did!" said Tim, bitterly, "Look what you made me do!" Rose let that ride. "What happened?" Water was still dripping from under the car and it seemed that the radiator was leaking. "Come in and have some tea with lots of sugar, I think you need it." He let her lead him in and sit him on the settee while she boiled the kettle and made tea. He had sped into the city area, failed to give way to the right at the main street and ploughed into a new Lamborghini!

Rose was suitably impressed. Trust Tim, in the throes of angry hatred against her, to choose a new Lamborghini to throw out of the cot! Everything of the best for Tim. If you are going to prove a point, choose a Lamborghini to destroy! Rose took pains to convince him that she had not for a moment doubted his love for her. It was all about Adam's rejected female friend settling in with designs on him. His artistically detailed description of her jealousy was diplomatically avoided and taken as the angry cries of love! He had to turn on her for even imagining he had designs on another woman.

Tim reminded her and her family of Don Quixote, striding out to tilt at windmills. Rose couldn't help likening herself to his little rotund Sancho Panza, trotting along behind the master. She has vivid memories of the wonderful holidays they took together every two years overseas – to England, Greece, France, Italy and America. They timed their holidays in England to include invitations received by Tim to functions like the centenary dinner at the Savoy of the exclusive 1800 club of which he was a member. On this occasion, he took Rose up to London having booked into a hotel near the Thames and the Savoy. There, she was able to dress in her long black evening dress and pearls and they walked along the Embankment to the Savoy. Margaret Thatcher was the Guest of Honour. Rose found herself in a group waiting to be presented to her when she arrived.

Lady Thatcher asked her where she came from and when Rose said Rhodesia she asked how things were there now. Rose said, "Just as we expected!"

Margaret Thatcher had the grace to look disconcerted, but she recovered and said "Oh, yes, I suppose it is.", and moved on. Many in Rhodesia had had great hopes that Margaret Thatcher would solve the political differences between Rhodesia and

Britain, but no such luck. Rhodesia went off the map! The dinner was excellent, of course, and the various glasses were filled with the best wines. At their table of eight or ten were empty seats where the women seemed to be alone, but the men kept joining them at different times and Rose found that parliament was sitting, and these were all M.Ps., except Tim, of course.

It was a delightful evening. Rose realised that she enjoyed the occasion but could not possibly countenance a life of that sort. She found it dull, trying to make small talk with the wives of strangers when they simply had nothing in common except an inborn snobbery and perpetual one upmanship which bored her to tears. That made her eat too much rich food and drink a copious amount of expensive liquor. She noticed that Tim, too, only enjoyed it in small doses and preferred his life in a colonial atmosphere. One of his uncles was Lord Grantchester, but it appeared that Tim had no desire to get in contact with him even though he, too, was in line for the title. Another uncle was Sir Charles Taylor, an M.P. That one they did visit in his flat in London, after Tim had lunched with him at Boodles and Rose spent the time shopping in Fortnum's and Harrods.

They met for tea in another big London hotel owned by Sir Charles who immediately ordered a bottle of port which the men drank as Rose finished her tea and cake and then joined them in a glass. Then they walked along a few blocks and up in the lift to a house sized flat, thickly carpeted throughout, and she met his diminutive wife, draped on the settee in a Chinese house-gown. This was Lady Taylor, tiny and fragile with a pile of fluffy golden hair, still lovely at the age of seventy-five.

Charles settled on the settee close to her after taking a

colossal bottle of best champagne out of the cabinet and opening it. The champers shot out all over the carpet and they ignored it as the glasses were filled. They knew how to celebrate seeing Tim again and meeting Rose. They drank and talked until Charles wanted to get up and fetch a book for Rose. He had crossed his legs and he tried unsuccessfully to unwind as he stood up. Connie said dryly "Are you sure you can get up, dear!" She had cancer, but no one knew it until she died suddenly, a month after they saw her. A week after that, Charles, too, died. It seemed that he couldn't live without her. There were five uncles, all of them wealthy and distinguished.

Rose and Tim were invited more than once to Lausanne in Switzerland for her to meet Uncle John, who stood them to a five-star hotel on the lake for five days the first time. He and his Canadian wife Peggy were both millionaires. Rose did her best to wear clothes that didn't look too cheap and let the side down for Tim. Peggy and all her friends wore such elegant, expensive clothes and jewels, so Rose got out her real pearls and gold bracelet Auntie Betty had given her. Arriving in Lausanne by train, they were collected by old Uncle John in his large black Jaguar and taken way up the steep city hill to Puilly where the car rolled into a double garage with automatic doors and alarms.

Inside was a lift to the upper floor where it seemed they owned a full house, not a flat. Two large lounges led to a wide veranda overlooking the lake and mountains. Peggy and John lived up on the hill but every morning, they motored down at seven for a swim in the warm indoor pool at the biggest and best hotel on the lake front which was next door to the one Rose and Tim were in. They met on the veranda at eleven, for drinks and lunch and Tim offered to stand them to Bucks fizz which they all enjoyed. Uncle John refused to let Tim pay for it, saying it was already on their tab. Their five days were lived in total luxury. There again, Rose knew in her heart that it was not the sort of life she would enjoy, and she felt no envy.

A group of their friends were invited to lunch at the same hotel, on the shaded piazza beside the colossal semi-indoor heated pool where John and Peggy bathed. The women were all dressed casually but expensively, still dripping with jewels. Rose was glad she had her bracelet and necklace on, and her mother's engagement ring which sported a solitaire one carat diamond.

The view was of the lake beyond the balcony near the esplanade, all along which the Swiss had planted palm trees.

The women concentrated on Rose because she was from Rhodesia and they wanted to establish exactly where she fitted into the scene and on what level of opulence. It was judgement day indeed. Living in sin didn't seem to lower her in their estimation, apparently, as probably they all had. Also, adultery seemed to leave them unperturbed. Rose had to admit to having no titled ancestors to her knowledge, but she did have wealthy Auntie Betty to talk about and her Q.C. husband, Uncle Fred. She seemed to have impressed them with her anecdote of having shot a rapist.

While talking flat out, she consumed course after course of delicious food, wiping her mouth with her napkin until she feared that all her lipstick was gone. So, once they were satisfied with their cross-questioning and chatted to each other, she took the opportunity to open her compact and apply some fresh colour. She was caught in the act by Peggy.

"That's a lovely colour, Rosemary, what is it?" Rose didn't know so she looked at the back of the tube, but it had been obliterated by age. Her lipstick was in a well-travelled and very scruffy plastic tube and she tried to put it away before they got a good look at it. However, Peggy was not going to give in so quickly. "Give it to me. Let me compare it with mine." Rose passed it to her and the more she looked at it the scruffier it looked!

Out came various tubes for comparison, all of them in gold or black tubes with Dior or Givenchy inscribed thereon and Rose blushed as they decided on the closest shade. From the way they looked at each other, Rose was sure they all had found the chink in her armour.

Everything was perfect, the food, the drinks, the hotel but Rose couldn't wait to be away once more. She felt overloaded with luxury and it was positively boring and fattening and the women appeared snobbish and self-satisfied.

Brought up on a dusty mine in the middle of Africa had made her a gypsy child, running barefoot and wild. The silence of the bush veld with the call of doves and the rustle of the wind in the trees appealed to something in her soul. To get on a horse and ride out into the country for mile after mile without seeing or hearing another human being was her idea of pleasure on the farm where she spent most school holidays unlike those who spent theirs at finishing schools in Switzerland. Nevertheless, to each, their own!

Tim was at home with any company he was in. He seemed to fit in with any plan Rose made or any holiday they shared. When they went to New York, the temperature was five degrees below zero and Rose was freezing. She was enveloped in several woollies, her long leather coat and boots, a woolen scarf, cap and fluffy fur ear muffs that looked most attractive to her. Tim said she looked like a bag lady!

He took her with him into the United Nations building where he had an appointment to see the Finnish V.I.P who was to preside over the handing back by South Africa of South West Africa. Tim, having taken two weeks leave to travel round South West Africa, getting to know the lie of the land, intended to try to accompany and assist Martti. Unfortunately, he took Rose up to the 36th floor with him and introduced her to the man without saying why she was with him.

A good looking, suave man eyed her up and down saying "Call me Martti" and politely led her to an enormous leather settee at the side of his impressive executive desk. She hadn't heard his surname when Tim introduced him, so Martti it was. He kept glancing at her speculatively, wondering what she was doing there.

Tim sat opposite him talking across the massive desk. Then Martti directed him past Rose where a large map of Namibia hung on the wall. Tim had a pointer and was talking to him about the various towns and the terrain, also about the South African presence there. Martti kept looking at Rose with a pensive stare and it struck her that he was still trying to work out why she was there? Trust Tim to leave him guessing. It amused him somehow. This was a sensitive subject politically, the crumbling edifice of white rule in Africa, and this was a diplomatic hot potato. There was a civil war raging in the future Namibia, but South Africa was handing over government because it's one-hundred-year mandate had expired.

South Africans had their own terrorist war to deal with against the Communist 'Freedom fighters', as they called themselves. By then, at least two thousand white farmers and their families had been slaughtered on remote farms. When the conversation included the apartheid government, Rose added her little bit, although she didn't really know what she was talking about. "I suppose this is all the fault of filthy, racist South Africa!"

He turned towards her and gave her a long, considering look: He raised an eyebrow and smiled. "Yes, I suppose it is", he said, and Rose felt rather pleased with herself. Tim ribbed her afterwards about it, calling Martti her boyfriend and making out that he didn't get the job because Ahtisaari couldn't take his eyes off her and didn't listen to a thing he said. Tim always did this, it amused him.

Back in Rhodesia, now Rhodesia-Zimbabwe, the new president, Bishop Muzorewa, the "Little Bish." as he was affectionately called by all, had been elected. However, in some shady deal at Westminster presumably, this election was nullified and a new one held. To oversee this "free and fair" referendum in Rhodesia, Sir Jonas Glynn-Jones, the retired Governor General of the Federation of Northern and Southern Rhodesia and Nyasaland, was sent out by the British Government from Goudhurst, England, where he had retired. He brought out all the retired District Commissioners who had returned to England when Northern Rhodesia became Zambia and the Federation broke up. Tim was one of these, but he had left England and returned to Africa. They were all his closest friends. Tim's wife's aunt was Lady Glynn-Jones, so Tim was related by marriage to Jonas.

Jonas had included six of Tim's best friends as overseers and they were all occupying rooms in the Monomatapa Hotel where Sir Glynn had a private suite. Later they would be scattered in the various areas of the country where there were polling stations. Tim and Rose had them over for lunch at his house and Rose got to know them.

Their stories about Northern Rhodesia were hilarious, particularly about a forester who had turned up and pounced on one of the wives there, and it had been 'to the woods, to the woods away'. They disappeared into the forest and didn't come back for a week. Her husband divorced her, and she married her woodsman. They were living in England near Exeter and Tim got their address so that he and Rose could visit them when next on holiday.

Then they mentioned one of Tim's closest friends, Mike, a D. C. stationed far across the country. He was still a bachelor and there were no eligible young women anywhere in his district. Tim had just married Jackie and Mike was bemoaning the fact that he was stuck there with no one. As luck would have it, two young, female, American tourists arrived who wanted to see the country and Tim phoned Mike saying he was sending them there.

Mike said he'd marry the first one he saw, and he did! Her name was Irene and when they came to stay with Tim, and Rose met her, she told Rose that her name was pronounced Eerayne! Mike was now high up in the United Nations, so Eerayne had married well, apart from which, he was one of the handsomest men Rose had ever seen and Eerayne was one of the plainest.

Jonas remained in Salisbury and Tim took him under his wing, inviting him to the house for meals and driving him to Marandellas where his only son had gone to boarding school at Peterhouse. Sadly, this boy had been kicked on the shin playing rugby and infection set in. He died age fourteen, and was buried at Zomba, in Malawi, where Sir Jonas Glyn-Jones was Governor General. Rose, of course, was included in Tim's activities, and she got to know Jonas very well. All the wives were at home in England, so she was the only woman there amongst them.

Jonas loved to dance, and he invited her to accompany Tim to the special dinners at Meikles Hotel where there was a large, sprung dance floor and a famous old Jewish pianist, Isadore Fisher, playing dance music every Saturday night.

While the others enjoyed their reminiscences and jokes about their years together in what was then Northern Rhodesia, Jonas danced with Rose. Neither of them had been there with the others in Northern Rhodesia. Jonas had moved Nyasaland as Governor General of the three territories and Rose was battling with husbands and divorces in Southern Rhodesia. Rose was delighted to be led around the floor in old fashioned waltzes and foxtrots. Jonas was short and slight, and she had a good close view of his face near hers. He was old and puffed a little as he whisked her about more energetically than she expected.

She enjoyed it immensely. Dancing like that is always thrilling. She wondered where he got the stamina, aged nearly eighty, until she was told of his fame on the sports fields in the past in Rhodesia. After the music stopped, he'd thank her with great courtesy and lead her back to her chair. One thing that fascinated her about Jonas was his salt and pepper eyebrows, thick and long, jutting straight out in front of his eyes like canopies. Some of the hairs curled and took off in interesting directions. She wondered why he didn't have them trimmed. His intensity and the bright, penetrating look in his twinkling eyes, from under those brows, stayed in her mind. She grew very fond of him and he seemed fond of her too. He certainly liked her company. Tim, of course, didn't fail to call him her boyfriend and say that he was besotted with her. It amused him to sit back and not dance himself.

The next time they went on holiday to England was for Catriona's wedding to her fiancé, Mike. This was to be a lavish affair with a marquee on the lawn at Shirley and Bobby's farm and about a hundred and fifty guests. Catriona said that as she was Tim's only daughter, he could afford to pay for a Rolls Royce to take her to the church at Mersham and she wanted to leave the reception in a balloon. She played up and demanded that Rose and Tim didn't stay at the farm as she didn't want any arguments there, so they went into a B&B in Folkstone and motored over every morning.

Rose offered to help, and Shirley asked her to iron Jackie's wedding dress which Catriona was going to wear. It was put in the guest cottage on the farm and Rose spent her time there ironing while all of them had tea together in the house. She also unraveled threads of the pieces cut off to narrow the dress and darned the patches of mould on it. No one came over and sat with her and she realised that Catriona had planned this. She still hated the idea of Rose being in her father's life. Tim was also aware of this although he didn't say anything. He arranged a short stay in Amsterdam the week of the Van Gogh centenary for the two of them after the wedding.

It was a package of six days with the choice of several five-star hotels, tickets to all the galleries and special dinners. Rose chose the Hotel Krasnapolski just by name alone.

Pictures showed the room where they would have breakfast as a colossal, glass domed hall with palm trees stretching up about three stories to touch the glass and iron patterned roof. This was a fabulous old hotel and the passages on the upper floors were wide enough to drive a car along. They were carpeted in thick, crimson cut-pile, and had cream and crimson, full length, Regency striped curtains for the windows on one side, and the rooms were on the other. This was one hotel that Rose really loved staying in. Against the wall, between each window there was a fragile, gilt, Louis Quinze chair. Although they had to book a room well in advance, there was seldom a sign of anyone else occupying the hotel, except at breakfast time in the fabulous centre hall where the food was placed on an enormous, long table down the centre. The bedrooms were large, with a room-size, curved, glass-fronted shower and the same Regency striped curtains and Louis Quinze chairs.

Huge bowls of fruit salad and piled dishes of fruit were placed all down the middle of the breakfast room, and at one end, was a pyramid of boiled eggs piled nearly a metre high. This fascinated Rose who imagined someone taking one out of the bottom and the whole lot taking off over the tiled floor.

Apart from all the bowls of cereal, there was every type of cold meat and cheese, bread, scones, croissants and toast. There was even a menu for ordering eggs cooked in any manner wanted, including eggs benedict and shirred eggs. Tea, coffee, cocoa, Ovaltine, and jugs of orange juice were served but the rest was self-service.

Loving hard boiled eggs, Rose decided to stock up with four eggs and some buttered rolls for their lunch in a park, perhaps, as they were going on foot to see the sights of Amsterdam.

It was a rather rash whim of the moment! She took her large handbag along to the table and slipped the eggs in. They were cold. The rolls, she collected when she next went up, buttered them and made Tim put them in his brief case, wrapped in some of the large paper napkins. A twist of salt and pepper in another napkin went in her bag too. Tim went along with everything Rose did as it always seemed to amuse him especially when there were somewhat disastrous consequences. In all the capitals of the world, Rose refused to go to any public toilet. She had devised a plan. Tim was to wait outside, window shop in the street somewhere as she casually walked into the Ritz or some other five-star hotel, looked about casually for a likely passage or lounge which would have a discrete sign and find the ladies room.

Afterwards she'd return and stand in the foyer, look at her watch, sit for a moment on an available chair, perhaps, then get up and look outside from the top steps. Seeing Tim, she'd greet him, and they would go off together as if it had been an arranged meeting place.

The egg lifting idea was a failure. It was an object lesson for those who decided to take up a life of petty pilfering! Before they found a place for a picnic lunch, Rose put her hand into her rather special leather handbag to find a lipstick and felt a strange sticky mess in the bottom. The eggs were not hard boiled! They had cracked and oozed over everything. Back to the hotel they went to clean up the mess.

For their special dinner, Tim chose a famous restaurant called "The Four Flies". That was a gastronomic experience, and every day they went to see Vincent van Gogh's original paintings and drawings in galleries in Amsterdam, collected from around the world for the occasion. Rose was delighted to be able to scrutinise his brushstrokes closely and see the original pen and ink drawings he transferred to canvas with a brush or palette knife. She went so close to examine the strokes on one occasion that a police guard with a gun ambled over and told her to move back.

It was a wonderful week. One event was memorable for a totally different reason. On the last morning, it happened. Rose woke and went to shower and dress for breakfast. Tim went in after her and spent an age in it. He hadn't spoken to her. She was dressed and ready to go by the time he burst out of the steamy clouds, stark naked and towelling himself dry. Without a word to her, he began throwing things about and shouting and she realised he was in a rage. She went to the door, opened it and waited, wondering as always what on earth had set him off, dodging the odd brush and other flying object. A gilt chair took off, but not in her direction.

Suddenly, jumping around like a demented pink spider on a hot stove, he ran out of the door, pushing past her, stark naked and all things dangling, picked up a little gilt chair and hurled it down the passage.

Rose was so wild with him, she was tempted to take the key and shut the door then head for the lift and go to breakfast, leaving him naked outside. At that moment, she just wished some people would come out of the lift and see the extraordinary sight. It was so hilarious she wanted to share it and she couldn't even dare to laugh. Then she suddenly felt sorry for him, and leaving him to get over it, went down to breakfast.

Half an hour later, there he was, dressed for the day, she was glad to see. Not a word was said about it and the day continued fair and warm, as if nothing had happened – but the memory of that colossal, pink, naked daddy-long-legs leaping around in a rage, dangling all before him, was so comical it was never to be forgotten.

Rose's diaries are full of unpleasant fallouts, delightful reconciliations and wonderful holidays all through the twenty-one years she and Tim were to be allowed before death took him from her. One year, the holiday overseas was over two months long. Over to London, Lilyvale Farm in Kent with Shirley and Bobby, using the Colt, their visitor's lodge, as a home from home, coming and going as they wanted and Rose was fascinated by Tim's relations. All of them were larger than life with equally extraordinary and extrovert adult children. Two of Shirley's sons followed in father's footsteps, Henry and Ben, as brilliant lawyers, Sam was a teacher and archaeologist and Seamus went to America where he made a fortune on the Stock Exchange. Once, Sam suddenly gave Rose a Roman farthing which she treasured. He was such a silent, reserved young man who had hardly spoken to her that it came as a surprise. Rose came to love all four of them.

Caroline had three girls and one son, Belinda, Araminta, Emily and Piers. All of them were delightful. Piers owned a picturesque mill in the country and ground special flours. His little children ran around naked in the wild garden and near the pond and stream leading to the water wheel that turned the machinery of the mill. It was worth a Constable painting and delighted Rose to visit there. Rose grew very fond of all of them over the years of being a de facto wife, 'de facto' much to her regret but it was impossible to risk living in the same house with Tim, chained to him by means of a 'de jure' marriage. She felt sad about it sometimes and wondered why she couldn't bear to part from him.

On another holiday, when Catriona had moved to England and was living with Mike before she married him, she phoned Rose and asked her if she should apply for a job as cook and Mike, the butler, for an American multimillionaire in Florida. Rose encouraged her; said go for it! Much to their delight, they both got the jobs and were flown first class to Palm Beach.

Rose and Tim flew to Miami from Heathrow that year, on Rose's birthday, 28th December and were met by Catriona and Mike who were working on Tarpon Island, which the Jewish millionaire owned, a Japanese bridge span off Palm Beach, Florida. Having booked a room in a hotel along Palm Beach front they spent the days on Tarpon Island, as the absent millionaire, Ray, was spending his non-Christian festive season in Aspen, Colorado.

The four of them spent five days in Orlando, at a special man-made lake surrounded by instant, fully grown palm trees, in a 'Spanish' hotel, one of several take-your-pick styles around the lake, eating paella and Spanish omelets to the thrumming of Spanish guitars. Created by Walt Disney for visitors to Disneyland, they caught the free transport provided every hour and were whisked to Disneyland. Everything technical amazed them with all the remote-controlled animals and half size cowboys and Indians warring, shooting guns and arrows, burning cabins and killing the occupants. They sailed by the scenes on a created river, where a colossal, fabricated, remote controlled elephant stood in the water, round a bend in the jungle area, raised its trunk, trumpeting and squirting water at them. The electrical wiring underground stretched over square kilometres.

It was impressive and the colossal golf ball, high on metal stilts, called Epcott Centre, took her breath away. They waited hours in a cue to go inside and be strapped in their seats which tilted sideways, where, in inky blackness, they seemed to be whisked through space, weaving between buildings and then past planets in space. They wore special glasses. Never did she think she was going to be so carried away in space by the sheer art and ingenuity of anything three dimensional. No wonder they provided sick bags! Even the seats swung with the action.

Finally, they sailed to the Bahamas, before travelling by Greyhound Bus to New York, stopping in Charleston and Washington on the way.

The ship to the Bahamas was called the Love Boat. They felt it was as common as dirt. As they crossed the gang plank, a ticket was handed to them and they passed a huge red heart on a stand with a sign 'The Love Boat' painted on it and there they had a picture taken and a ghastly photo was handed to them, with Tim wearing his 'Patience on a monument' expression. The ship was loaded with fat females wearing fat diamonds and rubies, who were on their way to gamble. The small island they docked at turned out to be nothing but a gambling den. The land seemed to be only a few feet above the sea, just a sandy little island with a few palm trees and a row of taxis with black drivers pushing in front of each other for passengers. Tim and Rose were whisked away at speed about seven kilometres through the sparse scrub on a bumpy, pot holed, sand road and the taxi stopped where there were a couple of small hotels advertising that they had casinos.

As neither of them were interested in gambling, they wandered about trying to find something worth seeing but it was a futile effort. They bought a few lurid, unreal postcards and could hardly wait for a taxi to drive them back for the return voyage. The return voyage was an experience was worth the whole trip for Rose.

The sea was rough, and the old tub was listing heavily. The passengers were carrying sick bags that were, revoltingly, made of clear plastic – with fat women hanging about on the stairways, looking green and filling them. Tim's face of thunder sustained Rose. She, at least, had nursed and could bear the gruesome sight. Tim was getting into a fouler mood by the moment. They went out onto the top deck where it was cold and drizzling. Later, as Rose was freezing, they braved the gangways and corridors to reach the dining room for dinner. Tim was losing his temper again as they tried to eat, with people making retching noises and plates sliding away as the ship heeled over. He finally got up from the table in a rage, ordering Rose to come out, they couldn't eat food like this. Rose regretfully followed him. As he stalked out through the door, there were two occupied one-armed bandits one side and portholes on the other, with benches below them and long curtains half enclosing them for some reason or other.

A woman was sitting at one machine and pulling the arm down, over and over, without any luck. Tim watched and when she moved away, he tried to take her place, but another man walked in and slid quickly onto the stool in front of him. Infuriated, Tim took a step back and moved to sit down on the window seat and wait. It was then Rose looked down at the seat. She was horrified.

"TIM! DON'T SIT DOWN!" The seat was covered with a pile of regurgitated dinner!

"WHY?" said he loudly. Scowling, Tim descended further. He wasn't going to be told what to do! Rose could hardly speak. By then, she was overcome by the thought of what would happen if he did sit in it. She was speechless with laughter.

She just pointed at it and tried to keep a straight face. Fortunately, Tim looked behind him and shot up. Just then, the man at the slot machine pulled the lever and won the jackpot! That was the last straw. Off he went, speechless with fury. It took a little while for Tim to see the funny side of that event. They spent the rest of the journey on the top deck, huddled against the steel front of the bridge, in the cold drizzle, peering out of the mist for the sight of land. Rose felt as if she were on the Titanic, but Tim simmered down. The cold drizzle put out his fire and he was able to greet his daughter and Mike when they docked and say they had a great time. Having stood the two of them to the day trip on the 'Love Boat', they looked so expectant that Rose and Tim had to enthuse.

The billionaire had taken over the whole of the Hilton Hotel for a week for his guests up in Aspen when he celebrated his 65th birthday. Rose and Tim watched a DVD on his huge cinema screen in his forty-seat cinema, sitting in luxury leather armchairs to watch. There was a stunt plane in the sky, doing loop-the-loops and sky writing in colour 'Happy 65th Birthday, Ray.

To fetch special salads for lunch, Catriona drove them in one of his limousines over the Japanese bridge, using a remote control to open the massive gates to the mainland. The bridge was only about twenty feet long. The road they turned onto, had a high hedge right opposite them and behind it was the golf club and links. A large sign faced the bridge:

'No Blacks and No Jews allowed,'

Rose was fascinated! This was America – the biggest nation in the world, imposing sanctions against Rhodesia for denying Black Rule!

All the taps in the bathrooms of the mansion were brass and in the colossal double length kitchen there was a central unit over which hung about twenty huge copper pots and pans. There were brass knobs on the doors and ten en suite bedrooms, several living rooms and dining rooms and brass catches and handles on the windows and brass taps. Two years later, when they left America and returned to England, Mike said he never wanted to see another piece of brass or copper in his lifetime. It was his job as butler, to clean all the copper and brass weekly.

Their employer stood Catriona and Mike, Tim and Rose to a special dinner theatre at the golf club he himself was barred from. Rose dressed in her most expensive black chiffon and silk, ankle length evening dress, found that her black pantyhose had a ladder, so off she rushed to find a shop, down a facsimile of Madison Ave. or Bond Street and joy of joys, there it was – an exclusive boutique for pantyhose!

Rose should have known – this was, after all, Palm Beach, Florida. She wandered in the darkened interior feeling the soft, cushioned carpet beneath her somewhat scruffy sandals. Peering about for some sign of life under the soft, hidden lighting, she saw a central, circular affair in the middle of the room with pantyhose hanging, rather quaintly, all round it.

Being late, she started riffling around it to find the ones she wanted. These were all lace topped or floral or stripy or frilly etc. At last! An ordinary pair! Rose unhitched them and turned around rapidly to find a little woman behind her looking at her as if she had seen a dog turd on the carpet. Undeterred and in a rush to get dressed, Rose said "How much is this pair?"

"Fifty-four, modom." The woman looked down her long nose. Rose couldn't understand American.

"Is that five dollars forty cents?"

"No, modom, that's Fifty-four DOLLARS!" She stared at Rose in disdain.

Rose thrust the gold-plated article into the woman's hands and went. She cobbled the hole in hers and it didn't show anyway. The dress covered it.

The evening out was fantastic. For a start, there was a table laden with help yourself starters. In the centre, was a huge glass bowl in ice, piled up with Beluga caviar. Rose couldn't believe her eyes. There was no limit to the number of helpings you could have. Two or three times, Rose went and refilled her side plate with scoops of caviar. Finally, realising she would be unwell if she consumed any more she ate a dainty amount of the rest of the dinner and enjoyed the play afterwards, feeling she was in the American equivalent of high society. The surfeit of caviar remained a precious memory.

When they decided to travel all the way up to New York in the Greyhound bus, everyone tried to put them off, saying they should fly, but Rose wanted to see the countryside. Reaching Charleston, they noticed that the outskirts housed the black people and as they reached the centre, the properties became the picturesque wooden houses, all two and three storied, with verandas decorated with fretwork, all centuries old and charming. Only a year or two later, most of these lovely houses were reduced to matchsticks in a violent cyclone onslaught. Most of old Charleston was destroyed. They were warned not to wander into the black areas because it was dangerous.

In Washington, Tim went to see some person at a government department and Rose wandered around on her own for the morning. Passing a park, she saw a young man dressed in army fatigues doing press ups, leaning on the low railing. He had his toothbrush tucked in his cap band and Rose stopped to speak to him, asking why he was there. It didn't take long for her to realise that he was no longer sane. Later, she was told he had fought in Viet Nam and there were many like him in America.

In New York it was five degrees below zero, but they read in the news that it was forty-five below in North Carolina and some poor old codger had driven himself to a supermarket, parked far away from the entrance, got out of the car and froze to death before he reached the door! That seemed to be impossible. It taught Rose something about sub-zero temperatures that she didn't know. New York seemed quite warm after that. Minus five, so Rose bought some fluffy blonde earmuffs and mittens which helped her cope. She wore a woolly scarf, several jerseys and a coat. Tim said she looked like a bag lady! Funny man! And thus, she met Martti Ahtisaari, way up in the United Nations building. They took a ferry over to see the Statue of Liberty and went up in the lift to the head where the pointed headdress was. It was so colossal that it was possible to walk along inside the points, but they refrained. Rose was afraid one might drop off when they were inside, and they were a long way from the ground. The next evening, they took the lift, up the fifty or more stories to the top floor of the Empire State Building. Out there, on a platform, you could walk round and see the whole of New York through plate glass windows. It was like being in an aeroplane. For as far as the eye could see, the city lights were glinting and the main thoroughfares with three or four lanes of traffic approaching and departing looked like sparkling diamond and ruby bracelets. It was a wonderful sight.

Over the road from their hotel, was Central Park and they walked through for some distance. It was late winter, so all the trees were bare and there were still little drifts of snow here and there. Rose got down and made a miniature snowman, scraping up enough snow to build it about eight inches high. Tim took a photo of her finishing it and told her that it looked more like a penis! They didn't stay too late because the New Yorkers had warned them that many murders had been done in the park at night.

Next morning, Rose went for a walk up the street and turned into a shop next to the hotel to try on a beautiful full-length sable coat she saw in the window, reduced to five thousand dollars. She was alone as Tim had gone to the bank and the sales women almost persuaded her to buy it. She looked at herself in the long mirror and felt very glamorous in it. Fortunately, she decided to wait until Tim came back and she could put it on and ask his opinion. Tim made no bones about it. "Darling, you are too short to wear a coat like that. It makes you look fat." That saved Rose five thousand dollars and when she really looked hard at the mirror image, she realised that he was right. All that beautiful, thick, shiny brown fur made too much bulk in the middle, around her ample bottom. So that was that.

New York seemed very safe to them, yet after they returned from seeing the Statue of Liberty, they boarded a train which travelled up Fifth Avenue to Forty-Eighth street where their hotel was, and they got off. Shortly after that, a gunman opened fire on the passengers and killed a couple of them. Rose was staggered at their lucky escape and learned a bit about the true nature of New York.

They flew back to England and went over from there to Holland to meet and be stood to a dinner party by her dear friend Ben. It was a farewell visit because he was living on borrowed time. His leukemia was killing him, and he had been given just months to live. As they talked to the others outside the restaurant before they left him and returned to their hotel, he gripped her shoulder in a special farewell. She turned and kissed him goodbye. She was very sad.

From there, they went to France, to Paris and a hotel close to the Arc de Triomphe, near where Tim's friend Rene had an apartment. They were going to meet his young wife, Ingrid and perhaps one or more of their three boys. None of the boys were there, as it turned out, so they were invited to spend a few days in the apartment in the boy's rooms. Ingrid was a beautiful woman, German and much younger than Rene. Born after the war, Rene nevertheless ribbed her about Hitler and called her Der Kaiser mutter, swearing blind that she had him right under her thumb and he dared not disobey! She and her brother in Germany owned and managed a company that manufactured sound barriers for highways and railways. Rene had been with

Tim in Malawi as he spent a year there as a Consultant to the U.N. He seemed to own containers and shipped the contents around the world.

They were both well heeled. The apartment was double storied and had three bedrooms and a large lounge, dining room, kitchen area, offices and private lift plus other rooms upstairs and a double garage. All this was a couple of blocks from the Arc de Triomphe and must have been extremely valuable. Just down the Rue Rennequin and a short walk away was a complete street of markets and pavement cafes with gay umbrellas and flower pots full of bright colours. This was the Paris of the Impressionists and right on the Beckers' doorstep.

They had a formidable hound called Casimir, a wirehaired terrier that spent his mornings at the market. He was a typical French dog-about-town and simply went to the front door and looked up at the handle; whereupon Ingrid or Rene would open it and he would bound down the stairs and out through the iron grille to the street. Then he was off to the marketplace to visit the butcher and the baker and spend some hours greeting other French dogs in the way French dogs do, sunning himself on the pavements and charming the people at the tables for soupcons of tasty pastries.

He was a beautiful dog, fluffy and white with big round patches of black or ginger and a long, long nose. He charmed everybody, even the butcher. When he was ready, he'd trot back to the apartments, through the grill, up the stairs and scratch at the door. Whatever calls of nature he had were done in the gardens. He didn't require a sandbox. He was, indeed, the perfect pet and a much loved one.

Ingrid went to market on the third day and came back loaded

with good things saying she was making a surprise dinner for Tim! An hour later, we were called to the table and 'Voila! Oooh, la, la!' there was a large, steaming bowl of ratatouille! Nobody had put Ingrid wise to the fact that Tim didn't eat the famous, exotic roast vegetable dish full of capsicum and olive oil. Rose watched as Ingrid filled a plate for him and served him first, his special treat! Watching him eat it, was a special treat for Rose. To cap it, having swallowed it all with murmurs of appreciation, he was urged to have a second helping. Rose watched as the second pile went down. She, of course, thoroughly enjoyed her dinner. Tim rose to the occasion with a forced show of pleasure. It was extremely funny, however it also showed how Tim could be the perfect guest. Rene took them to Chantilly one day and treated Rose to a special ice cream Chantilly, a long glass of ice cream and whipped cream eaten sitting on the grass under willow trees near the water's edge. Ingrid was working and couldn't come.

They went into the Bois de Boulogne and had a meal under the stars on their last evening together. Tim stood them to a dinner out and Ingrid drove them. Rene passed remarks about her intrepid driving – according to him, no one could beat the "Kaiser Mutter" when it came to weaving around the circle where several lanes of cars dashed madly round, hooting and literally bumping others out of the way. She streaked round grimly, in and out of the traffic with deadly accuracy until she peeled off on the far side to reach the tunnel called the bridge of the soul, where Princess Diana had been killed. Through they went, slowly round the curve where the great pillars had borne the force of the Mercedes crashing into them at high speed. It was a grim, forbidding place. Strangely named the place of the soul, three souls left their bodies there that night. The tunnel had an eerie feeling about it and they were glad to leave it. Rose felt subdued and saddened.

In the morning, Rose and Tim caught the train and travelled south east to Prague. There, their hotel was right in the centre of the quaint city with its twisted streets and great bridges over a wide river. They walked over the George bridge many times, as everything they decided to see seemed to be down under it or up the hill on the other side and even on it, where Tim bought a painting from one artist seated there. In the shops, tearooms, libraries, everywhere, there were young girls selling tickets to concerts and the theatre, and when Rose questioned them they usually said they were playing instruments in the orchestra. Many of them were Jewish.

The puppet theatre's version of Don Giovanni was delightful. The puppets all stood over a metre tall and the old puppet conductor with his bald pate and tufts if white hair at the side, was in a box conducting the full live orchestra. They performed the full opera. Within walking distance was the old Jewish centre and there they walked into the old cemetery and the mausoleum where they saw what appeared to be wall paper but turned out to be a record of all the names of the eighty thousand or more Jewish men, women and children killed there in the second world war. That was an experience that brought the horror deeply to their minds. There were pathetic little drawings done by the children, which brought tears and a deep sadness just thinking of them.

Altogether, of all the capitals they went to, Prague made the deepest impression. Paris, Stockholm, London, New York all had a character of their own, but Prague was a gem. Vienna, too, would have outshone Prague had they not gone there in August, not knowing that it was the month when everyone left the city because of the heat. There were no Lipizzaner horses – only the stables, and the Vienna Boys Choir was elsewhere. No operas could be seen except in Mozart's Theatre in der Wein, putting on their pot boiler 'Der Lustige Witwe' which was The Merry Widow. That was a pleasure, at least, because Rose had been in it in Reps Theatre in Salisbury, Rhodesia and knew everything they said although they sang in German. They had hoped to see Mozart's Don Giovanni and Magic Flute in the original theatre.

Back to Paris they went, visiting the Louvre, the Eiffel Tower and Montmartre, to see the artists and sit looking over the huge city and the river; to walk along the Rive Gauche, experience the soul of gay Paree up at the Moulin Rouge and stroll in the Bois de Boulogne. It was living the reality of a thousand songs and books everywhere they went. They went to see the tomb of Napoleon, of course, and it was there that Rose was caught short with no hope of finding a public toilet. The place was deserted, and vast concrete approaches surrounded it. Cars were parked all round and appeared to be there for the night. It was late at night.

Tim simply stood guard behind a car parked under a shady tree, turned his back on Rose and stared into space as she crouched down in the gutter to leave her calling card – carefully – as close to the front of the car as she could, hoping the driver would think it was from a large dog. A tissue had to suffice, folded up small and saved for a bin somewhere further along the street. Napoleon slept on regardless. She suggested that they get away as fast as possible before anyone came because she felt terribly embarrassed. Tim ignored the whole scene, just took her arm and said come on, and that was that!

London was the same. Rose had to be there and walk the streets, ably shown everything Tim knew so well, going to the famous old theatres to really feel the heart and soul. They saw every musical and play that was on, including The Mousetrap and Little Night Music. London Bridge and the Thames. Park Lane and the Ritz, Marble Arch and the underground – whisked here, whisked there, around on the circle line and off up long, long escalators out of the bowels of the monster city, jostled and hurried by a million strangers. That was an exhilarating sensation of being alive, mainly because Tim was there with her to show her and share everything. Tim was totally at home in London. His accountant was a Lord. Rose met him when she returned to their restaurant rendezvous for tea at Fortnums. It was there that he introduced her to their lobster bisque, even better than that in Paris.

His great friend was Personal Secretary to Elizabeth, the Queen Mother. They called at a mews flat near Buckingham Palace where, taken by surprise, he seemed to bar the door to them, but invited them to meet him at the palace later that morning. Rose had a distinct impression that he had someone there with him who he didn't want Tim to see. They went into Buckingham Palace through a side door Tim knew, and were ushered into a private suite, Rose was offered a sherry as they sat in the reception room, in a very comfortable lounge suite and talked. It amused Rose to see that the drinks were carefully written up in a book in the anteroom. Never did she think she'd see the interior of Buckingham Palace, even though it was through a side door.

He questioned her about Rhodesia and whether they liked Sir Humphrey Gibbs? She blotted her copybook by confusing Sir Humphrey Gibbs, the Governor of Rhodesia that Rhodesians admired, with Sir Garfield Todd, leftist ex-Prime Minister of Rhodesia that they couldn't stand and deported after finding him harbouring terrorists on his farm. Tim's friend was surprised to hear her say how detestable Rhodesians found him, because he was led to believe he was liked and admired, also, he added, he was a friend of the Queen Mother's! Tim just sat there and listened to her digging herself deeper and deeper into the mire. He knew perfectly well who Sir Humphrey Gibbs was. He was just being thoroughly entertained. He always told people "Rosemary is a veritable mine of misinformation!" It was part of his wicked sense of humour. Later, he reminded her of her gaffe about Sir Humphrey. Rose could have killed him! She immediately sent a letter of apology and an explanation to Buckingham Palace, to Tim's perplexed friend, assuring him that the Rhodesians had a lot of time for Sir Humphrey.

Rose adored Tim. Never could she take her eyes off him. His profile was perfect. She thought him the handsomest man she'd ever seen. Yet she had always avoided handsome men, knowing them to be vain and unfaithful, in the main. Tim was different. He openly enjoyed the attention other women lavished on him but didn't chase after them. A woman could sense the difference. Rose was proud of the way he sought her out in any room and automatically gravitated to her side. She was proud to walk into any theatre or even a restaurant or private party on his arm. Looking at a photograph of him, one sees a tall, well-shaped, slim man with a bald pate and grey hair above the ears, neatly brushed back, a patrician nose and blue, laughing eyes. Rose saw him through Rose-tinted glasses. That was love, of course!

Educated at Eton, his voice and every word he spoke had her constant attention. His rare sense of the ridiculous, and his witty remarks delighted her and her children too. Then, suddenly, without warning, he would come out with something particularly unpleasant and the bottom would fall out of her world. At first, she used to be so overcome with the sheer pain of being literally wiped out by his spite or unpleasantness that she'd become almost suicidal and want to scream as if she were being physically destroyed. He knew he behaved that way and regretted it. He even told her once that his wife, Jackie, had told him to 'piss off!' when he got like that - and she must do that too. Later there were times when she told him to "just fuck off!" It amused her to recall that when she did so, he would say mildly "Don't use that word!" quite ignoring the command to get out and stay out, he'd settle down on the settee and turn up the sound on the T.V. and that was that.

Of course, half their time together was spent horizontal. Neither could bear not to be cuddled up together, either watching T.V. or 'resting' after lunch or just simply indulging in some particularly pleasant variation of sleeping together. "Those whom God hath joined together." That was a reality in every sense of the word. They were a perfect match for nearly twenty years, until medications used to treat Tim's heart failure caused him to become like Ben - totally impotent. It was then that Rose was able to prove to him that love, true love, is not based on sex alone. His loss was hers as well, that was all, because they were one. Love would last right until death.

A final gesture of loving farewell came when Tim was

unconscious in hospital. When they first met, twenty-one years previously, he lay in her arms and said, "When I die, I just want to die in your arms." Unconscious and sedated, unable to speak or open his eyes, dying from a burst blood-vessel in his brain, he suddenly sat upright as if he were a Captain in the Queen's Guards once more. Rose was keeping a lone vigil at the bedside. He was sedated, and his eyes were closed but he knew she was there.

He laboriously lifted his arms in front of him, shaking at the effort, turned sideways and placed them on her shoulders. Then he laid his head on her bosom and she gathered him closely in her arms. There they stayed, locked together in a silent embrace and Rose felt him relax as though asleep. He died there, as he had wanted to, in her arms. Until death us do part, she thought, as she laid him back on the pillows and folded his hands on his chest.

That was in May,1999 and Rose recalled that Tim's health had begun to drag him down. He wasn't taking much notice of current affairs, even saying he wasn't interested in the Millennium celebrations. With his previous heart attacks and current angina, and the ominous feeling they gave him, he had distressed Rose by saying "I'm dying!" She said "We are all dying! You will only die once, and when you finally do, you probably won't even know it." She hoped it gave him courage. He couldn't abide sympathy.

The week before he died, an executive in British Embassy sent Tim up to the border of Zambia and Angola where twenty-eight thousand refugees were encamped. The Zambian Government had asked the British for a million pounds to pay the U.N., who were there in full force. The W.F.O. was there feeding them. U.N.H.C.F and all others were assisting in their fields and had to be reimbursed by the Zambians. Tim was sent up to assess the claim. He was to spend a week there and he really should not have agreed to go. He was literally dying on his feet! Rose had four phone calls from him from the five-star hotel in Lusaka, before he was driven up to the border and a last call from a farm where they stopped for lunch. Her last words to him were:

"Be careful where you walk"

"Why?"

"Well, with twenty-eight thousand refugees there, you might tread on a landmine or a lump of shit!" They laughed, and he said "They're calling me, I must go darling, I'll be back Tuesday. I'll call you. I've written you a letter." and he was gone. Tuesday came and no phone call from him. Rose was worried. She waited until ten a.m. With a sense of foreboding, she decided to ring the British Embassy and ask if Tim was still away. It was not like him not to contact her. She spoke to the man who sent him up there who said they hadn't been able to find out who to contact. He said Tim had been back from the border in time to go to the Embassy for a dinner and to give them details of his assessment. No doubt, as he talked, he ate too much of the special foods and drank a lot of wine. Thank goodness, he had told them all he had found because he had nothing down on a computer. It was all in his head.

Afterwards, apparently, he had felt a bit unwell, so he left the hotel and went for a walk in the dark street. He didn't return and in the early hours of morning he was found unconscious where he had blacked out and fallen. They carried him back to the hotel and the doctor was called. They thought he had been hit on the back of the head. They found he had medication to take for his heart but not how much and they rang the Embassy in Salisbury because he wasn't making sense. Until Rose phoned, nobody knew whom to contact. Rose gave them Adam's telephone number and the name of his heart specialist and she rang Peter Jack, his doctor. Peter didn't know the prescriptions. The specialist was away! They were to send Tim back as soon as the plane could pick him up. Adam, as official next of kin, became the one at the front of everything and Rose felt very heartsore that he spoke to Tim from the Embassy and she had no chance to be there and hear him or talk to him. Adam, when he finally reached him, said Tim was not making much sense, He was confused.

By a stroke of misfortune, the plane had been sent down to the low veld to pick up another emergency patient. The delay meant that Tim was in a coma by the time he reached the Avenues Clinic and he never came out of it. Two and a half days later, he died. The X rays showed a massive clot in the back of his brain from a burst blood vessel. Rose recalled him saying the night before he left "I've got such a dreadful headache!" She was worried about him insisting on this week in Zambia and said so, but he wouldn't listen or see his doctor. Also, she remembered that when they drove to Reps a day or two before, he went to park the car and was a while returning. He said he suddenly blacked out for a bit. Rose was cross with him for not going to see Peter Jack and telling him. Altogether, everything conspired to see Tim out of this world. It was his time to die.

At that moment of death, Rose felt deserted. It was as if her world had slipped away and she was alone on some high pinnacle with a black abyss all round her. Her heart died. It just shrivelled up inside her and seemed dead, but then it began to pain, literally, so she knew it was still there. And then began the most lonely and deadly days and nights of her life. As the months passed, Rose recalled that this was grieving, and she was glad she had grieved for Tim as deeply and so long.

In the first month, she still went through the motions of trying to live life in a normal way. She motored to Reps Theatre and went into the bar there, looking for her friends and his, the ones they had acted with and had a drink with - anything that would ward off the totally devastating lonely nights for a while. In the theatre bar, where Rose hardly drank more than a pink soda or a sherry but needed the company, she found three men who had lost their wives in the same month that Tim died, and she couldn't help gravitating to them because she knew exactly how bereft they felt. All women are motherly, it's just natural. Rose listened to hours of their misery and she sympathised. Little did she know that she was setting herself up for three proposals of marriage - two de facto and one de jure!

Let's call them Tom, Dick and Pat. Rose was shaken. She had just lost Tim! They had just lost their wives! How could they even bear to think of it?

Tom was pushy and common, which was a bad start. She had a surprise phone call one day. Did she remember him? They met at his son's house when his wife was alive? His son had business to do with Tim. Rose said that she did and was so sorry to hear of the sudden death of his wife. He was a millionaire and lived in a grand house that he bragged about and wanted Rose to share – not to marry me, mind, just for the company. She must come and see the house. Rose said she had seen it, remember. She and Tim had been invited to see it by him. She remembered Tim's private comments about the ghastly bar and the ducks on the wall, none of his observations flattering. He bragged about his money and about his wife who had been an 'air dresser and wonderful. He just needed the company, that's all, and she would never look back financially. He didn't want to marry her, he just wanted her to live with him and she could have everything she wished. Rose said she would when she had time and she was careful not to have time. He had a bad leg, phlebitis, the doctor said, and he suddenly died.

Dick, she knew very well. He was the senior clerk in the biggest legal firm in Salisbury and he sang in the operas and danced with Rose on stage. Dick the prick, one could have called him! He danced beautifully and he and his funny little wife, who came up to his navel when they did ballroom dancing together, were always in the bar on a Friday night and were inseparable. Yet more than once he had phoned Rose and suggested that he and she should get together in bed as his wife was away and Rose had told him to jump in a lake. Suddenly, his little wife had died, and Rose had sympathised, not expecting an immediate pounce. Rose put him wise to the fact that she was in mourning for Tim and would be for a long, long time. She couldn't possibly move into his very beautiful flat with him but thank you for asking.

Pat was an Irishman. For twenty years or more he had his legal practice in a small town near Salisbury. Then he sold up and joined the same firm in Salisbury that employed Dick. It was Dick who introduced Pat to Rose. He was sitting at the bar drinking heavily and crying crocodile tears into his double whiskeys. His wife had died of a brain tumour almost on the same day as Tim died of a clot on the brain. Rose couldn't bear to see this short, fat man with tears pouring down his face, downing glass after glass of whiskey. He seemed the most genuinely grieving person she had ever seen so she sat next him and started to talk to him - anything to stop him from cutting his throat! His wife, Gretel, she got to know very well in no time. He asked her to come to his house and he'd show her films of Gretel and albums full of pictures of her from before they married to the end - the dreadful end in hospital in Cape Town.

Nearly every day he phoned and invited her to everything he went to and they were many. He was a member of the Pioneer Society and the History Society, the Law Society and the Salisbury Club, so she met everyone important in the city and was wined and dined constantly. When there was nothing to go to, she was invited to lunch or dinner at his large house in the best suburb in the city, Arundel. He had an excellent cook who had been the gardener until Gretel had brought him into the house and taught him all her recipes. This short, fat man had two black Great Danes that were the biggest Rose had ever seen. They stood almost as high as his chest. As the dogs were not allowed in the sitting room, the bitch lay in the foyer and bit her nails...clunk...clunk, all evening. The Persian carpet stretched five by seven metres across the sitting room to reach the leather furniture

On went the T.V. to show pictures of Gretel, hour after hour. Four huge albums were discussed in detail, each holiday together and in Switzerland she saw Gretel's family and the churches they attended. He was a Catholic and so was Gretel. He had brought Gretel's ashes back to be buried in her brother's grave at a Catholic Mission where he'd been a priest. Rose was asked to accompany him to the mission for the weekend. There was a visitor's wing and separate bedrooms for each one. He asked her if she would sing the Ave Maria during the mass to be said on the Sunday in the chapel there. Rose was getting a little weary of Gretel by this time, but she felt even more drawn to Pat. Regardless of his heavy drinking and smoking, she felt so sorry for him she agreed to go. Off they went in his massive four-wheel drive, armed with several bottles of best wines and whiskeys, some for the priests. He sped along, smoking all the way and looking for all the world like Toad of Toad Hall with his large, pale green, weepy eyes peering over the dashboard. Being so short, he had to look through the steering wheel to see the road ahead.

In the back seat was his tall, good looking, black cook, Eric, who was also attending the funeral. When they arrived, an old priest met them and escorted them to the long building beside the central mission. Rose found herself placed in a tiny cell with a neat single bed, chair and small table in it. Other than a small window, a tiny mirror and crucifix, the room was bare, and the floor was concrete. Down the passage was a bathroom and around the corner was Pat's room. There seemed to be no other guests. Although there had been terrorists in the neighbourhood, this mission had never been attacked and she must not be nervous. There were no locks on the doors and she found that the black cook, Eric, had been given the room next to hers. Rose felt rather peculiar! The black cook, sleeping in a room next to her?! What on earth did this man, Pat, think she would put up with? She realised that she would embarrass a fine, decent, African man that she liked if she made a fuss.

Had it been an African nanny, she'd have been glad to have the company. She must just say nothing and put up with it.

Eric was not included in the evening drinking session that commenced at six, when all the priests gathered in a common room with benches around the walls and a well-stocked, large cupboard full of various bottles. Some of the priests were ancient and a particularly old one came in with an equally ancient nun which surprised Rose. They sat together and seemed almost like an old married couple. Rose was politely introduced but the conversation was all about Gretel, her brother and past events in their lives. Rose had a small whiskey and soda as the bottles emptied down the gullets of the rest, Pat included. He kept getting up and re-filling his glass as if he was trying to empty the bottle he had brought for all of them. Finally, a bell rang and they all emptied glasses and moved into the refectory next door for a simple meal. One priest remained to put all the bottles away and lock the cupboard. He then pocketed the key, after Pat had removed his one bottle to take to his bedroom for a bedtime spot.

He told Rose that they were not going to guzzle all his whiskey. Did she notice how they had pounced on it? The cupboard was kept firmly locked because the very old priest was an alcoholic and would polish off the lot if he could. Pat confirmed that the old nun and priest were a definite item. Rose thought back on her holiday with Tim in Bruges where she learned about Abelard and Heloise being there together. They went to bed early and thankfully, there was no sign of Eric, then or in the morning when Rose ventured into the bathroom for a hasty wash. He had kept well away like the gentleman he was.

The mass, the Ave Maria, sung without accompaniment

and the burial of the small box at the foot of a sandy, neglected and sunken grave at the other side of the mission, near some gum trees ended their stay. It was all rather R.C. for Rose and the Mission, she felt, probably harboured terrorists, as many Catholic establishments had. Apparently, Gretel's brother used to ride a motorbike through terrorist infested bush to visit the kraals and the catholic congregation who could not reach the mission for mass. He had hit a landmine and died in the explosion.

Rose thought back to her good friend Chris Hales who, aged twenty-seven, had been in an armoured car that hit a landmine buried on the side of the road and lost his eyesight. When she met him, he was a lawyer, having used part of his golden handshake from the army to purchase a house in Salisbury and take a law degree at the University, achieving a law degree. When Rose met him, his little boy of eight, Jonathan, was staying with him and his partner, Elisabeth. Rose used read to him once or twice a week when Liz was working, and she was fascinated when the little boy was seen tapping around the garden with his eyes closed, using one of the white sticks belonging to his father.

Chris told her that when Jonathan was three and they were sitting in the back of the car together travelling through the bush, they passed some wild animals. He grabbed his father's hand and flattened it on the window, saying excitedly:

"Look, Daddy! Look! Lions!"

Chris and Liz are still in the house, protected by a high wall and solid, iron gate, on an acre of land planted with the indigenous trees Chris loves and cannot see, in the garden he created. He knows every inch of his place and the position of everything, trees, little pool, rockery, fruit trees, Paths, driveway and gate. A letterbox bringing him tapes from St. Dunstan's in England, getting talking books and news tapes, freely sent and returned in a special cover. Both millions of blacks and a few whites still live there.

Now, their main problems are electricity, which goes off for weeks at a time and water. The taps run dry for months, let alone weeks. They rely on his two tanks, thoughtfully added by Chris at the back of the house to collect rain water. Chris still has three dogs. His large guard dog, Maud, is now dead but replaced by another large hound. The two Jack Russell dogs are still there. Time has passed, and Chris and Liz soldier on very bravely in Zimbabwe. They could go to England and receive the handouts that Britain gives those who suffered the loss of support from the mother country and the rest of the western world when they tried to maintain Rhodesia as the bread-basket of Africa. It's dangerous to stay in Zimbabwe because 90% of the population are out of work. The blacks thieve to survive, and life is cheap. Yet, because the clubs and bars Chris and Liz used to go to have closed, they consider it safe to go to the African Shebeen in Mbare and enjoy a night out there in the company of the local indigenous people.

But, off that line of thought and back to the saga of Rose and Pat. It was a mere three weeks since they were introduced when, suddenly, he leaned forward and held her hand. "Will you marry me?" he said, and Rose was stunned! The silence lasted for a few seconds. Then he launched into an almost legal reasoning about their compatibility as man and wife. Rose was lost for words! She had never thought of it. The reasoning was that they were both bereft and lonely and needed someone. They were both intelligent and had similar interests in theatre and art and life in general. It was a pity Rose was not a Roman Catholic, he said, but perhaps she would see the light later, and she didn't seem to object to his being one. Still Rose remained silent. Her mind was working in a different direction as he continued to hold the stage. She was stunned that he had leapt out of his deep despair over Heidi and floods of tears so suddenly. How extraordinary!

Her heart hurt suddenly as she thought of her loss of Tim. Was this man so dense that he didn't realise she was still in mourning? Why wasn't he in mourning? Why all the performance? Why did he suddenly want to get married again? He continued to hold her hand and discuss the arrangements. She could choose any bedroom she wanted. There was more than one en suite bathroom. He would prefer to remain in the room he had, but it was not compulsory. If she liked it better, he would move out of it. She could change anything she wanted in the whole house, except the lounge. There, he thought the carpet could not be bettered and the heavy suite and full-length curtains as well. Also, the original paintings on the walls must stay.

There was a pregnant pause and Rose realised he was waiting for her answer. She tried frantically to sum up her judgement of this bombshell but couldn't. He answered for her. She must think it over and not give him an answer straight away. He asked her if she would like a cup of coffee before he took her home and she said yes. With it, he provided a box of special chocolates and a choice of liqueur from his well-stocked cabinet and that was that – no hugs, no kisses etc. How peculiar, thought Rose. In a slight daze, Rose went home to think of it for quite a lot of the rest of the night and next day.

He didn't love her – that, she knew. There was no wild romance and heaven forbid! Could she bear to marry someone who hardly touched her? Why was she even asking herself? She knew the answer to that. He'd hit the nail on the head with many points he'd raised. It offered a place in the sun for her such as she'd never had before.

On the other hand, could she stand him? He insisted on putting away more whiskey than she'd ever thought a man could swallow and still drive a car as if he were sober. He insisted on taking out his cigarettes and lighting up as soon as he had stuffed his face with a large quantity of good food, then blowing a cloud of smoke towards her while she was still eating, which she found bad mannered. He soon appeared to her as being completely wrapped up in himself and totally selfish. She battled with the problem and tried hard to be practical but in the end, she had to admit that she just couldn't do it. She told him she was still grieving for Tim and hoped they could be friends. He didn't appear very upset about her decision! Somebody said to her "Once you have Pat for a friend, you have him for life. He continued to take her out and to dinners at home and at clubs and she found that wherever she went, he seemed to have to be there too.

Going to Capetown for Christmas with her daughter Sherrell and family, he persuaded her not to go by air but travel with him as he needed a co-driver. He went to stay with his nephew but angled for inclusion in her holiday arrangements and asked her to go to a New Year's Eve party with him and meet other friends of his at various places for meals. He bought her a beautiful bottle of Miss Dior for her birthday and wouldn't give up the constant wooing of Rose, hoping to change her mind.

He included Sherrell in a day trip to a winery in Franshoek and bought hampers for lunch. He continued to 'press his suit,' as the saying goes, and a lot of it was appreciated but somewhat exhausting. Still Rose tried to change her mind. She even discussed it with Sherrell whose answer was quite clear:

"Somehow, I just can't imagine calling that man father!"

One day, the phone rang, and a woman said "You don't know me. I am a friend of Pat's, and he has invited me to lunch today. I just wanted to ask you if you can tell me what is wrong with him? I went there on Sunday and he asked me if I wanted to lie down after lunch. He joined me, but he didn't do anything, he just lay there. Do you know why? He has asked me to marry him, but he never touches me." Rose was astounded! A stranger was asking her whether he was impotent! She wanted to laugh, it was so preposterous. She answered "I'm sorry, but I am afraid I know nothing about him below the belt. I have never seen any part of his anatomy below his belly button." The woman, Betty, apologise for asking and said she was a very sexy woman and didn't know whether she could marry a man who wasn't. He had given her a beautiful engagement ring, a big, yellow diamond that he said had belonged to his mother. How had Rose come to see his belly button?

Rose explained that his shirt had parted company over his fat stomach and peeping coyly out was a pink thing she thought was something else! His belly button extruded about an inch and it looked disgusting. She had told him he should have an operation on it, which he did.

Betty rang off and told Pat what Rose had said. Next morning, Pat rang her and told her it was true. He was impotent.

Betty had told him she couldn't marry him, and he took the diamond ring back from her.

Back in Rhodesia, Pat soon announced to Rose that she must come to dinner and meet Wilma. He had decided to marry Wilma who needed looking after as she was nearly blind. He was only sixty-two and she, going on for eighty but very spry and healthy otherwise. The yellow diamond now graced her hand. She was wealthy and owned a large flat on the ground floor which he was moving into as they prepared to sell up and go to Ireland as man and wife. He would get a pension in Ireland of four hundred punt and so would his wife, and that would be sufficient for them to live on. Rose realised then, why he was proposing to every woman he met, including her.

Shortly after that, she left Zimbabwe for good. The battle to ward off the intruders at night, even shooting at them to be safe, was getting her down. Creeping around the house with a gun in the early hours and peering out of windows trying to see a black man in the blackness and not getting to sleep, listening for sounds of a break in, was exhausting and nerve racking. She ended up living in the Cape Province in South Africa with her daughter, Sherrell, in the city of George, up on the Garden Route near Knysna.

Rose's son was living in Knysna and they gravitated to him. They didn't want to settle on his doorstep and George was only sixty kilometres away, and much less gold plated when it came to real estate.

They chose George because it was on the Garden Route and near the sea. Also, the Outeniqua mountain range swept down literally to the suburbs and there would be snow right down to the city in winter, yet the temperature never went below four degrees or over twenty-six degrees in summer. Their beloved Christopher was close. Their house was affordable and double storied and had a classic South African design. Also, it was high on a hill near a river in King George Park, north facing and overlooking the mountains. At last, Rose was living near her son and could visit her grandchildren. Thank God, they were there for some months, because, at end of 2005, Kit died in Johannesburg. He crashed his car into a tree driving to his cottage after a dinner party he had given for clients whose millions he was investing. He was killed almost outright. That was a deep loss for them and, what's more, Sherrell had to leave Rose alone in the house to work in England as it was impossible to find employment in South Africa now that the Government had changed, and all the jobs went to the black people.

However, for company, Rose had their little cat, Nougat. She was an extraordinary little cat, cross calico and tortoiseshell, and very beautiful. She was very motherly and seemed to think Rose and her daughters were her kittens. If there was an intruder outside at night, Nougat stared at the window and growled like a dog. When she came in from outside she meowed loudly and looked around for each of us. If Sherrell was upstairs she would go to the staircase and meow and Sherrell would oblige with a loud meow to let her know she was there. Nougat would either bound upstairs and join her or carry on calling her until she came down. Then she'd walk in front of her and lead her to her chair.

Nougat loved storms. They had the Outeniqua Mountains close to the city and the lightning and thunder when the storm clouds came over the mountains was quite frightening. Not for Nougat! She'd leap out of the window and sit on the arm of a chair on the veranda. The bolts of lightning and crashes of thunder made her sway from side to side and stare up at the sky. When the rain pelted down she'd be out on the lawn catching frogs. She didn't kill them, she'd scooped them up in her mouth and bring them in, deposit them carefully on the carpet and give them a prod to make them jump.

WHO ATE MY FROG? (I have my suspicions!)

She wouldn't eat anything but cat biscuits and the tomato sauce out of a tin of pilchards. Also, she didn't like milk or cream, only water which she drank out of a long, red glass vase Sherrell had on the dining room table. Sherrell was afraid she would break it, so she put it away. Nougat sat on the table and howled until Sherrell put it back. The day she did that Nougat reared up on her hind legs and hugged it. They all loved that cat. Sadly, when she was fourteen, she developed a cancer on her little pink nose and they had to have her put to sleep. She is missed to this day.

Despite having to live alone again and face the fears of intruders, all husbands, lovers and sundry others being long since deceased, Rose loved George. In summer, seldom did the temperature go above twenty-eight. The best climates in the world are recorded as being in George and Hawaii. Just over the Outeniqua mountain range, Oudtshoorn went from twelve below to a summer high of forty-five. However, that area provided beautiful scenery especially the pass known as Meiring's Poort, a place where Rose and Sherrell often went for picnics. It was always cool and shady there, with its sheer, granite canyon and seventeen little bridges over the winding stream.

The seven years spent in George were healing ones. Rose loved the house and the whole place. There were so many coves to go to and spend time at the beaches, and, over the Outeniqua Pass which was a scenic drive, and there were the ostrich farms and the wonderful Cango Caves to explore. Rose had her bridge club, a little group of friends that she had at home for tea and bridge or went to their houses and so the time passed. Nearly all her life she had lived in the bush or right next to the wild. The house backed onto bush land and the river and wild animals roamed there from time to time. There were no lions and elephants, but a huge bushbuck used to browse just outside the fence and a family of giant mongooses came in somehow and explored the garden. Dozens of guinea fowl roamed the streets near the river and came in daily to the garden.

The other birdlife were the ibis that settled on the ridge of the roof and sound off loudly. Called Ha de Da, that was their raucous call. These were not the sacred ibis from Egypt which were white. These were black with a beautiful sheen of pink and bronze on their backs. To sleep in Sherrell's bedroom upstairs, under the high eaves, was when the sound was deafening. Four or five settled there because it was a high, pitched roof and they quarrelled and laughed, wakening the dead at four a.m. Fortunately, Rose had a bedroom and a spare room plus full bathroom and separate toilet on the ground floor. There was a little private passage and a door into the dining room. It was so well designed that she thought she'd be there for the rest of her life. Upstairs, Sherrell had the big mezzanine bedroom and a lounge plus a walk-in wardrobe and full bathroom. There was another colossal mezzanine room opposite her. The lounge had no ceiling. It swept up to the rafters of the high roof.

All Rose had to do was get her residence and not have to leave the country every three or six months, returning to have her passport restamped with a temporary visa. Home Affairs was run by the blacks now and Rose still couldn't persuade them that she should have been given citizenship years before. They managed a two-year visa, finally.

Then, suddenly Rose had a bad experience. She thought she was going to die. It wasn't a pain but a mushrooming of what she described as black, fine gravel, rising from her chest to her throat and a feeling of dread and dying - weird, really. The doctor sent her for an X ray and that showed up three round gall stones. The surgery was done immediately, and Rose had no one to be with her. Another thing happened to her eyes. She went for new glasses and was sent to a specialist who said it was cataracts - replacement lenses or blindness, so that was done. She was by then over eighty-three and the only answer was to sell the house and emigrate once more.

All the members of her family were now in Johannesburg. Her son Christopher's children, Zoe, his daughter, and her husband Greg and their children, Sam and Grace, Dustin and his wife Lynne and their two girls, Isabella and Madison Rose. Also, Kit's other sons, Brett, James and Michael, her nephew, Gary Mason and his wife Carol, with their children, Shaun and the twins Brett and Lauren now married to David. There was no one left in George but herself.

Her wish to be with her children meant joining Jenny who lived on her little farm in New South Wales, Australia. Jenny came over to help her pack up everything and the house was sold. Sherrell was no longer there, so Jenny and Rose packed her things too. The removal firm sent a container to collect everything, including Rose's boudoir grand piano, and Jenny and Rose left. Her dear friends Don and Joy, Jehovah's Witnesses who had visited her every Saturday morning since Sherrell went to work in England, took them to the airport. She would miss them dearly, as well as the neighbours in King George Park, and all the lovely children.

So, at the age of eighty-four, Rose moved to Kyogle, an Aboriginal name that meant Turkey. One cannot help but ponder the significance! The house which has expanded to include Rose and Sherrell's goods and chattels is called "Cornfonteyn' as it has a large creek winding through the property called Cob o' Corn Creek. There are five birds in Cornfonteyn, a resident brush turkey named Uncle Pumblechook, a guinea fowl called Gavin and the three of us says Rose! There is also the two-minute tom cat, Sam. Two minutes of his time is all anyone gets on the lap.

Everything in Rose's life had changed every seven years and this was thirteen times seven. Her friends in George had been dying one by one so it was time to go. No use regretting the pension she should have been getting. There was no pension in Australia and no free medical aid for her either. She had almost no money, having been stripped of everything in Zimbabwe. She joked that she should have come in as a political refugee from Zimbabwe – get in a coracle and row herself to Christmas Island. Those boat people received a monthly allowance of about two thousand dollars and free medical aid. Joking aside, that is what she is! She's a political refugee and most interested to see what the next seven years has to offer!

Rose was plagued with skin lesions that appeared three years ago on her legs and fingers and nose. That was a logical result of a lifetime of being in the deadly rays of the sun in Africa, where, eighty years ago, they had never even heard of protective creams and merely were told to keep their hats on. Since then, everything has cleared up and she is in perfect health.

Years ago, Sherrell, Jenny and Rose sang in the Royal Albert hall, London. It was the special chorus of a thousand voices of combined choirs from all round the world, and they sang songs from the Gilbert and Sullivan operas. Despite her age, Rose can still reach top C and above. When Sherrell comes over for a couple of months holiday every two years, they take time to see the Theatre shows in Brisbane and Sydney. There, they saw 'My Fair Lady' performed at the Sydney Opera House, directed by none other than Julie Andrews herself and went up the Blue Mountains to stay with friends. They went to Cairns and up in the cable car to Kuranda a few years ago and to a coral island on the Great Barrier Reef.

Tim   Sher   Rose   Jenny   Bru
Australian Outback Spectacular

Jenny, Rose and Sher in cable car at
Kuranda, Cairns

Jenny with King
Parrots at
Lamington

Rose with Koala
Lone Pine

Rose is now ninety-one and she has finished her memoir. It's on the way to the publishers, so she and Jenny are going to South Africa in June, England and Greece in July. She wants her two daughters to see Delphi and Meteora. They will meet up with Sherrell in UK and spend a few days sight-seeing in Wales with Shannyn and Tom, the new man in her life. They have booked to go to the top of Mt. Snowdon in the train and over the border to the Cheddar Gorge. It will be great to get to know Tom and see their new house.

Then it's the Greek tour. They will be picked up in an air-conditioned coach complete with wheelchair as Rose is determined to see that they are not hampered by her lack of speed. They spend one night in Athens and Rose wants to go to a Taverna in the Plaka for some Greek food and drink, Retsina and Ouzo. A wheelchair is booked for the plane journeys too. That way they go into the departure lounge and onto the plane ahead of the first-class passengers and are taken to the plane in a special van and on a lift. There's no hauling of luggage up any steps and standing in queues and no trudging down long corridors and on the tarmac to get to the plane.

Jenny wrote a musical play for the One Voice Richmond Valley Choir Anzac Day centenary concert in 1915 and in-spanned Rose to design and paint the two sets, one of the beautiful Dardanelles where they fought and one of the sphinx and pyramids where they trained. So, there she was in her mid-eighties, painting sets in the men's shed, Casino. The choir sang the war songs and Patricia White, the choir director, wrote a moving poem about the Woman in White who stood at Circular Quay and greeted each troop ship returning the wounded to see if her son was amongst them.

At the end, a trumpeter sounded the Last Post and the choir sang Keep the Home Fires Burning. The play was performed to full houses in Kyogle and Casino and received standing ovations.

Coffee time but no sitting down while painting the decor for the first act of "Gallipoi - overe here, over there",

The formidable mountains of Gallipoli painted for the third act.

Tammy, Shannyn, Sherrell and Bert

Shirley, Kit,

Zoe Lynne Michael Dustin Brett James at Dustin and Lynne's wedding

EIGHTEEN

EPILOGUE

Rose's bucket list still has a lot in it. She would like to go to Japan in Cherry blossom time. She would like to go to Coober Pedy and stay in a hotel underground and see if she is lucky enough to scrape out an opal from somewhere. The next inch might unearth a fortune! This is opal-fever, like gold-fever. She wants to go up the Darling river on a paddle steamer and perhaps travel up north on the Ghan and see the 'town like Alice'. She'd like to go to Melbourne once again walk in the gardens at Government House where Tim was an A.D.C., catch a tram and see the houses in the old town. The bucket list is growing longer and longer.

But all these journeys depend on the company of her daughters, Sherrell and Jennifer, and hopefully, occasional additions of her step daughter, Gillian and some dear friends. Alone, nothing would be possible or fun.

Front section of the Australian homestead "Cornfonteyn"
on the Cob o' Corn Creek, Afterlee, Kyogle, NSW.

Printed in the United States
By Bookmasters